Financial Statements for Sr

Financial Statements for Smaller Companies

A guide to practice and the FRSSE

Fourth edition

Hazel Powling
Andrea Pryde
Isobel Sharp

Andersen

Croner.CCH Group Ltd
145 London Road
Kingston upon Thames
Surrey KT2 6SR
Tel: 0870 777 2906
Fax: 020 8247 1124
E-mail: info@cch.co.uk
www.cch.co.uk

© 2002 Croner.CCH Group Ltd

First Edition 1997
Second Edition 1998
Third Edition 2000

ISBN 1 84140 244 3

All rights reserved. No part of this publication may be reproduced or transmitted in any form or by any means, or stored in any retrieval system of any nature without prior written permission, except for permitted fair dealing under the Copyright, Designs and Patents Act 1988, or in accordance with the terms of a licence issued by the Copyright Licensing Agency in respect of photocopying and/or reprographic reproduction. Application for permission for other use of copyright material including permission to reproduce extracts in other published works shall be made to the publishers. Full acknowledgement of author, publisher and source must be given.

Material is contained in this publication for which publishing permission has been sought, and for which copyright is acknowledged. Permission to reproduce such material cannot be granted by the publishers and application must be made to the copyright holder.

Whilst considerable care has been taken in the preparation of this book, no responsibility for loss occasioned to any person acting or refraining from action as a result of any material in this publication can be accepted by the authors or publishers.

This book is based on legislation and regulation extant at 31 March 2002 and on the *Financial Reporting Standard for Smaller Entities* (Effective June 2002).

Appendix 5, *Financial Reporting Standard for Smaller Entities*, is reproduced with the permission of the Accounting Standards Board.

> **British Library Cataloguing-in-Publication Data**
> A catalogue record for this book is available from the British Library

Typeset by YHT Ltd, London
Printed in Great Britain by Headway Press, Reading

Contents

	page
Preface	ix

Chapter one
Recognising the smaller company in law and accounting

Introduction	1
Accounting standards in the 1970s	2
The small company in law	3
The 1980s and accounting standards	4
The 1985 research	4
The 1988 ASC statement	4
Accounting standards and the ASB	5
The CCAB Working Party	6
The structure of the FRSSE	9
Major issues	10
The need for a FRSSE	11
The review mechanism	12

Chapter two
Small companies and the law

Introduction	13
The Companies Act 1985	13
Small and medium-sized companies	15
Modified and abbreviated accounts	15
Accounting simplifications	16
Restructuring the schedules to the Act	16
Audit of financial statements	17
Future developments	19

Chapter three
Defining small and medium-sized companies and groups

Introduction	23
Public interest companies	23

Contents

Qualifying as small or medium-sized	24
Size criteria	26
Small and medium-sized groups	26

Chapter four
The exemptions and modifications available

Introduction	29
Modified directors' report and financial statements for small companies	31
Group financial statements exemption	34
Audit exemption	35
Abbreviated accounts	40

Chapter five
Policies and profit and loss account matters

Introduction	45
Unincorporated entities	46
A true and fair view	47
Relationship with other accounting standards	48
Accounting principles and policies	50
Reporting financial performance	51
Statement of total recognised gains and losses	53
Discounting	54

Chapter six
Assets

Introduction	55
Fixed assets and goodwill	55
Leases	63
Stocks and long-term contracts	66
Other debtors, debt factoring and consignment stock	66
Start-up costs	67
Share schemes	67

Chapter seven
Liabilities and shareholders' funds

Introduction	69

	Contents
Taxation	69
Retirement benefits	73
Provisions, contingent liabilities and contingent assets	75
Capital instruments	77

Chapter eight
Other accounting issues

Introduction	79
Foreign currency translation	79
Post balance sheet events	80
Related party disclosures	81
Consolidated financial statements and associated companies	82
Cash flow information	83

Chapter nine
Implications for auditors

Introduction	85
Assessing whether the company is entitled to the exemptions	86
Compliance with the Companies Act and the FRSSE	87
Can modified financial statements be true and fair?	87
Additional guidance to auditors	89
Reporting on modified financial statements	91
Reporting on abbreviated accounts	92
Group financial statements exemption	94

Appendices

Appendix 1 Example financial statements	97
Appendix 2 Example abbreviated accounts	117
Appendix 3 Illustrative wordings	127
Appendix 4 Small companies' disclosure checklist	135
Appendix 5 Financial Reporting Standard for Smaller Entities (effective June 2002)	209
Index	345

Preface

It is now two years since the third edition of this book was published and four years since the second edition. However, those expecting a fifth edition in 2004 may be disappointed. The steady updating rhythm of these recent editions is to be disturbed by two momentous events for accountants. The first of these is the expected new Companies Bill in the 2003/4 or 2004/5 parliamentary session of this government. This promises much change but not necessarily many alterations in the detailed rules on small company reporting, assuming the Bill follows closely the work of the independent Company Law Review Steering Group. That Group published its Final Report in July 2001. For small companies, the Group adopted the mantra of 'think small first'. It proposed that the criteria for defining a small company be increased to the maximum permitted under European law. This would lead to more companies being eligible to use the FRSSE (good news for book sales). A further major proposal would allow company law and the FRSSE to be integrated into one document, i.e., the one stop shop (good news for all).

The second significant change for accountants will be the move to use international accounting standards, as required by a forthcoming European Commission Regulation. While technically only required for listed groups, the use of international standards is expected to cascade through all UK companies. Whether it stops at the threshold of small companies or influences further editions of the FRSSE remains to be seen. But this whole process has meant that the ASB has not issued any new standards in the past year, apart from FRSSE 2002, and is not expected to issue other new standards in 2002.

All this means that the FRSSE 2002 is likely to have at least a two-year shelf life and, possibly, a bit longer. This new FRSSE makes significant changes to its predecessor, forcing this edition of the book to be updated in areas such as taxation, pensions, start-up costs and accounting policies, areas which affect all small company financial statements. Updating the book was not easy. The invaluable assistance of our colleagues Annette Davis and Ken Rigelsford was necessary, in particular, to assure that the disclosure checklist, found at Appendix 4, was properly updated. That our checklist

Preface

runs to over 70 pages illustrates that if we think small first there is plenty of scope to reduce the reporting burden on our small companies.

Let's all aim for a shorter next edition.

Hazel Powling
Andrea Pryde
Isobel Sharp
March 2002

Chapter one

Recognising the smaller company in law and accounting

Introduction

1.1 Small companies are a relatively new creation in company law. Introduced in the Companies Act 1981, which implemented the EU Fourth Company Law Directive, a small company was then defined as one in which for the financial year and the one immediately preceding it at least two of the following three conditions applied:

- its turnover did not exceed £1.4m;
- its balance sheet total did not exceed £0.7m; and
- its average weekly number of employees did not exceed 50.

But the debate over differential reporting has raged for at least 100 years. Over this time, people have argued that there should be different rules to reflect the different nature or size of companies.

1.2 The first great divide came in 1907 when the Companies Act of that year introduced private companies. The reason for doing so was to allow such private companies not to file their balance sheets with their annual returns because, using the words in the Committee's Report at that time, 'as they do not appeal to the public for subscriptions, there is no need for publishing their private affairs, and ... the disclosure involved in the filing of the documents would, or might, seriously prejudice their interests'.

1.3 By the time of the 1948 Companies Act, that exemption was considered too sweeping and so that Act introduced the 'exempt private company', which was exempt from public filing of financial statements. A company qualified as such, and was thus exempt from filing its balance sheet, if it met three conditions:

(1) principally that no body corporate was a holder of any shares or debentures in the putative exempt private company. Detailed rules on shareholdings were set out in Schedule 7 of the Act, the principal

thrust of which was to stop private companies whose shares were held by public companies being exempt from disclosure;
(2) the number of persons holding debentures were not more than 50; and
(3) no body corporate was a director of the company and neither the company nor any of its directors were party or privy to any arrangement 'whereby the policy of the company is capable of being determined by persons other than the directors, members and debenture holders or trustees for debenture holders'.

1.4 The next major step was the publication of the Jenkins Report in 1962. It recommended the abolition of the distinction between exempt and non-exempt private companies. As a result disclosure of financial information became identified with the comment that disclosure is the price to be paid for limited liability. When the 1967 Companies Act implemented this element of the Jenkins Report, it required all limited companies to file full financial statements, while allowing certain limited companies to reregister as unlimited ones to avoid this requirement. However, the 1967 Act permitted non-disclosure of certain items in the financial statements for shareholders, which were also the statements to be filed with the Registrar of Companies, for certain companies. For example, a company which was neither a holding company nor a subsidiary and whose turnover did not exceed £50,000 was exempt from disclosing its turnover for the financial year. So began differential reporting in earnest.

Accounting standards in the 1970s

1.5 In 1970, the UK's first accounting standard setting body began work. Established as a Committee of the Institute of Chartered Accountants in England and Wales, which had hitherto issued non-mandatory *Recommendations on accounting principles*, this Accounting Standards Steering Committee, on which members of other accountancy bodies participated, issued its first Statement of Standard Accounting Practice (SSAP1) *Accounting for the results of associated companies* in January 1971. The general rule which the Committee adopted was that standards were to be applied to all financial statements intended to give a true and fair view of financial position and profit or loss. But, exceptions to that general rule were given in future standards. SSAP3 *Earnings per share* issued in February 1972 was applicable only to listed companies. When a Statement of Source and Application of Funds was introduced into financial statements in August 1975, the relevant accounting standard, SSAP10, provided an exemption for companies with turnover or gross income of less than £25,000 per annum.

1.6 The highly controversial accounting standard, in which application to smaller companies was an issue, was SSAP16 *Current cost accounting* issued in April 1980. By this time, the Accounting Standards Steering Committee had been transformed into the Accounting Standards Committee, which was constituted as a creature of the six principal accountancy bodies in the UK and Ireland. In SSAP16, exemption was given from the need to prepare current cost accounts for companies which did not have any class of share or loan capital listed on the Stock Exchange and which satisfied at least two of the following three criteria:

(1) a turnover of less than £5m per annum;
(2) a balance sheet total at the commencement of the relevant accounting period of less than £2.5m as shown in the historical cost accounts; and
(3) the average number of employees in the UK or Ireland of less than 250.

Exemptions were also given for certain classes of company, including most wholly owned subsidiaries, charities, building societies, friendly societies, trade unions and pension funds. However, while SSAP16 was controversial and its application hotly debated, few disputed the general application of other accounting standards to smaller companies.

The small company in law

1.7 As previously noted, it was the 1981 Companies Act which divided private companies among those which were small, medium-sized and the rest. Prior to that Act, the government had published a Green Paper *Company accounting and disclosure* in September 1979. It had two major proposals for small companies. The first was to reduce significantly the amount of information to be disclosed by what it then termed the 'proprietary company'. The second major question was the possibility of an independent review of the financial statements for small companies, instead of an audit. As history now shows, it took a further 15 years for some exemption from audit to be given to companies. But the 1981 Act gave statutory effect to reducing the disclosure requirements for the financial statements filed with the Registrar of Companies for small and medium-sized companies. It also limited the information to be disclosed in the shareholders' financial statements, by giving exemption for certain specific items.

1.8 With the clear classification of companies according to size in company law and the increasing number and complexity of accounting standards in the 1980s and then 1990s, so the debate over establishing a clear set of rules for larger companies, popularly referred to as Big GAAP, and a set of accounting rules for smaller companies, Little GAAP, began in earnest.

The 1980s and accounting standards

1.9 In the 1980s the debate on the application of accounting standards to smaller companies continued, fuelled partly by the changes introduced in the 1981 Companies Act and partly by the continuing increase in the number of accounting standards. When the Accounting Standards Committee (ASC) reviewed its processes in 1983, its report *Review of the standard-setting process* reiterated the Committee's view that future standards should apply to all financial statements intended to give a true and fair view. However, the Report acknowledged that exemptions might arise as a result of applying a cost-benefit test. It recognised that in judging whether a standard should be applied universally, the following additional information could be helpful:

(1) the main purposes for which the financial statements of small companies are used;
(2) the burden imposed on small companies by accounting standards; and
(3) the level of compliance with existing standards.

The 1985 research

1.10 To find some of the answers to those questions, the ASC requested that a research study be carried out. The resultant publication, *Small company financial reporting* by BV Carsberg, MJ Page, AJ Sindall and ID Waring was published in 1985. One of the authors' major recommendations was that they did not 'believe that a case exists for exemptions from all accounting standards of all companies below a certain size or of all private companies'.

1.11 At this time, the government was also concerned about burdens on business and was taking various steps to investigate how those burdens might be reduced. Therefore, prompted by the continuing interest in the topic and the general political climate, in October 1996 the ASC set up a Working Party to investigate the application of accounting standards to small companies.

The 1988 ASC statement

1.12 The ASC accepted, in February 1988, the report of the Working Party which it had set up in 1986. The conclusion was that on the basis that company law requires small companies to present financial statements that give a true and fair view, the then existing standards had many benefits and few incremental costs. Accordingly, there appeared to be neither reason nor demand to reduce the application of accounting standards to small companies. In reaching that conclusion, the Working Party had consulted widely and most consultees supported this position.

1.13 That said, the ASC recognised that there could be situations in the future in which new standards would be inappropriate for small companies either on conceptual grounds or, more likely, for reasons of practicality. It was also recognised that applying all standards to all companies – the universality concept – could hinder the ASC from making progress in the regulation of large and publicly accountable enterprises. Therefore, the ASC undertook to continue to consider specifically each new accounting standard.

1.14 However, what the ASC meant by small was not the same as that defined in company law. In a paper released in July 1988, the ASC clarified what it would generally consider as 'small' for determining whether or not to apply accounting standards. The criterion adopted was that relaxations, as specified in accounting standards, would be available to companies if they were not public companies and met two or more of the following criteria:

(1) turnover does not exceed £80m;
(2) balance sheet totals do not exceed £39m; and
(3) average number of persons employed in the year does not exceed 2,500.

These criteria represented those adopted in company law for the definition of a medium-sized company but scaled up by a factor of 10. While the ASC accepted that these were arbitrary, they were its best attempt at determining what might be considered public interest entities and those which were not by virtue of their size.

1.15 As events turned out, these ASC definitions identifying which entities were considered to be publicly accountable were used on only two occasions. The first was in the revised SSAP13 *Accounting for research and development*; the second in SSAP25 *Segmental reporting*. Both standards are still extant and have not yet been replaced by standards of the FRS or international FRS variety.

Accounting standards and the ASB

1.16 In 1990, the ASC was replaced with the new Accounting Standards Board (ASB), no longer a creature of purely the accountancy bodies. Funded by the accountancy profession, the financial community and the government, the ASB develops, issues and withdraws accounting standards on its own authority.

1.17 While the ASB was allowed a brief honeymoon period by commentators during 1991 and 1992, the problem of the application of accounting standards to smaller entities remained unresolved and the piecemeal application was perceived as unsatisfactory. The ASB exempted small companies from its first FRS on cash flow statements. However, subsequent standards, such as FRS3 *Reporting financial performance* and FRS4 *Capital instruments,* which extended significantly disclosure requirements, did not contain specific exemptions. In this period also, corporate reporting requirements were being increased because of developments such as those emanating from the Cadbury Report on corporate governance matters. There was a general feeling of 'standards overload'.

1.18 Meanwhile, the momentum from government to reduce the burdens especially on smaller businesses continued. Therefore, in late 1993, the ASB asked the Consultative Committee of Accountancy Bodies (CCAB) to establish a Working Party with the following terms of reference.

> 'The Board like its predecessor the Accounting Standards Committee, examines, on a standard by standard basis, whether exemptions from all or part of the standard should be provided for certain types of enterprise on the grounds of size or relative lack of public interest. The Working Party is asked to recommend to the Board, on the basis of a wide consultation, appropriate criteria for making such exemptions.'

The CCAB Working Party

1.19 In its two and a half years of existence, the Consultative Committee of Accountancy Bodies (CCAB) Working Party issued two public papers:

- *Exemptions from Standards on Grounds of Size or Public Interest*, published in November 1994; and
- *Designed to fit – Financial Reporting Standard for Smaller Entities*, published in December 1995.

The 1994 paper

1.20 The November 1994 Consultative Document *Exemptions from Standards on Grounds of Size or Public Interest* can perhaps best be summarised as a proposed 'quick fix'. Its main proposals were that:

(1) with recent changes in company law, there should be no additional requirement for small companies to comply with the full body of

accounting standards;
(2) there should be a presumption that most small companies are exempt from accounting standards. Future standards should be reviewed on the basis of what is essential for small companies, using a number of specific criteria;
(3) exemptions from accounting standards and UITF Abstracts should be based primarily on size, using the Companies Act definition of a small company; and
(4) compliance with five particular standards and one UITF Abstract should continue for small companies.

1.21 The Working Party tentatively concluded that the following standards and one UITF Abstract should remain applicable for all companies:

- SSAP 4 *Accounting for government grants*;
- SSAP 9 *Stocks and long-term contracts*;
- SSAP 13 *Accounting for research and development*;
- SSAP 17 *Accounting for post balance sheet events*;
- SSAP 18 *Accounting for contingencies* (now subsumed in FRS12); and
- UITF Abstract 7 *True and fair view override disclosures* (now part of FRS18).

1.22 The results of the November 1994 consultation, which produced some 112 responses, were that broadly three quarters of respondents agreed that the arrangements, whereby accounting standards and UITF Abstracts apply to all entities with few exceptions, caused problems. The clear message to the Working Party was that the status quo was not an acceptable option.

1.23 The consultation also demonstrated that the use of the small company criteria in company law had support. While some commentators would have preferred the threshold to be much lower, others thought it should be at the medium-sized level or indeed applicable for all private companies.

1.24 However there was not clear support for the proposed 'quick fix' solution. Four recurring themes or issues were identified in examining the respondents' comments. The first was that the cost of considering and then complying with accounting standards was outweighing the potential improvement in information content in the financial statements. This issue had become very clear in the 1990s as the ASB's new Financial Reporting Standards were generally much longer and complex than the older SSAPs.

1.25 The second issue was that the standards themselves were in need of some refreshment. They had been developed by different people and committees over a period of some 25 years. While a codification exercise would benefit all users of accounting standards, it was recognised that this, while potentially of use in clarifying certain current difficulties, would not give a solution to the problems caused by the application of almost all standards to smaller entities.

1.26 Thirdly, while the quick fix solution did have some support, it was recognised that exempting smaller entities from some standards would solve some problems but in doing so would create others, particularly where there were interrelationships between different accounting standards.

1.27 The fourth issue, and perhaps the most serious one, was that guidance would still be necessary on measurement issues to determine whether financial statements of smaller entities gave a true and fair view. The absence of any form of guidance on measurement might lead to unacceptable treatments being adopted.

The 1995 paper

1.28 In considering the responses to the 1994 Consultative Document, the CCAB Working Party noted the ideas which the DTI was considering in its Consultative Document *Accounting simplifications*. The then proposal, which has now been enacted, was that company law should be revised so that all the accounting rules for small companies are given in one schedule. This was in contrast to the previous situation in which the legislation was drafted for all and then exemptions given, thus making it quite complicated for small companies to work out what applied to them and what did not.

1.29 The extension of this thinking into accounting standards resulted in the conclusion that piecemeal application of particular standards to smaller companies was a flawed approach. It involved accounting standards being formulated to fit *inter alia* the circumstances of the largest companies in the country and then a simple switch being applied as to whether these standards should be applied to small companies. Furthermore, it led to discussions on marginal cases. The piecemeal approach did not focus on what should apply to the generality of small companies. What was needed was a mechanism, such as a special Financial Reporting Standard. In short, it was clear that an accounting standard designed to fit small companies financial statements should be developed.

1.30 To prove that the proposed approach of a Financial Reporting Standard for Smaller Entities (FRSSE) was feasible, practical and capable of delivering benefits to smaller entities, a draft FRSSE was produced and issued for comment as part of the paper *Designed to fit – Financial Reporting Standard for Smaller Entities*. Published in December 1995, comments were sought by 29 March 1996. The responses were generally positive. The concept of a FRSSE received support from commentators such as the accountancy bodies, users such as the Inland Revenue and many more firms than the previous piecemeal application of accounting standards proposal had done.

1.31 The Working Party therefore recommended in July 1996 that the ASB should proceed with the development of the FRSSE. This proposal was accepted by the Board, which in December 1996 published its Exposure Draft of the FRSSE for comment by 14 March 1997. The final FRSSE was published on 4 November 1997. But it was not a painless process. A number of major issues had to be resolved and mechanisms put in place for the review of the FRSSE.

The structure of the FRSSE

1.32 There was no public dissension from the view that the ASB is the right body to issue the FRSSE. By virtue of SI 1990/1667 The Accounting Standards (Prescribed Body) Regulations 1990, the ASB is the body that issues applicable accounting standards to which companies must have regard. Furthermore, because the ASB presently carries out this task on behalf of all companies, the risks of Big GAAP and Little GAAP becoming unnecessarily out of step in the future would be reduced if there was a single body responsible for both. Therefore, with the ASB being considered the appropriate body to assume responsibility for the FRSSE, it was drafted in a similar format to that adopted for other Financial Reporting Standards.

1.33 While the FRSSE looks similar to other ASB publications, there are some differences. For example, other accounting standards place the 'Definitions' section before the Statement of Standard Accounting Practice. While other accounting standards have relatively few definitions because they focus on single topics, FRSSE 2002 defines some 90 terms. Therefore, the 'Definitions' section has sensibly been placed after the accounting guidance. But what this highlights is the absence of a generally accepted glossary of accounting terms in the United Kingdom at this time.

1.34 The International Accounting Standards Committee developed a glossary as part of its 1990s revision project. The new International Accounting Standards Board is expected to continue this. The UK's Auditing Practices Board similarly issued a Glossary of Terms when it carried out its codification exercise in 1995. The importance of a common lexicon is something which the accountancy profession has recognised in the past. Perhaps, in due course, when international accounting standards are used in the UK, the profession will at last have a comprehensive glossary.

1.35 A consequence of having so many terms defined in the FRSSE is that, within the text of the Statement of Standard Accounting Practice, terms which are explained in the 'Definitions' section are highlighted in bold text. It can be argued that the list of defined terms is excessive. While precise definitions may be necessary to curb the activities of loophole spotters or pedants, there is an argument that accounting standards are not written for, and are certainly not read by, the person who does not have any accounting knowledge (although standards are designed to benefit this community by producing consistent accounting practice). Therefore, on the presumption that the reader of the FRSSE has some accounting knowledge, definitions of terms such as 'consolidated financial statements' or a 'foreign entity' may be unnecessary.

Major issues

1.36 In developing the FRSSE, there were issues on which agreement was readily obtained and others which have proved controversial.

1.37 The FRSSE may be applied to all financial statements intended to give a true and fair view of the financial position and profit or loss (or income and expenditure) of all entities that are:
- small companies (or groups) as defined in companies legislation; or
- entities that would also qualify as such if they had been incorporated under Companies Act legislation, excluding building societies.

1.38 By restricting the scope in this way, the FRSSE continues the approach within the Companies Act 1985 whereby certain companies, such as those carrying on regulated activities under the Financial Services and Markets Act 2000 or insurance market activities, in which there is a public interest, are unable to take advantage of exemptions from disclosure. As building societies are not companies, they need a specific reference.

1.39 Furthermore, it is a logical extension of the availability of company law exclusions for small companies generally, such as those relating to the preparation of consolidated financial statements and from accounting disclosures, for there to be an accounting standard drawn up specifically for small companies principally to reduce the required level of disclosure.

1.40 More controversial have been the questions on whether:

- the FRSSE should be capable of application to small groups;
- there should be a requirement for cash flow information;
- there should be specific requirements for related party disclosures; and
- there is a need for any accounting standard on small companies.

The first three points are discussed in the later chapters dealing with specific issues. The fourth, and perhaps most serious, question is considered below.

The need for a FRSSE

1.41 Some respondents to the ASB's Exposure Draft raised the issue of whether there was a need for any accounting standard for small companies. While the FRSSE is in length approximately only 15 per cent of the guidance applicable to larger companies, it is still perceived by some as a burden. Some would prefer that small companies are required to follow only company law requirements.

1.42 Abolition of any accounting standard for small companies has not been an option available to the ASB to date for the following reasons:

(1) the evidence from the responses to the 1994 Consultative Document was that piecemeal application of only a few standards was not supportable as some guidance is needed in other areas to determine whether the financial statements of small companies give a true and fair view. What was considered unacceptable was the potential for an entity to report radically different figures dependent on whether or not it qualified for exemption and then dependent on which accounting measurement technique it chose to adopt;

(2) in recent years, the DTI and the ASB have looked at the combination of both requirements for financial statements. Therefore if a matter was covered by accounting standards and not required to be part of UK law because of an EU Directive, then the DTI would seek to eliminate that provision as part of its Accounting Simplifications project. As a result, if all accounting standards were removed at a stroke, then the system would be out of balance and the DTI might have to move quickly to put provisions back into law; and

(3) perhaps most seriously, the wrong message might be received by those involved in preparing relevant financial statements that all matters previously dealt with in standards could be disregarded. This might lead to those financial statements being challenged as not presenting a true and fair view. Furthermore, users of financial statements would not be confident that they had been prepared against a recognised template, leading to additional costs and confusion.

The FRSSE is the compromise. If its guidance is proven to be excessive as measured against the needs of the sector, it should be safely pruned back in future revisions. While its first two revisions in 1998 and 1999 have added more guidance, and thus words, it was to be hoped that the planned major review in 2000 and 2001 would result in some deletions. But this would have been a triumph of hope over experience in standard setting, where commentators tend to demand vociferously more guidance. Sadly, experience has triumphed once more. FRSSE 2002 is longer and more complex than its predecessor. Previously the FRSSE had 80 definitions, now it has over 90. FRSSE 2002 has three per cent more words than its predecessor. Those seeking a simpler rulebook will have to continue the good fight. The likely integration of the FRSSE with company law requirements and a move to base the FRSSE on international accounting standards provide opportunities to seek to streamline the rules.

The review mechanism

1.43 It was recognised in the 1995 CCAB paper, *Designed to Fit*, that any accounting standard for small companies would need to be responsive to changes in financial reporting practices for the generality of companies. For this reason the ASB established an advisory committee, the Committee on Accounting for Smaller Entities (the CASE), to assume responsibility for advising on financial reporting in smaller entities and thus for the FRSSE.

1.44 The official terms of reference for the CASE are:

(1) to review proposed accounting standards and UITF Abstracts, and proposals to revise or withdraw existing standards and Abstracts, including the FRSSE, and, in the light of the ASB's current policy, to recommend to the ASB how such proposals should apply to smaller entities; and

(2) to advise the ASB generally on such matters relating to smaller entities as the ASB may from time to time request.

1.45 As noted in *Designed to Fit* the FRSSE was seen as a small step forward in respect of amending GAAP as it applies to small companies. However its creation, and that of the infrastructure that supports it, was a big step forward for the UK accounting profession as it had for the first time created a different and distinct regime for small companies. The challenge for the CASE is to ensure that the FRSSE improves, that it meets better the needs of preparers and users of small companies' financial statements, and that the Working Party's aim of a document of some 30 to 50 pages with basic principles and clear requirements is achieved, without resorting to very small typeface.

Chapter two

Small companies and the law

Introduction

2.1 This chapter provides an overview of the company law applicable to financial statements of small and medium-sized companies and explains the origins of the exemptions now available to such companies. It also looks at some likely future developments. Chapter 3 then covers in more detail the criteria defining small and medium-sized companies while Chapter 4 provides details of the exemptions available.

The Companies Act 1985

2.2 The Companies Act 1985 (the 'Act') requires the directors of all companies to prepare financial statements for each financial year – s226. These should contain a balance sheet and profit and loss account which respectively give a true and fair view of the company's state of affairs as at the end of the financial year and of its profit or loss for the year.

2.3 In this book the term 'financial statements' is used in preference to the statutory term 'accounts' as the latter term has a variety of meanings in common usage. In contrast, financial statements are defined in accounting literature to mean the balance sheet, profit and loss account and other primary financial statements (cash flow statement and statement of total recognised gains and losses, where relevant) and related notes which together are intended to give a true and fair view. These statements and notes are those which are within the scope of the auditors' report. The directors' report is not part of the financial statements. The term 'annual report' is commonly used to mean the financial statements together with the directors' and auditors' reports.

2.4 The financial statements are produced for the shareholders, or members, of the company. The directors are responsible for sending financial statements to the members who will, in accordance with custom, formally approve them at an Annual General Meeting (unless the members have elected to dispense with such meetings). Certain other parties, such as debenture holders, may be entitled to receive the financial statements and attend the meeting at which they are due to be approved – s238. The directors are also required to file a set of financial statements with the Registrar of Companies – s242. These financial statements are then on public record and copies can be obtained, for a fee, by any interested party. As explained below such financial statements for filing may be the same as those prepared and sent to shareholders but in certain circumstances the directors may take advantage of certain exemptions in the Act and omit some accounting information from the public record.

2.5 The accounting provisions in the Act have developed over many years from sources as diverse as the recommendations of UK company law committees, attempts to deal with specific problems or perceived abuses, the implementation of EU Company Law Directives and government measures to simplify disclosure requirements as part of different deregulation exercises. The proliferation of accounting standards has also impacted, both directly and indirectly, on the volume of disclosure required under the Act. Indirectly, the requirement for financial statements to be true and fair requires regard to accounting standards which in recent years have become more detailed and complex. Directly, many requirements of accounting standards have been introduced into the Act's schedules detailing the requirements for financial statements as follows:

Schedule

4	Form and content of company accounts
4A	Form and content of group accounts
5	Disclosure of information: Related undertakings
6	Disclosure of information: Emoluments and other benefits of directors and others
7	Matters to be dealt with in directors' report
8	Form and content of accounts prepared by small companies
8A	Form and content of abbreviated accounts of small companies delivered to Registrar.

2.6 A major consequence of the evolution of company law has therefore been an inexorable increase in the required extent of disclosures and greater uniformity in the financial statements of companies, irrespective of their size.

2.7 Not surprisingly, this has led to something of a backlash, with the result that as part of the 1990s' Deregulation Initiative, the Department of Trade and Industry (DTI) began a review of the impact of statutory accounting requirements, with an overall aim of minimising the burdens imposed on companies, while at the same time ensuring that the information provided met the reasonable needs of users of financial statements.

2.8 Unfortunately, the present end product is confused and confusing. The following sections provide an overview of the development of company law affecting small companies and seek to explain the present hotchpotch of requirements.

Small and medium-sized companies

2.9 The discussion below refers to small companies and medium-sized companies. These terms are defined in the Act. The definitions are complex and are considered in detail in Chapter 3. For example, the legislation imposes restrictions on the ability of a company to take advantage of the exemptions when it is a member of an 'ineligible group' and provides transitional rules for when a company moves in or out of compliance with the size criteria from one year to the next.

2.10 However, it may be useful to be aware that the size criteria for a small company are currently turnover not more than £2.8m; balance sheet total (i.e., *gross* assets) not more than £1.4m; and average number of employees not more than 50. A company will be entitled to the exemptions available for small companies if it meets any two out of these three tests.

2.11 The equivalent thresholds for medium-sized companies are turnover not more than £11.2m; balance sheet total not more than £5.6m; and average number of employees not more than 250. The exemptions available to medium-sized companies are very limited compared with those for small companies. But both small and medium-sized companies may be exempt from the requirement to prepare group financial statements as more fully discussed in Chapter 4.

2.12 The exemption from audit currently applies only to 'very small' companies with turnover of less than £1m as more fully explained in Chapter 4.

Modified and abbreviated accounts

2.13 Both small and medium-sized companies are permitted to omit from the accounts prepared for filing with the Registrar of Companies certain aspects of the statutory financial statements drawn up and sent to members. Such 'reduced' financial statements are usually termed 'abbreviated

Small companies and the law

accounts' (not 'abbreviated financial statements' as they are not intended to give a true and fair view). In addition, small (but not medium-sized) companies meeting certain conditions may be able to take advantage of disclosure exemptions available for the financial statements drawn up for the shareholders. Financial statements drawn up on such a basis are usually termed 'modified accounts' or 'modified financial statements'. As explained more fully in Chapters 3 and 4, the concessions available are confusing; they are also subject to periodic changes.

2.14 Significant revisions to the requirements for the financial statements to be drawn up by small and medium-sized companies were introduced by SI 1992/2452 The Companies Act 1985 (Accounts of Small and Medium-sized Enterprises and Publication of Accounts in ECUs Regulations 1992. These regulations revised Schedule 8 to the Act dealing with the content of accounts which could be prepared for filing (which rather confusingly were then generally termed 'modified accounts' although as noted above this phrase now denotes financial statements prepared for shareholders which take advantage of disclosure exemptions). The principal changes introduced by SI 1992/2452 entailed the restructuring of Schedule 8, the introduction of certain disclosure exemptions for small companies' financial statements for members, and an increase in the turnover and balance sheet thresholds for companies to qualify as small or medium-sized.

Accounting simplifications

2.15 Another small step in the process of revising the required disclosures for financial statements prepared by small companies was introduced by SI 1996/189 The Companies Act 1985 (Miscellaneous Accounting Amendments) Regulations 1996.

2.16 The various accounting simplifications introduced by the 1996 Regulations applied to all limited companies, regardless of their size or business sector. Generally speaking the revisions were uncontentious and relatively minor. The consequent relaxations in accounting disclosures, in the main effective for periods ending after 2 February 1996, did not prove substantial in most cases.

Restructuring the schedules to the Act

2.17 In an initiative to find a more structured approach to the schedules within the 1985 Companies Act, the DTI issued in July 1996 a Consultative Document, *Accounting Simplifications: Re-arrangements to Companies Act Schedule on Small Company Accounts*. These proposals were enacted in

Audit of financial statements

SI 1997/220 The Companies Act 1985 (Accounts of Small and Medium-sized Companies and Minor Accounting Amendments) Regulations 1997 (the '1997 Regulations').

2.18 Up until this change, small companies had been able to take advantage of exemptions from disclosure available to them within Schedule 8 to the Act. The form that the exemptions took was that certain of the Schedule 4 disclosures could be dispensed with. The disadvantage of this structure lay in the fact that a company wishing to avail itself of the exemptions in Schedule 8 had first to go through the provisions for the generality of companies to identify those from which it could be exempt and those which it still needed to apply.

2.19 To remedy this situation the 1997 Regulations give the standard small company requirements, rather than presenting the requirements on an exemptions basis. The regulations did not include any significant amendments or reductions in the required disclosures for small companies. The intention was to preserve the right of small companies to:

- draw up Schedule 8 financial statements only; or
- add additional Schedule 4 requirements to the Schedule 8 minimum; or
- draw up full Schedule 4 financial statements.

2.20 The key implementation date for the 1997 Regulations was 24 March 1997. Companies preparing financial statements for accounting periods ending after that date were able to follow the revised Schedule 8 which sets out the requirements for the form and content of financial statements by small companies. Unfortunately reference is still needed to other schedules for matters such as disclosure of directors' remuneration. The new Schedule 8A sets out the requirements for small companies' abbreviated accounts prepared for filing purposes.

2.21 The requirements of Schedule 8 and Schedule 8A are discussed more fully in Chapter 4. Appendix 1 sets out example financial statements for a small company prepared in accordance with Schedule 8 and the FRSSE. At Appendix 2 there are example abbreviated accounts prepared in accordance with Schedule 8A. A disclosure checklist for a small company is provided at Appendix 4.

Audit of financial statements

2.22 One of the more far reaching changes affecting small companies was introduced by SI 1994/1935 The Companies Act 1985 (Audit Exemption) Regulations 1994. These regulations abolished the statutory requirement for the audit of financial statements of those small companies which meet the conditions within ss249A to E of the Act. By this one measure some 500,000 smaller companies were no longer required to have their financial statements audited.

2.23 Companies with an annual turnover of no more than £350,000 and meeting a number of other conditions were exempt from audit. However, those companies with turnover above £90,000 were required to obtain a report on their financial statements from a qualified independent accountant, thereby eliminating most of any benefit for all but the smallest companies. The availability of the exemption was also severely limited by the fact that it did not apply to a company that was, at any time during the financial year, a parent company or subsidiary. The intention here was that the exemption should apply only to 'stand-alone' small companies rather than to those which were part of a larger group.

2.24 But within two years the DTI made further changes in the form of SI 1997/936 The Companies Act 1985 (Audit Exemption) (Amendment) Regulations 1997. The principal effect of these changes was to amend the threshold for total audit exemption to £350,000 and thus remove the requirement for a report from a qualified accountant (except in the case of charities where it was retained pending further consultation).

2.25 The 1997 amendments also made a slight relaxation of the previous rule that parent companies and subsidiaries could not take advantage of the exemption. Such companies may now do so provided that the group as a whole meets the size test for the audit exemption.

2.26 In April 2000, the DTI published the results of its consultation on The Statutory Audit Requirement for Smaller Companies and announced a decision to increase the audit turnover threshold in two stages, from £350,000 to £1m, and then to £4.8m, the maximum permitted under EU Law. Statutory Instrument 2000/1430 The Companies Act 1985 (Audit Exemption) (Amendment) Regulations 2000 came into effect on 26 July 2000 and duly raised the threshold to £1m. The DTI postponed action on the £4.8m threshold (which may affect an estimated 75,000 additional companies) pending the outcome of the full Company Law Review, which is discussed below.

2.27 The detailed requirements for the audit exemption are considered in Chapter 4.

2.28 Whilst this measure to exempt companies from audit undoubtedly removed certain burdens from smaller companies, it did not impact on the form that their financial statements should take nor reduce the compliance costs directly associated with financial statements preparation. The financial statements of companies taking advantage of the audit exemption provisions still need to be drawn up in accordance with the requirements of the Act and accounting standards. Most small companies will therefore seek the services of a professional accountant to achieve this.

Future developments

The Company Law Review

2.29 On 26 July 2001, the Company Law Review Steering Group published its final report on the reform of company law. This Group was established in 1998 to consider a fundamental review of the framework of core company law and how it could be modernised to provide a simple, efficient and cost-effective framework for the regulation of companies.

2.30 The recommendations of the Steering Group were wide-ranging and will now be considered more fully by Government, leading to further consultation before a new Companies Bill is presented to Parliament, probably no sooner than 2003. Therefore, the recommendations of the Company Law Review Steering Group may be augmented, altered or deleted over the next few years. However, some of the changes, such as the turnover threshold for audit exemption, could be changed sooner by way of Statutory Instrument.

2.31 The key recommendations which may affect reporting by smaller companies are:
- the delegation of all requirements governing the form and content of small companies financial statements to a Standards Board so that all small company reporting requirements may become part of a revised FRSSE;
- simplifying the format and content requirements for small companies financial statements and making legislation on private companies easier to understand;
- extending the small company accounting regime so that companies who meet two out of the following criteria are classed as small: turnover no more than £4.8m (currently £2.8m); balance sheet total no more than £2.4m (currently £1.4m); or no more than 50 employees (as now);
- abolition of the category of 'medium-sized' companies;
- raising the audit threshold to bring it into alignment with the small company accounting regime; and
- removing the option of filing abbreviated accounts at Companies House.

Small companies and the law

The Independent Professional Review

2.32 The Company Law Review Steering Group initiated a debate on whether a lighter, less costly form of assurance, namely the Independent Professional Review (IPR), should replace the audit for companies with a turnover between £1m and £4.8m. Companies below this threshold would be totally exempt. The IPR would provide a limited level of assurance to the effect that the reviewer is not aware of any material modifications that need to be made to the financial statements for them to be in conformity with accounting standards.

2.33 The Company Law Review Steering Group stated in its Final Report that they had been unable to reach a firm conclusion on the IPR and that responses were mixed. At the time of the Final Report, the Auditing Practices Board (APB) was still performing field trials. Therefore, the Steering Group recommended that the audit requirement be removed in the £1m to £4.8m bracket in any event and that the DTI should draw a policy conclusion as to whether to require an IPR in that range on the basis of the APB trials and any other relevant considerations.

2.34 The APB published the results of its field trials on 19 November 2001 and concluded that in some circumstances IPRs, compared with audits, can reduce costs quite significantly, although the APB also indicated the difficulties of performing reviews based largely on analytical procedures in unsophisticated businesses.

2.35 The Government had not yet announced any policy decisions on the IPR at the time of writing.

International harmonisation

2.36 International harmonisation of accounting standards is likely to bring profound changes to financial reporting requirements in the UK. The European Commission has proposed that all European Union companies listed on a regulated market should prepare their consolidated financial statements in accordance with International Accounting Standards (IAS) by 2005. Although this has no direct impact on small, unlisted companies, including those which may adopt the FRSSE, convergence with IAS will nonetheless be the major force which will drive the direction in which accounting in the UK develops. At the time of writing there are many uncertainties about how the EC proposal, which is expected to be finalised sometime in 2002, will be implemented in the UK.

2.37 Once finalised, this EC Regulation will apply only to the consolidated financial statements of listed groups. However, member states will have the option to permit or require the use of IAS for unlisted groups

Future developments

and individual company financial statements. The DTI is expected to consult on this issue after the EC Regulation is published.

2.38 It is argued that having two concurrent accounting regimes, IAS for some and national rules for others, would lead to confusion amongst users of financial statements, additional expense in the preparation of subsidiary financial statements and more cost for accountants learning both systems. This could be avoided by using IAS as the basis for all accounting in the UK.

2.39 However, IAS may impose an unacceptable burden on small businesses as it does not have any special rules for small companies. A number of approaches to this problem have been considered, including the development of an international accounting standard for smaller entities to simplify the requirements of IAS. The International Accounting Standards Board (IASB) has identified this as a research project and is considering the need for separate guidance for smaller entities. Given the present popularity of the FRSSE, strong UK resistance is expected to any proposal which may require small companies to have regard to all IASs. On the other hand, the FRSSE, because of its focus on basic rules, could probably be made IAS compatible, without causing serious changes in practice. A better route would of course be for the IASB to produce the IFRSSE, which would be the model for small company reporting worldwide and which could then be introduced in the UK together with any necessary company law rules. At the time of writing, it is expected that the IASB will set up a special committee in mid-2002 to look *inter alia* at small company reporting issues.

Chapter three

Defining small and medium-sized companies and groups

Introduction

3.1 The Companies Act 1985 ('the Act') makes four important concessions to companies which fall within the definition of 'small' or 'medium-sized'. These concern the ability to circulate 'modified financial statements' to shareholders, file 'abbreviated accounts' with the Registrar of Companies, avoid the need to prepare group financial statements and avoid the need to appoint auditors. Full details of the exemptions appear in Chapter 4. This chapter discusses the definitions of small and medium-sized companies and groups.

Public interest companies

3.2 Certain classes of company in which there is a public interest are specifically excluded from being able to take advantage of the provisions relating to the preparation of modified or abbreviated accounts. A company is excluded by s247A if it is, or was at any time during the financial year to which the financial statements relate, either:

(a) a public company;
(b) a person who has permission under Part IV of the Financial Services and Markets Act 2000 to carry on one or more regulated activities;
(c) a person who carries on insurance market activity; or
(d) a member of an ineligible group.

3.3 An ineligible group is defined in s247A as one which includes a parent or subsidiary which is either:

(a) a public company;
(b) a body corporate, other than a company incorporated under the Act, which can offer its shares or debentures to the public;
(c) a person who had permission under Part IV of the Financial Services

Defining small and medium-sized companies and groups

and Markets Act 2000 to carry on a regulated activity; or
(d) a person who carries on an insurance market activity.

3.4 These restrictions are very important and non-compliance with them has resulted in abbreviated accounts being rejected by the Registrar of Companies. It is clear that a subsidiary of a publicly quoted group, however small, would be unable to file abbreviated accounts. However, as a consequence of (b) above, the existence of a foreign fellow subsidiary with the power to offer its shares to the public would also invalidate entitlement to the exemption, even in a small group headed by a private company. Another example where the Registrar has rejected abbreviated accounts is where the company concerned was regulated under the Financial Services Act 1986, the predecessor to the Financial Services and Markets Act 2000.

3.5 Section 247A of the Act stipulates that a company cannot take advantage of the small and medium-sized company exemptions if it 'is, or was at any time within the financial year' in one of the categories described at **3.2** above. It is generally recognised that the 'is' relates to the time at which the financial statements are prepared. Accordingly, if the company becomes ineligible after the balance sheet date, but before the financial statements are prepared then it would not be able to take advantage of the exemptions, such as filing abbreviated accounts, even if it had not been ineligible throughout the financial year to which the financial statements relate.

Qualifying as small or medium-sized

3.6 A company, which does not trigger the 'public interest' exclusion, will 'qualify' as small or medium-sized in the financial year to which the financial statements relate if it meets the relevant size criteria in the year in question and the preceding year – s247. It will also be 'treated as qualifying' if:

(1) it qualified in the preceding year; or
(2) was treated as qualifying in the preceding year under (3) below; or
(3) it qualifies in the financial year to which the financial statements relate and was treated as qualifying in the preceding year under (1) or (2) above.

3.7 The effect of these rather confusing requirements is that:

(1) a company will qualify if it meets the size criteria in two consecutive years; and
(2) if a company fails subsequently to meet the required conditions in a single future year its qualifying status will not be lost in that year.

However, if the failure occurs in a second consecutive year the status will be lost. The company would then have to meet the criteria for two consecutive years before the status is regained.

3.8 The following table illustrates the impact of these provisions.

Year	Meets size criteria in year	Qualifies
1*	X	N
2*	✓	N
3	✓	Y
4	X	Y+
5	✓	Y+
6	X	N
7	X	N
8	✓	N

+ = treated as qualifying

*NB This does not denote the company's first and second years of trading. There is a specific provision for a company's first year of trading.

3.9 A newly incorporated company qualifies as small or medium-sized in its first financial year if it meets the required conditions in respect of that year, notwithstanding the general rule that a company must meet the criteria in two consecutive years to qualify as small or medium-sized – s247.

3.10 Parent companies (including intermediate parent companies) are subject to a further restriction – s247A(3). A parent company can only be treated:

(1) as a small company in relation to a financial year if the group headed by that company qualifies as a 'small group'; and
(2) as a medium-sized company in relation to a financial year if the group headed by that company qualifies as a 'medium-sized group'.

3.11 This restriction would prevent a 'shell' parent company with no turnover or employees taking advantage of the exemptions where it has more substantial subsidiaries. The definitions of small and medium-sized groups are considered below.

Defining small and medium-sized companies and groups

Size criteria

3.12 Small and medium-sized companies must satisfy at least two of the three criteria in the following table in order to qualify as such:

Size criteria for small and medium-sized companies	
Small company	Turnover – not more than £2.8m Balance sheet total – not more than £1.4m Average number of employees – not more than 50
Medium-sized company	Turnover – not more than £11.2m Balance sheet total – not more than £5.6m Average number of employees – not more than 250

3.13 Turnover is defined as:

'the amounts derived from the provision of goods and services falling within the company's ordinary activities, after deduction of: (i) trade discounts; (ii) value added tax; and (iii) any other taxes based on the amounts so derived' – s262(1).

3.14 When comparing turnover, if the financial year of a company is not a period of 12 calendar months then the maximum figure for turnover set out within the table above should be proportionately adjusted – s247(4).

3.15 'Balance sheet total' is the sum of all the assets, without any deduction for liabilities – s247(5).

3.16 The average number of employees should be determined on a monthly basis. That is to say, the number of full and part-time employees with a contract of employment in each month of the financial year should be totalled and divided by the number of months to arrive at the average – s247(6).

Small and medium-sized groups

3.17 The criteria for determining whether a group qualifies as a small or medium-sized group are of relevance for the following reasons:

(1) there is an exemption available to the parent company of a small or medium-sized group permitting it not to prepare group financial statements for a financial year in relation to which the group headed by that company qualifies as a small or medium-sized group and is not an ineligible group – s248; and

Small and medium-sized groups

(2) a parent company's own entitlement to be treated as small or medium-sized is restricted by reference to these criteria as discussed above.

3.18 The definition of an ineligible group for the purposes of the exemption from preparing group financial statements is not identical to that for the purposes of permitting companies to prepare modified and abbreviated accounts. For the group financial statements exemption a group is ineligible if any of its members is:

(a) a public company or body corporate which has the ability under its constitution to offer its shares or debentures to the public;
(b) a person who has permission under Part IV of the Financial Services and Markets Act 2000 to carry on a regulated activity; or
(c) a person who carries on an insurance market activity.

3.19 While this list looks superficially similar to the one in paragraph 3.3 above, the significant difference is that it is only concerned with the status of the companies within the reporting group rather than looking to whether the parent company of that group is itself a member of an ineligible group. So for example, a sub-holding company which is a subsidiary of a US listed company would not be able to file abbreviated accounts but would be able to take advantage of the group financial statements exemption provided that it met the size tests and was not ineligible for any other reason.

3.20 A group will qualify as small or medium-sized in the financial year to which the financial statements relate if it meets the required size criteria in the year in question and the preceding year. A group will also be 'treated as qualifying' in certain circumstances which follow the same rules as those discussed in paragraphs 3.6 to 3.9 above.

3.21 The size criteria for small and medium-sized groups are set out in the following table – s249(3):

Size criteria for small and medium-sized groups	
Small group	Turnover – not more than £3.36m gross (or £2.8m net) Balance sheet total – not more than £1.68m gross (or £1.4m net) Average number of employees – not more than 50
Medium-sized group	Turnover – not more than £13.44m gross (or £11.2m net) Balance sheet total – not more than £6.72m gross (or £5.6m net) Average number of employees – not more than 250

Defining small and medium-sized companies and groups

3.22 The gross criteria are applied by aggregating the relevant amounts from the financial statements of a parent and its subsidiaries without making the normal consolidation adjustments. The net criteria are applied after making consolidation adjustments and are likely to be relevant when there is significant intra-group trading which will be eliminated from the figures for consolidation. A group may qualify under either the gross or the net criteria (i.e., it may use the most advantageous method) – s249(4).

3.23 The balance sheet total refers to the total of all assets (both fixed and current) and is not the same as 'net assets'.

3.24 Section 249(4) provides that the aggregate figures shall be ascertained by aggregating the relevant figures 'determined in accordance with section 247' for each member of the group. However, this does not appear to pick up the requirement of s247(4) that the maximum figure for turnover shall be proportionately adjusted where the company's financial year is not in fact a year. Neither is the requirement of s247(4) repeated in s249. Consequently, it appears that, for the purposes of the definition of small and medium-sized groups, no adjustment should be made where the period is not 12 months. However, this seems likely to be an oversight and common sense suggests that the maximum figure for turnover should be proportionately adjusted for periods which are not in fact a year.

3.25 The amounts in respect of subsidiaries should be based on their financial statements for financial years that are coterminous with those of the parent company or, where this is not the case, the last financial year ending before the year-end of the parent company – s249(5). If those figures cannot be obtained without disproportionate expense or undue delay, the latest available figures should be used – s249(6). Again there is no specific provision to deal with the situation where the length of the subsidiary's accounting period is different from that of the parent.

3.26 Where the group has made an acquisition during the year, the issue arises as to whether only post-acquisition turnover of the acquired company should be brought into account. This appears to be right in terms of the net criteria, which are intended to be net of normal consolidation adjustments.

3.27 Section 248(1) states that a company may take advantage of the exemption for a financial year '... in relation to which the group ... is not an ineligible group'. This would seem to relate to the time at which the financial statements are being prepared. Accordingly, the test in s248(1) (unlike s246(3) which states that a company is ineligible if it 'is, or was at any time within the financial year') seems to be one to be applied at the financial statements approval date.

Chapter four

The exemptions and modifications available

Introduction

4.1 The Companies Act 1985 (the 'Act') makes four important concessions to companies which fall within the definition of 'small' or 'medium-sized':

(1) small (but not medium-sized) companies may prepare 'modified financial statements' – s246(3) and a 'modified directors' report' – s246(4) for circulation to members;
(2) small and medium-sized companies may file 'abbreviated accounts' with the Registrar of Companies which take advantage of exemptions (which are more extensive for a small company than for a medium-sized company) – s246(5), 246A(3);
(3) parent companies of small and medium-sized groups are exempted from the requirement to prepare group financial statements – s248(1); and
(4) some small companies are exempt from audit – s249A, subject to more restrictive size tests and other conditions.

4.2 By using s246 and Schedule 8, a small company can produce a modified directors' report and financial statements for circulation to its members. As with any company, it is entitled to include more information than the required minimum. There is a layer of detail which may then be omitted from the accounts prepared for filing with the Registrar of Companies. A medium-sized company cannot take advantage of the exemptions in the preparation of its financial statements for circulation to its members but can file abbreviated accounts with the Registrar, although the detail which may be omitted is much less than for a small company. The permutations are shown in the following table.

The exemptions and modifications available

	Small companies		Medium-sized companies	
	To members	For filing	To members	For filing
Full financial statements (no exemptions)	✓	✓	✓	✓
Modified financial statements – s246(3) and Schedule 8	✓	✓	X	X
Abbreviated accounts – s246(5), s246(6) and Schedule 8A(extensive exemptions)	X	✓	X	X
Abbreviated accounts – s246A (very limited exemptions)	X	X	X	✓

4.3 There are relaxations of disclosure requirements which apply to small and medium-sized companies automatically even if they prepare full financial statements in accordance with Schedule 4. All small and medium-sized companies are exempt from the requirements of:

(1) paragraph 36A of Schedule 4 which requires financial statements to disclose whether they have been prepared in accordance with applicable accounting standards and give particulars of any material departures from those standards, including reasons – s246(2), s246A(2). Nevertheless, this should be regarded as good practice for all companies. Financial statements prepared in accordance with the FRSSE should state that they have been so prepared;

(2) s390B relating to the disclosure of remuneration received or receivable by the company's auditors and their associates in respect of non-audit work – SI 1991/2128(4); and

(3) Part VI of Schedule 7 relating to policy and practice on payment of creditors. A company required to make these disclosures would be a public company or a subsidiary of a public company and so a member of an ineligible group.

4.4 There are also requirements which apply in theory to small companies but are very unlikely to be encountered in practice. For example, Schedule 7 requires disclosures about employment of disabled persons for companies where the average number of employees exceeded 250 for the year. A company might qualify as small by reference to the turnover and asset criteria but still have more than 250 employees. But this is unlikely.

4.5 The exemptions from disclosure considered below in respect of

Modified directors' report and financial statements for small companies

modified financial statements are those to which a company is entitled when it has elected to prepare modified financial statements and disclosed that it has done so.

Modified directors' report and financial statements for small companies

4.6 Small companies are able to take advantage of certain exemptions from disclosure when preparing the financial statements and directors' report for circulation to members. If group financial statements are prepared for a small group they may also be prepared on the basis of these disclosure exemptions. Financial statements which take advantage of such exemptions are usually termed 'modified financial statements' or 'modified accounts' (not to be confused with 'abbreviated accounts' which are relevant for filing purposes only).

4.7 There are no corresponding exemptions from disclosure for medium-sized companies.

4.8 Example financial statements taking advantage of the small company exemptions are set out in Appendix 1 and a full disclosure checklist for such financial statements is in Appendix 4.

Modified financial statements

4.9 A small company may take advantage of all or any of the various disclosure exemptions available in s246(3) and through the adoption of Schedule 8 for its individual financial statements. Schedule 8 effectively combines various sub-headings which are required under the formats within Schedule 4 (applicable to companies not meeting the definition of a small company, or those which have elected not to follow Schedule 8) to the Act. For example:

(1) intangibles other than goodwill may be combined;
(2) tangible fixed assets, other than land and buildings, may be combined;
(3) amounts to be reflected as shares in group undertakings may be combined with those for participating interests, and similarly loans to group undertakings may be combined with loans to undertakings in which the company has a participating interest (in both fixed and current asset investments);
(4) raw materials, work in progress and finished goods may be combined as an item 'stocks' to be shown above 'payments on account';
(5) other debtors may be combined with called up share capital not paid, prepayments and accrued income;
(6) debenture loans, payments received on account, bills of exchange

The exemptions and modifications available

payable, other creditors including taxation and social security, and accruals and deferred income may be combined as 'other creditors' on the face of the balance sheet (although any convertible loans or creditors in respect of taxation and social security should be separately disclosed in a note to the financial statements);
(7) provisions for liabilities and charges (such as pensions and similar obligations) need not be sub-analysed between the different kinds of provision; and
(8) 'other reserves' need not be analysed into its components (such as the capital redemption reserve).

4.10 In addition, certain of the detail required to be given by way of note under Schedule 4 may be omitted. The following notes are among the more significant of those required under Schedule 4 but which are not required for small companies taking advantage of the exemptions in s246 and adopting Schedule 8.

Paragraph	Notes not required by s246(3) and Schedule 8
Schedule 4	
27(3)	Difference between book value and replacement cost of stock
40	Detail as to number, the price paid and period exercisable where there are contingent rights to the allotment of shares
41	Details of debentures issued in the year
44	The analysis of land and buildings between freehold and long and short leasehold
47	The separate disclosure of deferred taxation from other provisions for taxation
48(1)	Analysis of debts falling due in more than five years may be in aggregate rather than for each format heading
48(2)	Terms of repayment and interest rates for certain debts
48(4)(b)	The nature of security for secured debts
51(2)	Separate disclosure of the aggregate amount outstanding on loans provided by way of financial assistance for purchase of own shares
53(2)	Analysis of interest payable into bank loans and overdrafts, and other loans
54	Analysis of tax charge and details of circumstances affecting tax

Modified directors' report and financial statements for small companies

55	Segmental analysis of turnover (but must instead state the percentage of turnover attributable to geographical markets outside the UK, if any)
56	Particulars of staff (i.e., average numbers, analysis of wages, social security costs etc)
Schedule 5	
4	Financial year ends of subsidiary undertakings – s246(3)(b)(i)
Schedule 6	
1(1)	Directors' emoluments, long-term incentive scheme benefits and pension contributions may be shown as a single aggregate figure instead of three separate figures – s246(3)(a)
1(2)(b)	Number of directors exercising share options and receiving shares under long term incentive schemes – s246(3)(b)(ii)
2	Details of highest paid director's emoluments – s246(3)(b)(iii)
7	Excess retirement benefits of directors and past directors – s246(3)(b)(iv)

4.11 Where a small company has taken advantage of any of the exemptions in preparing individual financial statements it may also take advantage of all or any of the exemptions, as outlined above, in drawing up group financial statements – s248A. Whilst many companies take advantage of the exemption from preparing group financial statements some may elect to prepare them for the benefit of members. This is discussed further below.

4.12 Where the directors have taken advantage of the provisions available to small companies under s246(3), the balance sheet should contain above the signature required by s233 a statement that the financial statements have been prepared in accordance with the special provisions of Part VII of the Act relating to small companies – s246(8). Where the financial statements have also been prepared in accordance with the FRSSE, such a statement would typically take the following form:

'The financial statements have been prepared in accordance with the special provisions relating to small companies within Part VII of the Companies Act 1985 and with the Financial Reporting Standard for Smaller Entities (effective June 2002).'

4.13 Issues concerning whether modified financial statements can be true and fair are discussed in Chapter 9.

The exemptions and modifications available

Modified directors' report

4.14 Section 246(4) also allows small companies exemptions from certain of the disclosures normally required within the directors' report. The report for a small company need not give the following information which is otherwise required under s234 or Schedule 7:

(1) a fair review of the development of the business;
(2) the amount which the directors recommend should be paid as dividend;
(3) market value of land and buildings if substantially different from book value;
(4) details about employee involvement;
(5) particulars of important events affecting the company which have occurred since the end of the year;
(6) an indication of likely future developments in the business;
(7) an indication of the activities of the company in the field of research and development; and
(8) an indication of the existence of branches outside the UK.

4.15 Where the directors have taken advantage of the exemptions in s246(4), the directors' report should contain above the signature required by s234A a statement that the report has been prepared in accordance with the special provisions of Part VII of the Act relating to small companies – s246(8). Such a statement would typically take the following form:

> *'This report has been prepared in accordance with the special provisions relating to small companies within Part VII of the Companies Act 1985.'*

Group financial statements exemption

4.16 Section 248 provides that a parent company need not prepare group financial statements if the group headed by that company qualifies as a small or medium-sized group. The criteria for entitlement to this exemption are considered in Chapter 3.

4.17 As discussed in Chapter 9, the Act previously provided that where directors elected to take advantage of this exemption they were required to obtain a report from the auditors confirming that they were able to take advantage of the exemption. However, this requirement was removed for financial statements approved by directors after 2 February 1996 – SI 1996/189.

4.18 Section 230 provides an exemption whereby a company's individual profit and loss account may be omitted when group financial statements are prepared. However, it appears that this exemption may not be available when a small or medium-sized group prepares group financial statements voluntarily. This is because the exemption in s230 refers to circumstances where 'the company is required to prepare and does prepare group accounts in accordance with the Act' and it is not completely clear whether a company can be said to be 'required' to prepare group accounts simply because the directors have chosen not to take advantage of an exemption which is available. However, it is rare for such groups to prepare statutory group financial statements. Non-statutory group financial statements (even if audited) would not cause a problem.

Audit exemption

4.19 Section 249A exempts certain companies from the requirement for their annual financial statements to be audited. There are separate requirements for charitable companies involving a lower turnover threshold and in certain circumstances the ability to obtain a report from a reporting accountant rather than an audit report. The conditions applicable to charities are not discussed further in this book.

4.20 A company which is able to take advantage of the exemptions can, if directors so decide, still have its annual financial statements audited. Indeed, providers of finance may still insist on a company having its financial statements audited (or there may be terms in loan agreements to that effect) especially where the company has a limited track record or the lender is concerned about the financial position of the entity. There are also safeguards for shareholders who can require an audit in certain circumstances.

4.21 Whenever a company intends to take advantage of the exemptions it should make sure that there is nothing in its Articles that requires audited financial statements to be presented to the members. If there is, the Articles will need to be changed before the company can take advantage of the exemption.

4.22 A company which meets the relevant condition in relation to a financial year is exempt from the requirements of Part VII of the Act relating to the audit of financial statements in respect of that year. The exemption is from:

(1) the requirement in s235 that the company's auditors must report to the members on the annual financial statements which are to be placed before the company in general meeting (and s238 and s239 (right to receive or demand copies of financial statements and reports)

The exemptions and modifications available

have effect with the omission of references to the auditors' report);
(2) the requirement in s241 to lay a copy of the auditors' report before the company in general meeting; and
(3) the requirement in s242 to deliver a copy of the auditors' report to the Registrar.

Qualifying for the exemption

4.23 A company (other than a charity) will be exempt from audit in respect of a financial year if:

(1) it qualifies as a small company in relation to that year for s246 (i.e., it would be entitled to file abbreviated accounts);
(2) its turnover for that year is not more than £1m; and
(3) its balance sheet total (i.e., gross assets) for that year is not more than £1.4m – s249A(3).

4.24 As explained in Chapter 3, a company may be able to take advantage of the small company exemptions when its turnover or balance sheet total exceeds the size criteria in the year in question (e.g., because it met the criteria in the previous year). The turnover test for the audit exemption is additional to qualification as a small company for the purpose of s246 and is in relation to turnover in the year in question and only in relation to that year. Accordingly, it is not possible to reach a view on whether a company will be eligible to take advantage of this exemption until after the year is completed.

4.25 Section 249A(6) provides that where the company's financial year is not in fact a year, the maximum figure for turnover should be proportionately adjusted.

4.26 'Balance sheet total' for the purpose of s249A(3) is defined in the same way as in s247, i.e., the total of all assets before the deduction of liabilities rather than net assets. As with the turnover test above, this test is additional to qualification as a small company for the purposes of s246. The test is in relation to the balance sheet total at the end of the year in question and only in relation to that year. Again, it is therefore not possible to reach a view on whether a company will be eligible to take advantage of this exemption until after the year is completed.

4.27 Section 249B provides a list of cases where the exemption is not available. Some of these overlap with the circumstances which would prevent the company from qualifying as a small company. For example, the company cannot be a public company, one carrying out an insurance market activity, or a person carrying out a regulated activity under the

Financial Services and Markets Act 2000. However, a number of additional restrictions apply solely for the purposes of the audit exemption.

4.28 The most significant of these restrictions is the requirement that a company is not entitled to the exemption in respect of a financial year if, at any time within that financial year, it was a parent company or a subsidiary undertaking. However, there are two potentially significant exceptions to this general rule:

(1) a dormant parent company or subsidiary undertaking will not invalidate the exemption. For this purpose 'dormant' is as defined in s249AA; and
(2) a parent company or subsidiary undertaking will not invalidate the exemption provided that the entire group qualifies as a small group and meets the turnover and balance sheet criteria for the audit exemption. For this purpose the tests are applied in a similar way to those defining a small group in that they can be met on a net or gross basis. The group's aggregate turnover may be no more than £1m net (or £1.2m gross) and the group's aggregate balance sheet total may be not more than £1.4m net (or £1.68m gross).

4.29 It is important to appreciate that for this purpose the group is any group of which the reporting company is a member. It is not just the group headed by the reporting company. The effect of this is that the audit exemption is not available to a subsidiary of any group which exceeds the size tests. This was the deliberate intention of the legislation which was targeted at small owner-managed businesses rather than small subsidiaries within larger groups.

4.30 In addition, the exemption is not available if the company was at any time within the financial year:

(1) an appointed representative under s39 of the Financial Services and Markets Act 2000; or
(2) a special register body as defined in s117(1) of the Trade Union and Labour Relations (Consolidation) Act 1992 or an employers' association as defined in s122 of that Act.

Companies with an overseas parent

4.31 A UK company with an overseas parent will be able to take advantage of the exemption from audit if it complies with the above conditions. However, before 26 July 2000, a subsidiary of an overseas parent was ineligible for the exemption even if it met the above conditions, because an overseas parent company was not included in the definition of a parent company within the Act. Statutory Instrument 2000/1430, which

The exemptions and modifications available

applied from 26 July 2000, amended the wording of the exemption to include bodies corporate that are not incorporated under the UK Act.

Shareholders' objections

4.32 There are safeguards for shareholders. Any member or members holding not less than 10 per cent in nominal value of either:

(1) the aggregate of issued share capital; or
(2) one class of issued share capital,

can take steps to require the company to obtain an audit of its financial statements for that year – 249B. The members wishing to require an audit must deposit a notice in writing at the registered office of the company not later than one month before the end of the financial year concerned. This means that the members concerned may need to serve the notice before they know whether or not the company qualifies for, let alone intends to take advantage of, the exemption from audit.

4.33 If the company does not have share capital, these steps can be taken by not less than 10 per cent in number of the company's members.

Directors' statement

4.34 To qualify for the audit exemption the balance sheet must include a special statement by the directors – s249B(4). This must state that:

(1) in the year in question, the company was entitled to the exemption under subsections (1) or (2) of s249A or subsection (1) of s249AA;
(2) no member or members have deposited a notice in the specified manner requiring an audit; and
(3) the directors acknowledge their responsibility for ensuring that the company keeps accounting records which comply with s221 and for preparing financial statements which give a true and fair view of the state of the company's affairs as at the end of the financial year and of its profit or loss in that financial year, in accordance with s226 and which otherwise comply with the Act in relation to financial statements, so far as is applicable to the company.

4.35 This statement should appear in the balance sheet above the signature approving the financial statements on behalf of the board (required by s233). However, if the company has taken advantage of the small company exemptions outlined above, this statement should appear above the statement required by s246(8). Such a combined statement could be as follows:

Audit exemption

> **Directors' statement**
>
> In preparing these unaudited financial statements advantage has been taken of the exemption under section 249A (1) of the Companies Act 1985. Members have not required the company to obtain an audit under section 249B(2).
>
> Company law requires the directors to prepare financial statements for each financial year which give a true and fair view of the state of affairs of the company and of the profit or loss of the company for that period and which comply with the provisions of the Companies Act 1985. The directors are responsible for keeping proper accounting records which disclose with reasonable accuracy at any time the financial position of the company and to enable them to ensure that the financial statements comply with the Companies Act. They are also responsible for safeguarding the assets of the company and hence taking reasonable steps for the prevention and detection of fraud and other irregularities.
>
> The financial statements have been prepared in accordance with the special provisions relating to small companies within Part VII of the Companies Act 1985 and with the Financial Reporting Standard for Smaller Entities (effective June 2002).

4.36 The statement of directors' responsibilities contained in the second paragraph above should be made even if it is already made elsewhere (e.g., in the directors' report).

4.37 The form of statement illustrated above would appear in the financial statements circulated to shareholders (excluding the last paragraph if advantage had not been taken of the 'modified accounts' exemption). It is then necessary to consider whether the same statement should also appear in any abbreviated accounts filed with the Registrar of Companies (abbreviated accounts are discussed later in this chapter). While the interaction of the relevant sections of the Act is complex, it appears that the requirement for this statement to appear on the balance sheet also applies to the 'copy balance sheet' filed with the Registrar (i.e., the abbreviated accounts). This is certainly the interpretation reflected in guidance issued by Companies House.

4.38 However, the statement by the directors that they acknowledge their responsibility to prepare financial statements which give a true and fair view could easily lead to confusion when included in abbreviated accounts which are not required to, and will not, give a true and fair view. The following alternative statement would be appropriate for abbreviated accounts:

The exemptions and modifications available

> Directors' statement
>
> These abbreviated accounts are derived from unaudited financial statements. In preparing the unaudited financial statements advantage has been taken of the exemption under section 249A(1) of the Companies Act 1985. Members have not required the company to obtain an audit under section 249B(2).
>
> Company law requires the directors to prepare financial statements for each financial year which give a true and fair view of the state of affairs of the company and of the profit or loss of the company for that period and which comply with the provisions of the Companies Act 1985. The directors are responsible for keeping proper accounting records which disclose with reasonable accuracy at any time the financial position of the company and to enable them to ensure that the financial statements comply with the Companies Act. They are also responsible for safeguarding the assets of the company and hence taking reasonable steps for the prevention and detection of fraud and other irregularities.
>
> The abbreviated accounts have been prepared in accordance with the special provisions relating to small companies within Part VII of the Companies Act 1985.

4.39 In addition to amending the opening paragraph to make a distinction between the unaudited financial statements and the abbreviated accounts, the reference to the FRSSE has also been removed as the abbreviated accounts will not have been prepared in accordance with the FRSSE. However, as discussed in paragraph 4.43 below, it would be usual to make reference to the FRSSE in the accounting policy notes.

Abbreviated accounts

4.40 Abbreviated accounts are accounts prepared by either small or medium-sized companies for filing at Companies House. Such accounts are permitted to contain less information than those produced for shareholders. However, full or modified financial statements still need to be prepared for circulation to shareholders.

4.41 The ability to prepare modified group financial statements taking advantage of Schedule 8 was introduced in 1997 and such financial statements can be sent to members and filed with the Registrar of Companies. However, there is no facility to file abbreviated group accounts taking advantage of Schedule 8A. If an eligible group does not take advantage of the exemption from preparing group financial statements, it must deliver to the Registrar the full or modified group financial statements

Abbreviated accounts

which it prepares for the members. Therefore, practice is usually to prepare non-statutory group financial statements for private circulation in addition to the statutory company-only modified financial statements and company-only abbreviated accounts for filing.

4.42 It is a requirement of the Act that abbreviated accounts should contain, in a prominent position on the balance sheet, above the signature required by s233, a statement that they have been prepared in accordance with the special provisions of Part VII of the Act relating to small companies. This requirement is identical to that in respect of modified financial statements and so the statement may be worded in an identical way to that illustrated above. However, it will not refer to the accounts having been prepared in accordance with the FRSSE because the abbreviated accounts will not be prepared in accordance with that standard even if they are derived from modified financial statements which have taken advantage of the FRSSE. The statement will therefore usually be as follows:

'The abbreviated accounts have been prepared in accordance with the special provisions relating to small companies within Part VII of the Companies Act 1985.'

4.43 Although abbreviated accounts for a small company will not be prepared 'in accordance with the FRSSE' it is thought to be useful for users to know that they are an abbreviated version of financial statements prepared in accordance with that standard. Although most of the disclosures required by the FRSSE will be omitted from the abbreviated accounts, users may be interested to know that assets, liabilities, income and expenses have been measured in accordance with the requirements of the FRSSE. Also, the abbreviated accounts are required by Schedule 8A to disclose the accounting policies adopted and in this context it is logical to include reference to the FRSSE. Accordingly, in a footnote to paragraph 2.3 of the FRSSE the ASB comments that if abbreviated accounts are prepared, the statement referring to the FRSSE should be included with the note of accounting policies so that it is reproduced in the abbreviated accounts. This footnote was added first in FRSSE 2000.

4.44 The required minimum content of abbreviated accounts will depend on whether the company is small or medium-sized.

Small companies

4.45 If the company is a small company then the exemptions relating to small companies within s246(5) and Schedule 8A permit it to file abbreviated accounts comprising only an abbreviated version of its balance sheet and certain specified notes. The abbreviated accounts for a small

The exemptions and modifications available

company therefore do not need to contain a directors' report, a profit and loss account or disclose the auditors' remuneration.

4.46 The abbreviated balance sheet, indicating on the face the name and signature of the director signing the accounts on behalf of the Board, needs to show only those items to which a letter or Roman numeral is assigned in the formats within Schedule 8. The following matters must be disclosed on the face of the balance sheet or in an accompanying note:

(1) the aggregate amount of debtors due after more than one year; and
(2) where Format 2 has been used, the aggregate amount of creditors due within one year and the aggregate amounts of creditors due after more than one year (this information is already disclosed in Format 1).

4.47 Of the detailed information required by Schedule 8, Schedule 5 and Schedule 6, only the following need be disclosed.

Paragraph	Required Disclosure
Schedule 8	
36	Accounting policies
38	Share capital
39	Particulars of allotments
40	Fixed assets (but only in so far as it relates to those items that do not have Arabic numerals)
44(1) and (2)	Particulars of debts and the amount secured (but not the nature of security given)
51(1)	Basis of conversion of foreign currency
51(2)	Corresponding amounts for previous financial year
Schedule 5 4 6	All information *except*: Financial years of subsidiary undertakings Shares and debentures of the company held by subsidiary undertakings
Schedule 6	Part II Loans, quasi-loans and other dealings in favour of directors Part III Transactions, arrangements and agreements with officers other than directors (But not Part I Directors' emoluments, pension contributions and compensation for loss of office.)

4.48 A cash flow statement is not a Companies Act disclosure requirement but a requirement of an accounting standard (FRS1), applicable only to financial statements intended to show a true and fair view. Since abbreviated accounts do not purport to show a true and fair view, a cash flow statement may be omitted. Moreover, FRS1 specifically exempts from its requirements any company that would be eligible to file abbreviated accounts as a small company. Somewhat optimistically the FRSSE has included the suggestion that those applying the FRSSE should present a cash flow statement by way of voluntary disclosure. Where such a statement has been included in the financial statements for shareholders it may be omitted from the abbreviated accounts sent to the Registrar.

4.49 An example set of abbreviated accounts for a small company is set out in Appendix 2.

Medium-sized companies

4.50 The reductions in the level of disclosure for the abbreviated accounts of a medium-sized company, available under s246A, are far more limited than those applicable to small companies. A medium-sized company may file abbreviated accounts comprising a full (that is, unmodified) balance sheet, all notes to the accounts, the directors' report and an abbreviated version of its profit and loss account. The profit and loss account abbreviations available are as follows:

(1) the figures for turnover and cost of sales may be combined into one figure for gross profit or loss (items 1, 2, 3 and 6 in Format 1, and items 1 to 5 in Format 2 within Schedule 8); and
(2) the analysis of turnover by markets and by classes of business may be omitted.

4.51 Paragraph **4.48** above notes that the abbreviated accounts for a small company may omit the cash flow statement even if it is voluntarily included in the financial statements sent to shareholders. The abbreviated accounts will also omit almost all of the disclosures required by accounting standards because it is clear that the accounts do not need to give a true and fair view. Unfortunately the position is not so clear in the case of abbreviated accounts for a medium-sized company.

4.52 For small companies, the Act specifies positively what must be included in the abbreviated accounts and in the absence of a requirement for a true and fair view this list is taken to be comprehensive. But for a medium-sized company the content of the abbreviated accounts is specified in terms of what may be omitted by comparison with the full financial statements sent to shareholders. Some argue that this drafting means that the only difference between the full financial statements and the abbreviated accounts should be the matters specified in paragraph **4.50** above.

The exemptions and modifications available

4.53 However, there is no requirement for the abbreviated accounts to show a true and fair view as confirmed by legal advice which is referred to in APB Bulletin 1997 No 1. Accordingly, such accounts need not include disclosures which are not required by the Act and so may omit disclosures which are voluntary or required only by accounting standards. Abbreviated accounts for a medium-sized company may therefore omit the cash flow statement. More contentiously, it appears that they could omit related party disclosures required by FRS8. However, on this latter point it must be remembered that the statutory disclosure requirements of Parts II and III of Schedule 6 concerning loans and other transactions with directors and officers apply to the abbreviated accounts.

Chapter five

Policies and profit and loss account matters

Introduction

5.1 The guidance within the Statement of Standard Accounting Practice of FRSSE 2002 is organised into discrete sections as follows.

(1) Scope
(2) General
(3) Profit and loss account
(4) Statement of total recognised gains and losses
(5) Fixed assets and goodwill
(6) Leases
(7) [Withdrawn]
(8) Current assets
(9) Taxation
(10) Retirement benefits
(11) Provisions, contingent liabilities and contingent assets
(12) Capital instruments
(13) Foreign currency translation
(14) Post balance sheet events
(15) Related party disclosures
(16) Consolidated financial statements
(17) Date from which effective and transitional arrangements
(18) Withdrawal of the FRSSE (effective March 2000)

This format was designed to facilitate revisions. Sections may be revised or withdrawn and others left unamended. For example, section 7 on intangible assets was withdrawn in the March 1999 revision of the FRSSE and its content amalgamated into the section on fixed assets.

5.2 The Standard is set out in a logical order with matters of general application, the profit and loss account and the statement of total recognised gains and losses being considered first. Thereafter topics are tackled in the order in which they generally appear in a vertical balance sheet.

Unincorporated entities

5.3 A perennial issue for standard setters in the UK is that while the standards apply to all financial statements intended to give a true and fair view of the financial position and results of all entities, a large proportion of entities complying with accounting standards also comply with detailed accounting rules in company law while others, the unincorporated entities, are not subject to that legal regime. To ensure that the accounting standards make sense for all entities, rules are often introduced which overlap with those in company law.

5.4 Dealing with unincorporated entities therefore presented something of a challenge to the authors of the FRSSE. Should the FRSSE repeat accounting rules to be found in company law? Should unincorporated entities be ignored completely on the grounds that the number of sole traders, partnerships and other unincorporated entities preparing 'true and fair' financial statements is relatively small? What has been followed is a middle course. Paragraph 1.1(b) of the FRSSE introduces a new piece of guidance for unincorporated entities. They:

> 'should have regard to the accounting principles, presentation and disclosure requirements in companies legislation (or other equivalent legislation) that, taking into account the FRSSE, are necessary to present a true and fair view'.

5.5 One effect of this sentence is that unincorporated entities, wishing to prepare true and fair view financial statements, should adopt, to the extent that is applicable to them, one of the formats in company law for the profit and loss account and balance sheet with appropriate additional note disclosure. Some items will clearly be not applicable. For example, in a partnership's financial statements there will be no share capital but there should be information on the partners' accounts. Similarly, having regard to the company law formats would mean that assets would generally be ordered from the least liquid to the most liquid, in other words from intangible assets through to cash. A structure which added property and debtors together and motor cars and investments together would fall foul of the above requirement. However, minor rearrangements such as placing tangible fixed assets before intangible fixed assets would probably not affect the ability of those financial statements to give a true and fair view. However, if the matter is minor, often the best advice is to follow the requirements and avoid the question being raised.

5.6 The reference to 'other equivalent legislation' is designed for unincorporated charities. They will naturally look to the Charities Act for guidance, rather than company law.

A true and fair view

5.7 Experience suggests that the number of unincorporated entities wishing to prepare true and fair financial statements is relatively small compared to the number of companies who are required to do so. Just short of a million companies are entitled to adopt the FRSSE. Therefore, the above device of inserting one sentence to require unincorporated entities to have regard to matters of accounting principles, presentation and disclosure in company law is surely an example of the tail not wagging the accounting standards dog. In future editions of the FRSSE, company law and accounting standards requirements may become integrated into the 'one-stop shop'. This development awaits the enactment of the Company Law Review.

A true and fair view

5.8 Section 2 of the FRSSE should be the most powerful in the document. It contains four elements:

(1) the requirement to present a true and fair view;
(2) that regard should be had to the substance of any arrangement or transaction, or series of such, into which the entity has entered;
(3) to do so, consideration should be given as to whether new assets or liabilities have arisen or existing ones have been changed; and
(4) where applying the provisions of the FRSSE would be insufficient to give a true and fair view, then further explanation should be given in the notes to the financial statements.

5.9 The second and third elements are designed to bring the general requirements of FRS5 *Reporting the substance of transactions* into the FRSSE. Inspired by FRS5, accountants no longer talk of something being sold. The former asset is now derecognised because there are no longer rights or other access to future economic benefits controlled by the entity as a result of past transactions or events. The latter is unlikely to win a Plain English prize and fortunately the full glories of FRS5 are not repeated in the FRSSE. If the rules can be communicated more directly to users of the FRSSE, then that is likely to lead to the document being easier to follow, more consistent accounting and perhaps the financial statements being more comprehensive to the readers. Meanwhile, there is of course a valid reason for including this extra guidance in Section 2. It reinforces the need to have regard to the substance of transactions and supports the guidance on consignment stock and debt factoring in Section 8 of the FRSSE.

5.10 The fourth element, paragraph 5.8(4) above, is potentially very useful. It is extremely unlikely that accounting standards can give specific guidance on all transactions or arrangements likely to occur in practice.

Policies and profit and loss account matters

Furthermore, it is often recognised that they should not try to do so. Accounting standards should be written so that they deal with perhaps 80 per cent of cases, leaving those at the margins to be dealt with sensibly, having regard to generally accepted accounting principles and the overriding requirement to give a true and fair view. In drafting the FRSSE, which is essentially a précis of existing accounting requirements, some existing requirements were dropped or otherwise subsumed. Therefore, it is recognised that the fourth point will be useful in ensuring adequate explanation is given of the transactions or arrangements concerned and the accounting treatment adopted.

Relationship with other accounting standards

5.11 The FRSSE's Preface makes clear that reporting entities using the FRSSE are exempt from other accounting standards and UITF Abstracts, unless they are preparing consolidated financial statements. It continues:

'Financial statements will generally be prepared using accepted practice and, accordingly, for transactions or events not dealt with in the FRSSE, smaller entities should have regard to other accounting standards and UITF Abstracts, not as mandatory documents, but as a means of establishing current practice.'

5.12 The relationship with other accounting standards was one of the confused and contentious areas in the development of the FRSSE. It is therefore useful to consider the background.

5.13 Some commentators on the *Designed to Fit* paper suggested that, in the absence of guidance on particular transactions in the FRSSE, regard should be had to any or all guidance provided in the accounting standards applying to larger entities. This approach was presumably proposed to ensure that there would be identical accounting between larger and smaller entities. In particular, there would not be divergences of practice between the way a transaction was accounted for in a company with a turnover of £2.5m compared to a similar transaction in a company with a turnover of £3m, the former qualifying as a small company and the latter not.

5.14 Such cases at the margins are always difficult to deal with. But, they are not new. For the FRSSE, it mirrors the different treatments available in company law. For example, the company with the lower turnover can file abbreviated accounts, which are significantly less detailed than the financial statements for the shareholders. For the company with the larger turnover, which qualifies as a medium-sized company, the exemptions available in the filed accounts are very few. Company law also gives significant exemptions in respect of the shareholders' financial statements for small companies.

Relationship with other accounting standards

5.15 The Working Party and the ASB rejected the approach of requiring all other SSAPs, FRSs and UITF Abstracts to be followed where these provide guidance on transactions not covered in the FRSSE. If that route had been taken, then the FRSSE would not have achieved its purpose of reducing the burden on small companies. The burden would in fact have been increased as such companies would have had to comply with the FRSSE and then check all other authoritative accounting guidance. However, such guidance cannot be completely ignored. The courts, if asked to determine whether financial statements give a true and fair view, will presumably wish to know that the accounting practices adopted were acceptable. Thus, in the absence of specific guidance in the FRSSE, preparers and auditors should consider what is established and accepted practice. Hence the words in the Preface were included.

5.16 In using the statement in the FRSSE's Preface it is important to recognise that it is a two part entreaty. The first point is to establish accepted practice. As part of that process regard should be had, secondly, to other authoritative accounting statements. Paragraph 28 of Appendix IV to the FRSSE usefully recognises that over time Little GAAP may diverge from Big GAAP as new rules are established applying to larger entities. As both sectors applied essentially the same set of accounting rules on implementation of the FRSSE, what was accepted practice in one sector became the same in the other. An oft-quoted example of a divergence which may appear in the future is in accounting for financial instruments where the current proposal of marking to market fixed interest instruments might be considered onerous and unnecessary in respect of smaller entities. Another area in which there may be some divergence at present is on accounting for share options. UITF Abstract 17 provides that under certain circumstances a charge should be made to the profit and loss account when at grant date the exercise price of an option is less than the share value at that date. For listed companies, establishing share value at grant date is easy: there is a market in shares. For smaller (and indeed other private) companies, it is very difficult, simply because shares are rarely traded. Accordingly, instead of trying to follow slavishly UITF 17 accounting, simple disclosure of these share option arrangements may be viewed as a sensible approach.

5.17 Where the current tensions are likely to be is in the entreaty to consider accepted practice and thus other authoritative accounting statements, which is not limited to matters of accounting treatment and could be said also to apply to disclosure. However such an approach would run contrary to much of what the FRSSE is seeking to achieve, namely a significant reduction in the disclosure and compliance burden on smaller

Policies and profit and loss account matters

entities. It therefore is reasonable to presume that there should not be enthusiastic use of the above entreaty solely on disclosure matters. The key consideration should be paragraph 2.2 of the FRSSE that adequate explanation is given in the notes to the financial statements of transactions or arrangements on which specific guidance is not given in the FRSSE.

Accounting principles and policies

5.18   The financial statements should state that:

'they have been prepared in accordance with the Financial Reporting Standard for Smaller Entities (effective June 2002)'.

This statement may be included in the accounting policies note or, where the company is taking advantage of the exemptions for small companies in legislation, as part of the statement required to be given on the balance sheet. As discussed in Chapter 4, where abbreviated accounts are prepared, the ASB has recommended that the statement should be included with the note of accounting policies so that it is reproduced in the abbreviated accounts.

5.19   Individual accounting standards have usually contained a requirement that the reporting entity sets out its accounting policy on the topic which is the subject of the individual standard. This is in addition to FRS18 *Accounting policies,* which contains the general rule that the accounting policies that are material in the context of the financial statements should be disclosed. In the past there has been double counting on accounting policies, leading to disclosure of policies on items which are not necessarily material to the financial statements in question or even in some cases visible. Therefore, to encourage preparers to focus on the major accounting policies, the FRSSE focuses on the general requirement in FRS18 and has dropped all the detailed requirements on individual topics from the other accounting standards.

5.20   The publication of FRS18 has created a number of changes in FRSSE 2002, including:

(1)   a reference to estimation techniques for the first time;
(2)   an explicit requirement to review regularly accounting policies so that they remain the most appropriate; and
(3)   a need for directors to consider going concern.

Estimation techniques take almost a page to explain in the FRSSE's 'Definitions' section. In short, they are a subset of accounting policies and

Reporting financial performance

are methods used by entities to estimate monetary amounts. Methods used to calculate the amount of overheads in work in progress are estimation techniques. If an entity varies its methodology to include a different balance of overheads as attributable to work in progress, this is a change in an estimation technique. In most cases, such changes have little impact on reported results. They are mere refinements. But, if they have a material impact, they should be disclosed. FRSSE 2002, like FRS18, requires a description of such a material change and, where practicable, the amount by which the results for the current year have changed.

5.21 The need to review regularly accounting policies should be a statement of the obvious to all good accountants. However, it is helpful to have this requirement in 'black and white' just in case others argue 'but it's always been good enough for us in the past'. The ASB, however, wishes to guard against companies chopping and changing their policies with alarming frequency. The impact of changes on comparability of financial statements over the years must be considered. As before, prior periods have to be amended for changes in policy, changes have to be explained and justified, and the impact on current and prior periods disclosed.

5.22 The requirements for directors to consider whether there are any significant doubts over going concern and to disclose whether they have assessed a period of less than one year from the date of approval of the financial statements are new in FRSSE 2002. Their inclusion makes accounting rules consistent with matters for auditors in the Auditing Standard, SAS 130.

5.23 The final policy topic is perhaps one of the most cherished by British accountants, namely the ability to override a specific provision of company law or an accounting standard to ensure that a true and fair view is given in the financial statements. If the override is used, full and detailed disclosures are required, not only in the period in which the override is first used but also in subsequent financial statements if the departure continues.

Reporting financial performance

5.24 FRS3 *Reporting financial performance* was made mandatory in respect of financial statements relating to accounting periods ending on or after 22 June 1993. The Standard aimed to highlight a range of important components of financial performance and therefore required the profit and loss account to contain information on the activities of reporting entities analysed among:

- continuing;

Policies and profit and loss account matters

- discontinued; and
- acquisition activities.

5.25 FRS3 thus requires a layered format to be used for the profit and loss account such that the results of a company or group are analysed between continuing and discontinued operations down to the level of operating profit. The analysis of turnover and operating profit, at least, are required to be shown on the face of the profit and loss account. The analysis of the other statutory profit and loss account format items must be given in the notes if they are not disclosed on the face of the profit and loss account.

5.26 The FRSSE continues to apply many of the features of FRS3. However, the FRSSE does not require the same level of analysis or the tiered approach to the profit and loss account as is required under FRS3. There is no requirement to analyse the profit and loss account between continuing and discontinued activities, nor do the results relating to the acquisition of subsidiaries or separate businesses need to be separately disclosed, either on the face of the profit or loss account or in the notes to the financial statements, other than as required under the Companies Act.

5.27 One of the significant impacts of FRS3 has been the virtual abolition of the use of extraordinary items in UK reporting. Instead the focus of attention has moved to whether or not certain items meet the definitions within paragraph 20 of FRS3 and so be regarded as exceptional items which fall below the operating profit line.

5.28 The conditions for regarding an item as a non-operating profit exceptional is restricted in the FRSSE to the same items as in paragraph 20 of FRS3, namely:

(1) profits or losses on the sale or termination of an operation;
(2) costs of a fundamental reorganisation or restructuring having a material effect on the nature and focus of the reporting entity's operations; and
(3) profits or losses on the disposal of fixed assets.

5.29 The positioning of such exceptional items below operating profit is more important for listed companies than for small ones. But this is not to say that a measure of sustainable earnings is not an important feature for entities of any size. One of the basic methods of valuing a business is on the basis of its projected stream of anticipated future income. This can still be achieved since the FRSSE continues to recognise that those matters which are exceptional or outside the company's normal operating activities should be separately and clearly disclosed either on the face of the profit and loss account or in the notes to the financial statements.

Statement of total recognised gains and losses

5.30   FRS3 made it clear that the profit to be reported in the profit and loss account on a disposal of a revalued asset should be calculated as the difference between proceeds and net book value rather than historical cost. The method of calculating the profit on the disposal of a fixed asset is the same under the FRSSE as currently required in FRS3.

5.31   Paragraph 3.4 of the FRSSE deals with the accounting treatment for a profit or loss on disposal of an asset and purchased goodwill written off to reserves on previously acquired businesses now being sold or terminated. Such goodwill has to be round-tripped through the profit and loss account, following the requirements of FRS10 *Goodwill and intangible assets*. This must be a case of another hump on the FRSSE camel. While it cannot be denied that small companies dispose of such businesses from time to time, it is difficult to imagine that this is a routine transaction reflected in 80 per cent or 90 per cent of financial statements of such companies. It is a matter which could have been handled as and when it arose in cases where the goodwill was material.

5.32   In contrast to the above point, paragraph 3.5 of the FRSSE on extraordinary items is succinct and reflects that such an event would not arise in practice.

Statement of total recognised gains and losses

5.33   The FRSSE requires a statement of total recognised gains and losses (STRGL) to be presented, with the same prominence as the profit and loss account, showing the total recognised gains and losses and its components. These components should be the gains and losses that are recognised in a period in so far as they are attributed to shareholders.

5.34   Where the only recognised gain or loss in the year is as a result of the items in the profit and loss account the big change from FRS3 is that no additional sentence or statement need be made. For companies which have not revalued assets during the year, a separate gains statement has generally not been needed and a statement to the effect that there is no statement has added nothing to the financial statements.

5.35   Given that small companies generally do not revalue fixed assets or record other gains or losses not recognised in the profit and loss account, a strong case could be put forward for dropping the requirement for a separate statement of total recognised gains and losses in the FRSSE. On drafting of the FRSSE the Working Party did not propose this to the ASB, although it did drop FRS3's requirements to give:

Policies and profit and loss account matters

- a note of historical cost profits and losses; and
- a reconciliation of movements in shareholders' funds.

5.36 Perhaps the reasons for retaining the STRGL are partly political. The STRGL is one of the four primary financial statements as currently reported by UK companies. However, the future of the STRGL is uncertain. The ASB issued a Discussion Paper *Reporting financial performance: proposals for change* in June 1999 following a Position Paper developed by the G4+1 group, an international body of standard setters. This was followed by FRED22 in December 2000. These papers propose that a single performance statement should replace the profit and loss account and the STRGL, effectively combining them in one statement.

Discounting

5.37 The Exposure Draft of the second revision of the FRSSE published in July 1999 included a general discussion on discounting. It was proposed that, rather than dealing with discounting on a piecemeal basis, the effect of discounting future cash flows should be taken into account when measuring the amounts to be recorded as long-term assets or liabilities. However, this more general requirement to apply discounting where its impact would be particularly significant was opposed by respondents commenting on the Exposure Draft. This provision has therefore not been included in the third version of the FRSSE published in December 1999.

5.38 However, discounting is required in relation to provisions when the effect would be material. It is also permitted in respect of deferred tax balances. Thus the FRSSE is consistent with Big GAAP. But the ASB has not ruled out discounting of long-term assets. Within Appendix IV of the FRSSE on development of FRSSE 2000, it was noted that preparers may apply discounting techniques in a wider context if the financial statements would otherwise fail to show a true and fair view. In short, discounting should be adopted where necessary to give a true and fair view.

Chapter six

Assets

Introduction

6.1 Chapter 5 noted that the FRSSE is now organised into 18 discrete sections in its Statement of Standard Accounting Practice. Chapter 5 covered sections 1 to 4 of the FRSSE discussing general matters and those associated with the profit and loss account and the statement of total recognised gains and losses. This chapter discusses the FRSSE's next three sections which deal with assets.

Fixed assets and goodwill

6.2 Section 5 of the FRSSE on fixed assets and goodwill discusses seven topics, the key requirements of which are discussed below.

Research and development

6.3 While many smaller entities do not undertake research and development (R&D) activities, for those that do, the accounting is often a contentious matter. The major provisions of SSAP13 *Accounting for research and development* have therefore been incorporated in the FRSSE. Following a policy of capitalisation means that the immediate write-offs are avoided, thus protecting realised and distributable profits in early years of new projects. The key requirements in the FRSSE on accounting for research and development are:

- to write off pure and applied research expenditure as incurred;
- to permit the capitalisation of the cost of development expenditure and amortise over the useful life; and
- otherwise to write off development expenditure as incurred.

6.4 Development expenditure may be deferred to the extent that its recovery can be regarded as assured. This assurance is measured by reference to five criteria, for example there must be a clearly defined project with separately identifiable expenditure and the technical feasibility of the

Assets

project should be reasonably certain. These criteria requirements are discussed in more detail in paragraph 5.3 of the FRSSE.

6.5 The present relief in SSAP13 from the requirement to disclose the amounts charged to profit and loss account, which is available to companies meeting the criteria for medium-sized companies in which the financial thresholds are multiplied by a factor of 10, is retained for small entities as defined in the FRSSE. Specific disclosures are required only where the capitalisation route is adopted. That said, for any company in which R&D activities are significant, an accounting policy may be needed and some discussion in the directors' report may be advisable.

Other intangible assets and goodwill

6.6 The guidance on other intangible assets and goodwill has been taken from FRS10 *Goodwill and intangible assets* which became effective for accounting periods ending on or after 23 December 1998. The FRSSE's provisions on goodwill are an example of an area in which dealing with groups has meant potentially more complexity within the document. The key requirements in the FRSSE are:

- positive purchased goodwill should be capitalised and amortised over its useful economic life, subject to a maximum of 20 years;
- purchased intangibles should be capitalised and amortised over their useful economic lives, subject to a maximum of 20 years;
- internally generated goodwill and intangibles should not be capitalised;
- goodwill and intangibles should not be revalued; and
- negative goodwill should be capitalised up to the fair value of the non-monetary assets acquired and released over the lives of those assets. Any excess negative goodwill should be recognised over the period expected to benefit from it.

6.7 Where an intangible asset is acquired as part of the acquisition of an unincorporated business, it should be recognised separately only if its value can be measured reliably. Otherwise the intangible asset will be accounted for as part of the goodwill.

6.8 The useful economic life of both goodwill and intangible assets should be reviewed at the end of each reporting period. Where a change is necessary the carrying value at the date of change should be amortised over the revised remaining useful life.

6.9 One significant simplification between the FRSSE and FRS10 is that the FRSSE has set a maximum of 20 years for the length of the useful economic life of goodwill and intangible assets. This contrasts with FRS10, which only presumes a maximum life of 20 years but then requires annual impairment testing where asset lives are longer. If the FRS10 rules had been

Fixed assets and goodwill

introduced, then many more words would have been needed in the FRSSE to explain impairment testing. The ASB has wisely decided that since goodwill and intangibles with lives in excess of 20 years in small companies' reporting are rare the additional complexities are unnecessary. But if such a rare occasion arises in which longer or indefinite life is justified, then the override provisions can be used.

6.10 If a small company is preparing group financial statements, then it must comply in the consolidation with FRS10. Transitional provisions apply in respect of consolidation goodwill on implementation of the previous version of the FRSSE. This permits smaller entities to leave previously written off goodwill against reserves in place (i.e., there is no requirement to capitalise it as an asset to be consistent with the new requirements). Although FRS10 requires that goodwill which remains eliminated against reserves should be separately disclosed, the FRSSE has no similar requirement.

Tangible fixed assets

6.11 The section on accounting for tangible fixed assets is consistent with FRS15 *Tangible fixed assets*, but simplifies the Standard considerably to be more appropriate to smaller entities. The key requirements are:

- to recognise tangible fixed assets at cost;
- to write down tangible fixed assets to their recoverable amount if necessary;
- to capitalise only directly attributable costs, including finance costs;
- generally to charge subsequent expenditure to the profit and loss account as incurred;
- to revalue assets held at valuation at least every five years;
- to recognise revaluation losses in the STRGL if caused by changes in market price, otherwise to charge them in the profit and loss account; and
- to recognise revaluation gains in the STRGL unless reversing a loss previously charged to the profit and loss account.

6.12 The rules on initial measurement largely set out the requirements in FRS15. The FRSSE includes the requirement that during extended periods in which there is no active development, capitalisation of costs should be suspended.

> For example, if a house building company adds to its landbank of sites available for future development, then finance costs cannot be capitalised in respect of the landbank. It is only when the company has commenced the process of building houses on that site that capitalisation of finance costs can commence.

Assets

6.13 Capitalisation of costs must cease when substantially all the activities that are necessary to get the asset ready for use are complete, even if the asset has not yet been brought into use.

6.14 Subsequent expenditure should be capitalised only where it improves the condition of the asset beyond its previously assessed standard of performance, with the amount being recognised as an addition to the fixed asset cost. Such expenditure will include, for example, modifications to increase the economic life, capacity or quality of the output of the fixed asset.

6.15 The implementation of FRS12 *Provisions, contingent liabilities and contingent assets* has stopped the practice of providing for repairs of fixed assets. Instead, the assets have to be depreciated over the useful economic lives of their component parts, with repairs being capitalised and depreciated over the life of the new component, probably until the next routine maintenance. The FRSSE includes the principles of FRS12. Therefore, subsequent expenditure incurred to replace a component part should be capitalised. It is perhaps regrettable that these somewhat contrived rules on repairs (or subsequent expenditure as it is known) had to be included in the FRSSE. The old 'repairs' provision being built up over time was understandable and identifiable to users. The FRS12 style rules do not change the profit and loss account impact but somewhat conceal the balance sheet numbers. Small companies will need to consider whether the components approach must be adopted in their business where appropriate, or whether the pattern of their repairs bill is such that they can take the 'hit' as the repairs are incurred.

6.16 Tangible fixed assets may be carried at valuation rather than cost. Where such a policy is adopted the valuation should be carried out by an experienced valuer at least every five years. Unlike the provisions in FRS15, this valuer does not have to be external to the company but he or she should have recognised and relevant recent professional experience and knowledge of the market. Thus estate agents may be able to value their own premises. But other directors are unlikely to have the necessary skills to be able to value their properties.

6.17 In the intervening four-year period a valuation is only required where it is likely that there has been a material change in value. This poses the 'chicken and egg' problem. Interim valuation is needed if there has been a change in value, but unless a valuation is carried out, how is it known whether there has been a change in value? In practice, the answer must be that if the directors are in doubt regarding an asset value they should obtain another valuation.

Fixed assets and goodwill

6.18 A policy of revaluation must be applied to a 'class' of assets rather than individual assets. A class of assets can be a smaller group than the Companies Act headings of:
- land and buildings; and
- plant and machinery.

6.19 A 'class' of tangible fixed assets is defined as being separable because they are similar in nature, function or use in the business. The classes adopted should however be appropriate to the business concerned.

6.20 It is important that the classes selected are not *too* narrow. It would be acceptable to distinguish between different types of property, for example between hotels and industrial properties. It is probably acceptable to revalue a general office property but not to revalue a nearby workshop. On the other hand, valuing one office property in one part of the UK and leaving another at cost would be unacceptable.

6.21 Transitional arrangements were introduced in the 2000 edition of the FRSSE for previously revalued tangible fixed assets. The transitional provisions allow two choices where an entity decides not to adopt a policy of revaluation but historically carries some of its tangible fixed assets at valuation. The two choices are to:

(1) retain the current book values. Where this option is adopted the entity must disclose:
- that the transitional provisions have been applied;
- that the valuation has not been updated; and
- the date of the last revaluation; or

(2) restate the carrying value of the previously revalued tangible fixed asset to depreciated historical cost. The restatement will be accounted for as a change in accounting policy.

Depreciation

6.22 The rules on depreciation have been taken from FRS15 and replace the SSAP12 based rules that were in the first two editions of the FRSSE. The key requirements are:
- tangible fixed assets should be depreciated;
- the depreciation method should reflect as fairly as possible the pattern in which the asset's economic benefits are consumed; and
- components depreciation should be applied where the tangible fixed asset comprises two or more major components with substantially different useful economic lives.

6.23 The depreciation method and rate should be disclosed separately for

Assets

land and buildings and other tangible fixed assets. The useful economic lives and residual values should be reviewed regularly. Where there is a change in the useful economic life on an asset, the carrying value of the asset should be depreciated over the remaining useful economic life. This is consistent with the rules on goodwill and intangible assets.

> For example, a piece of machinery costing £1m has a useful economic life of ten years. At the end of six years its carrying amount in the financial statements is £400,000. A review of its useful economic life has highlighted that the machinery only has a remaining life of two years before it will need to be replaced. The annual depreciation for the remaining two years will be £200,000p.a. (£400,000 / 2 years).

Write-downs to recoverable amount

6.24 All fixed assets, both tangible and intangible, and goodwill should be recorded at no more than their recoverable amount. Recoverable value is defined as the higher of that which can be obtained from selling the asset or continuing to use the asset in the business (value in use). Any write-downs necessary to reflect a decrease in recoverable amount should be charged to the profit and loss account. However, a loss resulting from changing market prices that represents a reversal of a revaluation gain in respect of a revalued asset should be recognised in the STRGL instead.

6.25 If the recoverable amount of a fixed asset subsequently increases, as a result of a change in economic conditions or the expected use of the asset, then the carrying amount should be written back to the lower of recoverable amount and original depreciated value. Any such write back may take place in respect of tangible fixed assets. Where the increase is in respect of goodwill or intangible assets the write back may only take place if the increase has arisen from a subsequent external event which has reversed the original event in a way that was not originally foreseen. Write backs are expected to be rare events.

Website development costs

6.26 The FRSSE does not include specific guidance on accounting for website development costs as this was seen as an area where the UITF Abstract 29 *Website development costs* was 'too detailed a matter for inclusion in the FRSSE'. The principles of the UITF Abstract are of course included in the FRSSE in other specific areas, for example the guidance on accounting for research and development, tangible fixed assets and start up costs. Therefore, should website development costs be an issue in a smaller entity, it should be possible to reach easily the same answer as Abstract 29 provides, without the need for explicit guidance in this area.

Fixed assets and goodwill

Impairment reviews

6.27 The FRSSE does not contain specific guidance on impairment reviews. FRS10 requires annual impairment reviews where a life for goodwill or intangible assets exceeds the presumed 20 years. The guidance in the FRSSE however has instead adopted a maximum of 20 years. FRS15 similarly requires annual impairment reviews to be carried out where an asset life in excess of 50 years has been adopted. The FRSSE does not contain any similar guidance, nor set a 50-year maximum for tangible assets. The Development appendix to FRSSE 2000 indicated that this was an area that would be kept under review. The ASB took the view that small companies could be trusted to adopt long lives for assets only where justified. Introducing annual impairment reviews would be unduly onerous for smaller entities. However, the ASB made it clear that it would revisit this issue if the FRSSE's relaxation from FRS15 was being abused. While this paragraph does not reappear in FRSSE 2002's Development appendix, it would be unsafe to assume that this means any change of mind at the ASB. Evidence of significant abuse would lead to a rethink in this area.

6.28 Although the FRSSE does not specifically address the need for impairment reviews to be carried out, the principle, that assets should not be carried at amounts in excess of their recoverable values, applies. Where it is obvious that a fixed asset has suffered an impairment then the FRSSE would require the asset to be written down to its recoverable amount. The guidance in FRS11 *Impairment of fixed assets and goodwill* may be helpful to establish whether an impairment has occurred and the general process involved in carrying out such a review.

6.29 FRS11 includes some practical examples of the type of events or circumstances that may indicate that an impairment may have arisen. Examples include:

- a significant decline in a fixed asset's market value during the period;
- a major loss of key employees; and
- ongoing operating losses or net cash outflows.

6.30 The following example illustrates the principles.

> A company is operating from two small factories. The first factory was recently acquired on the outskirts of a new business park. The second factory is situated on an industrial estate constructed over 20 years ago.
>
> The first factory produces organic food products at high margins and recent sales figures have indicated that the market is expanding. The second factory produces meat pies at low margins. Recent operating

Assets

> results have shown a decrease in market share with many suppliers competing.
>
> The indicators of low margins, decreasing market share along with the poor location and condition of the factory all lead to the possibility that there may be an impairment. An impairment review should be carried out on the business operating from the second factory. An impairment review will compare the carrying value of the assets with their recoverable amount, being the higher of net realisable value and value in use.
>
> It is possible that the land on which the second factory is situated is worth more than its value in use. Perhaps it is ripe for redevelopment by a supermarket or suitable for a new housing development. In this instance the assets may not necessarily be impaired but obviously the future usage of the factory would need to be considered carefully.

6.31 A common sense approach should be applied when carrying out an impairment review for companies reporting under Little GAAP. For example, it may be appropriate for the directors to have discussions with surveyors to assess the likely carrying value of the business assets and produce a 'back of the envelope' type calculation rather than a more complex review which may be appropriate under FRS11. The methodology of FRS11 may be relevant but should be applied in a sensible manner.

Investment properties

6.32 The discussion on investment properties has been taken from SSAP19 *Accounting for investment properties*. The key requirements in the FRSSE are:

- to include investment properties at open market value;
- not to charge depreciation except for property held on short leases; and
- to recognise changes in market value in the STRGL and not the profit and loss account unless the deficit is expected to be permanent.

Government grants

6.33 The discussion on accounting for government grants is based closely on the requirements in SSAP4 *Accounting for government grants*. The requirements in the FRSSE are:

- to match the income with the expenditure towards which the grant is expected to contribute;
- only to recognise the grant in the profit and loss account once all conditions for its receipt have been satisfied;
- to provide for potential liabilities to repay grants only where repayment

is probable; and
- to require a grant in respect of expenditure on a fixed asset to be taken to a deferred income account and credited to the profit and loss account as the asset is amortised.

Leases

6.34   The section on accounting for leases in the FRSSE is unusual in one respect. There are reasonably extensive disclosure requirements for both lessees and lessors in the FRSSE. The key requirements in respect of accounting for leases by a lessee are:

- a hire purchase contract should be accounted for on a basis similar to that for either finance or operating leases depending upon the nature of the contract;
- a finance lease should be recorded in the lessees balance sheet as an asset and depreciated over its useful life (or lease term if shorter) and a corresponding liability should be set up;
- the finance charge associated with a finance lease should be charged over the lease term at a constant rate on the remaining obligation (but the straight-line method may be a reasonable approximation, see paragraphs 6.35 to 6.37 below);
- under an operating lease, the rental should normally be charged on a straight-line basis over the lease term regardless of the pattern of payments; and
- reverse premiums and similar incentives should be spread on a straight-line basis over the shorter of the lease term or the period to the review date on which the rent is first expected to be adjusted to prevailing market value.

6.35   The CCAB Working Party included a simplification in the first draft FRSSE in respect of the allocation of finance charges. However, this was missing from the final FRSSE. The simplification in the draft FRSSE was in respect of rentals payable under finance leases. In SSAP21 *Accounting for leases and hire purchase contracts*, these are apportioned between the finance charge and the reduction of the outstanding obligation for future amounts payable. The finance charge is then allocated to accounting periods over the lease term to produce a constant periodic rate of charge on the remaining balance of the obligation. The Guidance Notes to SSAP21 allows this to be done on an actuarial basis or on the sum of the digits basis. The draft FRSSE took this one stage further by recommending that finance charges should be charged on a straight-line basis over the lease term. For those who wished to adopt a different basis or continue with the SSAP21 calculations, then this would have been allowed.

Assets

6.36 In the final FRSSE the principal requirement is as in SSAP21. Finance charges have to be allocated to accounting periods to produce a constant periodic rate of charge on the remaining balance of the obligation for each accounting period, or a reasonable approximation thereto. As a concession, the ASB has added a sentence to paragraph 6.4 which states:

'*the straight-line method may provide such a reasonable approximation.*'

6.37 However, this is hardly a concession. Presumably, the only time in which a straight-line method may be used is where the lease is simply not material in the context of the financial statements. In such cases, accounting standards generally do not have to be considered as the *Foreword to Accounting Standards* makes clear that they need not be applied to immaterial items. Therefore, this additional wording in paragraph 6.4 of the FRSSE hardly appears to constitute a concession from the ASB.

6.38 The FRSSE requires that commitments under operating leases be analysed between those leases expiring in the next year, those expiring in years two to five and those expiring over five years from the balance sheet date. This is a requirement of SSAP21 but is not a company law requirement.

6.39 Accounting for sale and leaseback transactions is also covered in Section 6 of the FRSSE. Any apparent profit or loss arising should be deferred and amortised over the shorter of the lease term and the useful economic life of the asset where the transaction results in a finance lease. If the transaction was effected at fair value and results in an operating lease then the amount should be recognised in the profit and loss account immediately. Additional guidance is provided where the transaction has not been effected at fair value.

6.40 The key requirements in respect of accounting for finance leases by a lessor are to:

- record a debtor for the net investment in the lease; and
- recognise the gross earnings, normally based on a constant periodic rate of return on the net investment recorded.

Where a lessor has assets under operating leases, those should be recorded as fixed assets and hence depreciated accordingly as discussed in paragraphs **6.22** and **6.23** above. Operating lease rental income will normally be recognised on a straight-line basis over the lease term.

6.41 The publication of UITF Abstract 28 *Operating lease incentives* has resulted in just four additional words being added to the FRSSE. UITF

Abstract 28 addresses the way in which lessees and lessors should account for incentives given by the lessor to the lessee. The publication of this new Abstract was largely to provide guidance on the accounting required by the lessor as a result of such transactions with existing rules for lessees in UITF Abstract 12 *Lessee accounting for reverse premiums and similar incentives*. The rules in UITF Abstract 12 were included in the FRSSE as described above in the last bullet point to paragraph **6.34**.

6.42 The FRSSE now requires, although previously this may have been regarded as best practice, an incentive given by the lessor to the lessee to be spread in the lessor's books. The incentive should be spread straight-line over the shorter of the lease term or the period to the next review date on which the rent is first expected to be adjusted to prevailing market value. As explained above, this mirrors the existing requirements for lessees. This should be brought to the attention of any smaller entity acting as lessor and providing such incentives as the extension of the spreading requirements to lessors is included, presumably for neatness, in the 'accounting by lessees' section of the FRSSE.

6.43 In December 1999, the ASB published, together with other international accounting standard setting bodies, a Discussion Paper *Leases: Implementation of a new approach*. The Discussion Paper was developed by the so-called G4+1 Group of international standard setters, who published an earlier Discussion Paper in 1996 *Accounting for leases: a new approach*. The 1999 Discussion Paper is broadly consistent with the earlier proposals but develops further lessor accounting. Its principal focus is to end the distinction between finance and operating leases.

6.44 Work has been undertaken by the ASB to assess the scope of this project and the detailed issues involved, including the principles that should determine the extent of the assets and liabilities that lessees and lessors would have or retain under leases. Due to the new role that International Accounting Standards will have on UK listed companies, the ASB is in close liaison with other national standard setters. In the meantime, the ASB is continuing its work in this area, considering issues raised by respondents but focusing initially on lessee accounting. The IASB is keeping abreast of the ASB's progress and has the project on its long-term agenda. However, it seems likely that it will be a few years before a comprehensive International Standard is published on the topic. Perhaps it is time for those interested in small company reporting to start lobbying for a simple regime in the FRSSE, and for a bigger gap to develop between Big GAAP and Little GAAP.

Assets
Stocks and long-term contracts

6.45 The principal requirements of SSAP9 *Stocks and long-term contracts* are incorporated in the FRSSE. Furthermore, SSAP9's guidance notes on practical considerations in calculating stocks and long-term contracts are repeated in Appendix III to the FRSSE. This is a topic on which there have been consistent requests for guidance. The key requirements of the FRSSE on stocks and long-term contracts are:

- stocks should be recognised at the lower of cost and net realisable value;
- long-term contracts should be assessed on a contract by contract basis;
- turnover and related costs should be recognised in the financial statements for ongoing long-term contracts; and
- attributable profit should be recognised in respect of long-term contracts where its outcome can be assessed with reasonable certainty.

Other debtors, debt factoring and consignment stock

6.46 The FRSSE does not include the requirements of UITF Abstract 4 *Presentation of long-term debtors in current assets* that debtors due after more than one year should be disclosed in the notes to the financial statements except in those instances where the amount is so material in the context of the total net current assets that it should be disclosed on the face of the balance sheet so that readers do not misinterpret the financial statements. These requirements have been dropped presumably because it is essentially a disclosure matter. However, this is a case in which if there was such an example of a highly significant long-term debtor in a small entity's balance sheet it would need to be clearly explained for the financial statements to present a true and fair view of the state of affairs of the company.

6.47 Factoring of debts is a relatively common activity among smaller companies. Factoring improves cash flow and, depending on the arrangements, may leave the task of debt collection to another party, thus allowing the proprietors of the business to focus on obtaining new sales and generally running the business. The FRSSE contains the guidance extracted from FRS5, which explains when the debtors should be retained on the company's balance sheet, when they might be considered as sold to the factor and when a linked presentation should be adopted.

6.48 Also incorporated from FRS5 is paragraph 8.5 on consignment stock. Consignment stock is stock held by one party but legally owned by another. The stock is held on terms which enable it to be sold in the normal course of business or for it to be returned unsold to the legal owner. Stocks are often held on a consignment basis in the motor dealership industry. Consignment stock should be recognised in the dealer's balance sheet and a corresponding liability set up where in substance it is an asset of the dealer.

Start-up costs

6.49   A paragraph has been added to FRSSE 2002 on accounting for start-up costs. This is based on the requirements in UITF Abstract 24 *Accounting for start-up costs*. The key point is to remember that start-up costs are not a 'special' cost that requires a departure from normal accounting principles. Therefore, where start-up costs do not meet the criteria for recognition as assets under another specific requirement of the FRSSE (e.g., tangible fixed assets) then they should be written off immediately to the profit and loss account.

Share schemes

6.50   In the Exposure Draft of FRSSE 2002 issued in June 2001 the appendix outlining the development of the Exposure Draft noted that the UITF Abstracts that relate to accounting requirements for share schemes are not considered to be *'sufficiently relevant to smaller entities to warrant inclusion in the FRSSE'*. The Development appendix to FRSSE 2002 states that the Board hopes to conduct further research into the relevance of share scheme accounting for smaller entities. This comment was made in response to a number of specific comments made by respondents to the Exposure Draft on the extent to which share scheme arrangements are used by smaller entities. If research shows that share scheme arrangements are being widely adopted by small companies then it is likely that the ASB and its Committee on Accounting for Smaller Entities will give further consideration to the appropriate reporting of such arrangements.

Chapter seven

Liabilities and shareholders' funds

Introduction

7.1 Following on from Chapter 6 on assets, this chapter covers the four sections in the FRSSE associated with liabilities and shareholders' funds, namely taxation, retirement benefits, provisions and capital instruments.

Taxation

7.2 The FRSSE includes the broad principles of FRS16 *Current tax*, although it simplifies the disclosure requirements. FRSSE 2002 has also simplified the quite prescriptive disclosure requirements that were in the previous version of the FRSSE. The requirement is now simply that 'material components' of the tax charge or credit should be shown. However, the FRSSE continues to require disclosure of 'special circumstances' that affect the overall tax charge or credit.

7.3 FRS16 was developed because of the abolition in April 1999 of advanced corporation tax (ACT) and the restrictions on reclaimability of tax credits introduced in 1997. It requires incoming dividends to be recognised at the amount received or receivable without adding any attributable tax credit. The previous version of the FRSSE required that incoming dividends should be grossed up for the attributable tax credit as originally required under Big GAAP. However, any withholding tax deducted at source should be included. These requirements are mirrored in FRSSE 2002 and are based on the principle that there is a difference in economic substance between tax credits and withholding tax. Any withholding tax suffered should be shown as part of the tax line.

7.4 Outgoing dividends will continue to be shown exclusive of the attributable tax credits, but to match the incoming dividends treatment, they will be inclusive of any withholding tax. The rules on the treatment of ACT have been deleted since, as stated above, it has now been abolished.

Liabilities and shareholders' funds

7.5 The FRSSE makes it clear that tax will normally be recognised in the profit and loss account. However, where tax is attributable to amounts recognised in the statement of total recognised gains and losses, the tax should follow this treatment. If in doubt, the answer will be the profit and loss account.

Deferred tax

7.6 The accounting requirements for deferred tax are based on those in FRS19 *Deferred tax*. The detailed disclosure requirements in FRS19 have not been included in the FRSSE. Instead the FRSSE concentrates on the disclosure of 'material components'.

7.7 FRS19 was published by the ASB in December 2000. The principal effect of the Standard is that the UK has moved closer to a full provision basis to be more in line with international practice although there continue to be a number of significant differences. The FRSSE incorporates some of those differences, such as not providing deferred tax on revaluation gains and losses unless there is a binding sale agreement in place at the balance sheet date. At the time of preparing the original FRSSE, there were calls for small companies not to provide for deferred tax and adopt the so-called flow through method. This would have meant a much simpler regime for small companies although the ASB obviously did not believe that the benefit outweighed such a divergence of practice in this area. Research carried out by the ICAEW found that only one company that had adopted the FRSSE made a provision for deferred tax. The approach taken with FRS19 appears to be that Big GAAP has been simplified for smaller entities, without perhaps full consideration being given to whether it meets the majority of the criteria for inclusion in the FRSSE.

7.8 The new requirements for accounting for deferred tax remove the subjectivity that existed under the partial provisioning basis that previously applied. The FRSSE now requires that deferred tax should be recognised in respect of all timing differences that have originated but not reversed at the balance sheet date. Deferred tax should be based on the average tax rates that would apply when the timing differences are expected to reverse (based on tax rates and law that have been enacted by the balance sheet date). Timing differences are defined as:

> *'Differences between taxable profits and the results as stated in the financial statements that arise from the inclusion of gains and losses in tax assessments in periods different from those in which they are recognised in financial statements.'*

7.9 The definition helpfully goes on to include an example based on the

Taxation

comparison between the depreciation charged in the financial statements for a tangible fixed asset and the capital allowances that the company might receive in respect of that asset. The difference between these two amounts at each balance sheet date means that there will be a timing difference between when items are included in the financial statements and the tax assessment. Ultimately these timing differences will reverse over time.

7.10 Where an entity receives capital allowances in excess of depreciation, a timing difference is created. The reversal happens in the future and is illustrated numerically below.

	20X1	20X2	20X3	20X4	20X5
Financial statements					
Opening balance of asset	100	85	70	55	40
Depreciation	15	15	15	15	15
Closing balance of asset	85	70	55	40	25
Tax accounts					
Opening balance of asset	100	75	56	42	31
Capital allowance	25	19	14	11	8
Closing balance of asset	75	56	42	31	23
Timing difference					
Capital allowance	25	19	14	11	8
Depreciation	15	15	15	15	15
Difference – originating (reversing)	10	4	(1)	(4)	(7)
Cumulative difference	10	14	13	9	2

Deferred tax should be recognised on allowances for the cost of a fixed asset before or after depreciation is allocated in the profit and loss account. Once all the conditions for retaining the allowance are met, the deferred tax should be reversed. For example, one particular type of capital allowance, the 'industrial building allowance' (IBA), is repayable only if the building is sold within 25 years of purchase. Therefore, where an asset is subject to IBAs, deferred tax should be provided until the expiry of the 25 years has been met.

Liabilities and shareholders' funds

7.11 Deferred tax should not be provided for in respect of permanent differences because there will never be a catch up between the financial statements and the tax assessment in respect of the item. Permanent differences arise where items of expenditure charged in the financial statements are, for example, disallowable for tax purposes or where items that obtain tax relief do not impact on the financial statements.

7.12 Deferred tax should not generally be recognised on revalued assets. However, if at the balance sheet date the company has entered into a binding sales agreement and the asset is reflected at the selling price in the financial statements then the effect of deferred tax should be taken into account. There is one exception to this general rule and this is where it is considered *'more likely than not'* that any gain will be rolled over into a replacement asset. 'Rollover relief' can be claimed in several tax jurisdictions when the proceeds of sale of certain 'qualifying' assets (e.g., land and buildings) are reinvested in similar assets. The related tax on the gain on sale is rolled over into the replacement asset and the tax becomes chargeable if and when the replacement asset is sold. Although generally the deferred tax effect of revalued assets will not therefore be accounted for, there is a requirement to disclose the amount of tax that would be payable or recoverable if the assets were sold at their current valuation.

7.13 The FRSSE includes only one paragraph on accounting for deferred tax assets. This states that they should only be recognised where *'it is more likely than not that they will be recovered against the reversal of deferred tax liabilities or other future taxable profits'*. A deferred tax asset can therefore be used to reduce or eliminate a deferred tax liability, without consideration of future taxable profits, provided that the asset and liability can be offset under tax legislation.

7.14 Where a deferred tax asset cannot be recovered against the reversal of deferred tax liabilities, it will be necessary to consider whether there are other suitable future taxable profits. Although the FRSSE repeats the guidance from FRS19 that the existence of unrelieved tax losses provides strong evidence that there may not be future taxable profits, no additional guidance is provided. FRS19 (paragraph 28) provides that *'historical information about the entity's financial performance and position may provide the most objective evidence'* as to the existence of suitable future taxable profits. FRS19 (paragraph 30) goes on to state that if the trading losses have resulted from an identifiable and non-recurring cause and the entity has usually been profitable, with any past losses being easily off-set by income in later periods this would be evidence of suitable taxable profits. These paragraphs might be useful for a small company trying to assess the recoverability of a potential deferred tax asset.

Retirement benefits

7.15 The FRSSE does not require the discounting of deferred tax assets and liabilities although it permits such a policy provided that it is applied consistently. This appears to be another example of taking Big GAAP, instead of looking at a small company's needs. Many users of the FRSSE will not be familiar with Big GAAP and this sentence may have limited meaning to them. The Exposure Draft to FRSSE 2002 acknowledged that it was unlikely that many FRSSE preparers would adopt such a technique although it was still included in the latest FRSSE update.

Value added tax

7.16 The FRSSE includes the principal requirements of SSAP5 *Accounting for value added tax* that turnover shown in the profit and loss account should exclude VAT on taxable outputs. The FRSSE also makes clear that irrecoverable VAT on, for example, fixed assets should be included in their cost where practicable and material, the latter phrase being a direct import from SSAP5.

Retirement benefits

7.17 In small entities, defined contribution schemes are far more popular than defined benefit schemes. The accounting in respect of the former is straightforward, with the amount charged to the profit and loss account being the contributions payable in the period. The FRSSE has taken a rather strange approach in its Section 10 on accounting for defined benefit pension arrangements. The accounting rules have been included in an appendix rather than in the main section. The development of the Exposure Draft appendix explained that the *'number of smaller entities using defined benefit schemes is not sufficient to justify the inclusion of existing (SSAP24) and proposed (FRS17) requirements in the Statement of Standard Accounting Practice itself'*. In fact only one out of 200 eligible smaller companies disclosed the use of a defined benefit scheme in surveys carried out by ICAS and ICAEW. This is perhaps another area where the requirements of Big GAAP have been included in the FRSSE without considering the criteria for its inclusion. The first criteria set out in the first section of the FRSSE dealing with its status lays down that the ASB *'has had, and will continue to have, regard for'* whether the requirement is *'likely to be regarded as having general application...'*. Despite this, rules on accounting for defined benefit schemes are included in the FRSSE, albeit in an appendix which follows the basic approach of FRS17 *Retirement benefits* published in November 2000.

7.18 FRS17 has two years of transitional provisions where only disclosure requirements are necessary. The FRSSE has taken a similar approach with

Liabilities and shareholders' funds

the first disclosure requirements becoming effective for periods ending on or after 22 June 2002 (i.e., the effective date of FRSSE 2002).

7.19 For the two transitional periods (i.e., accounting periods ending before 22 June 2004), the pension cost for defined benefit schemes should be calculated under the existing rules using actuarial valuation methods. The objective here is to arrive at a regular pension cost each year that is a substantially level percentage of the pensionable payroll. Any variations from the regular cost are spread forward and recognised gradually over the average remaining service lives of the employees.

7.20 Although the accounting will therefore be based on the requirements consistent with previous versions of the FRSSE, as stated above, there are additional disclosure requirements based on the provisions of FRS17. It should be noted that the actuarial valuation previously used is unlikely to be suitable for use under the new provisions. Even if that valuation uses the projected unit method, it is unlikely to comply with the new requirements in all respects, such as the use of fair values for investments and the use of a high quality corporate bond rate to discount liabilities. Assumptions will also have to be updated to reflect the circumstances at the balance sheet date. Therefore it will be necessary to instruct actuaries to prepare a suitable valuation to meet the transitional disclosure requirements. An example of the transitional disclosure requirements are included in Appendix 3 of this book.

7.21 For accounting periods ending on or after 22 June 2004 the accounting will change to reflect the effect of the transitional disclosure requirements. This will be accounted for as a change of accounting policy and therefore a prior year adjustment will be required. However, the two years of transitional disclosures will mean that the impact of the new policy will have already been calculated and hence there will be no need for the company to go back to previous periods to make any reassessment.

7.22 The main effects of the new rules on accounting for defined benefit schemes are that:
- assets should be measured at their fair value at each balance sheet date;
- liabilities should be measured on an actuarial basis using the projected unit method and discounted at a rate equivalent to the current rate of return on a high quality corporate bond of equivalent currency and term to the scheme liabilities (e.g., AA rated);
- the profit and loss account should show the relatively stable ongoing service cost, interest cost and expected return on assets;
- fluctuations in market values should be recognised immediately in the statement of total recognised gains and losses; and

- the balance sheet should show the deficit or recoverable surplus in the scheme.

7.23 A full actuarial valuation will be required at least every three years although the actuary will need to be involved at each balance sheet date. Any surplus will be recognised in the company's balance sheet to the extent that it is able to recover the surplus either through reduced contributions or refunds.

Provisions, contingent liabilities and contingent assets

7.24 Section 11 is based on the provisions of FRS12 *Provisions, contingent liabilities and contingent assets.*

7.25 A provision should be recognised when the following conditions have been satisfied:

- it is probable that a present obligation exists as a result of a past event;
- a transfer in economic benefit will be required; and
- a reliable estimate of the transfer can be made.

7.26 The key requirements in the FRSSE on accounting for provisions once the above conditions have been satisfied are:

- a provision should represent the best estimate of the obligation at the balance sheet date;
- where the time value of money is material, the provision should be discounted to represent the present value of the expected expenditures;
- the unwinding of the discount rate should be shown as a financial item, disclosed separately from interest;
- where a reimbursement of some or all of the obligation can be obtained this should be recognised only where its recovery is virtually certain and disclosed as a separate asset; and
- the profit and loss account may be presented net of any recovery.

7.27 As noted in Chapter 6, the practice of providing for repairs of fixed assets has been stopped. Instead, the assets have to be depreciated over the useful economic lives of their component parts, with maintenance costs being capitalised and depreciated over the life of the new component, probably until the next repair. Routine minor repairs should be expensed as incurred.

7.28 The FRSSE makes it clear that components depreciation should be used only for major components with substantially different useful economic lives.

Liabilities and shareholders' funds

> For example, the tyres on a motor car would not be a different component from the rest of the vehicle simply because the tyres have to be replaced every two to three years.

7.29 Where components depreciation is adopted the asset is split up into its component parts. Each individual component is depreciated over its useful economic life. Where an asset undergoes routine maintenance that restores the component its replacement cost is added to the fixed asset cost.

> For example, a helicopter costing £1m is depreciated over 15 years. At three-year intervals the company is required by law to carry out a full overhaul of the helicopter, at a cost of £150,000. It is assumed that over the life of the helicopter there will be four overhauls at the end of year 3, 6, 9 and 12. Accounting for this overhaul for the first four years under the new rules would be as follows.
>
> The two components of the helicopter should be recognised from the outset. The first component at a cost of £850,000 with a life of 15 years, and the second component at a cost of £150,000 with a life of three years.
>
> At the end of year 3 the cost of £150,000 would be removed in a similar fashion to accounting for a disposal and the overhaul expenditure incurred, added to the cost of fixed assets as the maintenance work leads to an asset with renewed service potential. The new cost of £150,000 will be depreciated over three years up to the date of the next overhaul at the end of year 6.

7.30 Although applying components depreciation rather than providing for such costs may not have a material effect on the amount that is charged through the profit and loss account it could impact on the tax cash flows. The Revenue now accepts that provisions correctly made under FRS12 are generally tax-deductible except where there are specific tax rules to the contrary. For example, provisions for capital expenditure are not tax-deductible.

7.31 In common with FRS12, the FRSSE requires that contingent liabilities and contingent assets should not be recognised. A contingent liability does not meet the definition of a provision in the FRSSE and recognition of a contingent asset may result in the recognition of profit that may never be realised.

7.32 The FRSSE requires that the following should be disclosed for contingent liabilities, except where their existence is remote, and for contingent assets which are probable:

(1) a brief description of the nature of the contingent item; and
(2) where practicable, an estimate of its financial effect.

7.33 The FRSSE does not reflect the FRS12 requirements that an indication of the uncertainties relating to contingent liabilities or the possibility of any reimbursement is disclosed.

Capital instruments

7.34 The five paragraphs in the FRSSE on capital instruments clearly represent a significant reduction from the comparable 40 or so which appear in FRS4 *Capital instruments*. FRS4's requirements to analyse shareholders' funds between the amounts attributable to equity interests and those attributable to non-equity interests are not in the FRSSE.

7.35 The main requirements in the FRSSE on capital instruments are to:

- classify as liabilities all capital instruments which contain an obligation to transfer economic benefits, other than shares;
- allocate finance costs over the term of the debt at a constant rate on the carrying value;
- state borrowings initially at the fair value of the consideration received, with the subsequent additions of finance costs and reductions for payments made;
- treat an arrangement fee that represents an additional cost of finance in a similar way to finance costs. Otherwise, it is charged to the profit and loss account (see example below); and
- accrue dividends (unless ultimate payment is remote) that are calculated by reference to time and show any excess over the amount paid or payable separately in shareholders' funds.

7.36 The presentation resulting from accounting for an arrangement fee as part of the finance costs can cause confusion in the balance sheet.

> For example, an entity incurs an arrangement fee of £15,000 to secure a facility of £500,000 for a period of five years.
>
> The £15,000 would be classified as issue costs and the debt is recorded at its net proceeds, in this case £485,000.

7.37 This approach, while conceptually elegant, is often criticised. Directors look at their balance sheet, knowing they have a £500,000 loan

Liabilities and shareholders' funds

to repay but see only £485,000 in their balance sheet. In their view, the arrangement fee is exactly that and is a cost of that period. Therefore intuitively they might prefer to write-off the arrangement fee in the year and then record the loan at its full amount.

7.38 The FRSSE allows the intuitive approach to be adopted. The only exception is where the arrangement fee represents a significant additional cost of finance when compared with the interest on the facility.

> For example, if in the above example interest was being paid at eight per cent per annum, the expected rate which a company of this size would pay on such a facility over such a period, the arrangement fee may be taken to the profit and loss account immediately.
>
> If, on the other hand, the arrangement fee was £100,000 and the interest rate was only four per cent then it can be seen that in effect the arrangement fee represents interest. In this case, the spreading rule would apply.

Chapter eight
Other accounting issues

Introduction

8.1 The main section of the FRSSE has four sections that deal with other accounting areas. These are: the treatment of foreign currency translation; accounting for post balance sheet events; the disclosure of related parties and transactions; and the preparation of consolidated financial statements. The inclusion of a cash flow statement is discussed in a special section of the FRSSE dealing with voluntary disclosures. All five areas are discussed below.

Foreign currency translation

8.2 Section 13 of the FRSSE incorporates the principal requirements of SSAP20 *Foreign currency translation*. This section has proved relatively uncontroversial, although the desire to cope with provisions on foreign entities, such as branches, being incorporated into the financial statements of the investing company has meant that a further two pages of guidance have been included in the Standard.

8.3 The key requirements in the FRSSE on accounting for foreign currency transactions are set out below.

- Foreign currency monetary assets and liabilities should be translated at the closing rate at each balance sheet date.
- Foreign currency non-monetary assets and liabilities, and revenue and costs arising from foreign currency transactions, should be translated at the exchange rate in operation at the date of the transaction (with no further retranslation). Where exchange rates have not significantly fluctuated during the period an average rate may be applied.
- Where there are related or matching forward contracts in respect of trading balances, the fixed rate of exchange in the contract may be applied to those balances. This is an option, not a requirement.
- Foreign exchange gains and losses on settled transactions and unsettled

monetary assets and liabilities should be reported as part of profit or loss from ordinary activities in the profit and loss account for the period.
- Special hedging provisions may be appropriate where foreign currency borrowings are used to finance, or provide a hedge against, foreign equity investments. Where specific criteria are met, as set out below, the investment can be retranslated at the closing rate at each balance sheet date with the resulting gain or loss taken, via the statement of total recognised gains and losses, to reserves. The corresponding gain or loss on the retranslation of the foreign borrowings will also be recognised in the same way to the extent that it matches the exchange difference on the equity investment.

8.4 The special hedging provisions set out above may only be applied where specific criteria are met, being:

(1) the exchange difference on the borrowings may only be taken to reserves to the extent that they match the foreign equity exchange differences recognised in reserves. Any excess exchange difference on the borrowings should be recognised in the profit and loss account for the period;
(2) the foreign currency borrowings used to finance or hedge the foreign equity investment should not exceed the expected amount of cash that the investment is expected to generate; and
(3) if such an accounting policy is adopted then it should be applied consistently from one period to the next.

8.5 The FRSSE includes accounting guidance on incorporating the accounts of foreign entities into those of the investing company. These rules will be applicable, for example, where the small company has overseas branches. If a small company is preparing group financial statements, it also follows these rules.

8.6 The FRSSE does not include any specific disclosure requirements in relation to foreign currency transactions.

Post balance sheet events

8.7 Section 14 of the FRSSE deals with post balance sheet events, which are those events, both favourable and unfavourable, that occur between the balance sheet date and the date on which the financial statements are approved. Their treatment depends on whether they are 'adjusting events' or 'non-adjusting events'. In this respect the FRSSE is consistent with SSAP17.

Related party disclosures

8.8 Adjusting events are those which provide additional evidence of conditions existing at the balance sheet date. They include events that because of statutory or conventional requirements are reflected in financial statements. Adjusting events require changes in the amounts to be included in financial statements. SSAP17 provides helpful examples of adjusting events, some of which are reproduced below:

(1) the subsequent determination of the purchase price or of the proceeds of sale of a fixed asset purchased or sold before the balance sheet date;
(2) a property valuation that provides evidence of an impairment at the balance sheet date; and
(3) an amount received in respect of an insurance claim which was in the course of negotiation at the balance sheet date.

8.9 A non-adjusting event is one that concerns conditions that did not exist at the balance sheet date and so does not result in changes to the amounts stated in the financial statements. A material non-adjusting post balance sheet event should be disclosed if non-disclosure would affect the understandability of the financial statements. Some examples of non-adjusting events are:

(1) losses of fixed assets or stocks as a result of a catastrophe such as a flood or fire;
(2) the decline in the value of property if it can be demonstrated that the decline occurred after the year end; and
(3) the purchase or sale of fixed assets.

Related party disclosures

8.10 One of the more controversial topics in the development of the FRSSE has been related party disclosures and the extent to which the provisions of FRS8 *Related party disclosures* have to be reflected in the FRSSE.

8.11 In the drafting of the original FRSSE the CCAB Working Party agreed that there should not be any explicit related party disclosures. However, the ASB disagreed, having noted that such disclosures were often more important in respect of smaller entities than others.

8.12 The ASB therefore decided to include the disclosure requirements in respect of related parties in the FRSSE. There are some simplifications compared with FRS8.

8.13 Disclosure is required of related party relationships, as well as the nature and value of the transaction with the related party in respect of the following types of transactions:

Other accounting issues

(1) the purchase, sale or transfer of assets or liabilities;
(2) the provision or receipt of services; and
(3) the provision or receipt of financial support.

8.14 The disclosure net is wide. Transactions and balances with associated companies will be caught. Transactions with members of the close family or any partnerships, companies, trusts or other entities in which they have a controlling interest will be disclosable. Furthermore, what might be considered personal arrangements which individual shareholders or directors undertake on behalf of the company may need to be disclosed.

> For example, where a company's overdraft facility is secured by a personal guarantee from a company director, disclosure would be required. Paragraph 15.2 of the FRSSE specifically addresses such a relationship.

8.15 By way of a footnote to paragraph 15.1, the FRSSE makes clear that materiality should be judged in terms of its significance to the reporting entity. This is a significant relaxation compared with FRS8, which requires materiality also to be judged in relation to the other party where that party is, for example, a director or closely connected with a director. Of course, materiality has both a qualitative and quantitative aspect to it. However, this relaxation should avoid some unnecessary pain and cost in seeking to determine whether transactions, while clearly immaterial to the reporting entity, might be material to the other party.

8.16 In addition to disclosing details of related party transactions, the FRSSE also requires disclosure of the existence of a controlling party. The disclosure is not dependent on whether there have been any transactions between the two parties. The very existence of the control relationship must be disclosed. It is likely that this requirement will affect many, if not most, small companies.

Consolidated financial statements and associated companies

8.17 The FRSSE may be adopted by small companies preparing consolidated financial statements. However, if they do so they must also comply with the accounting practices and disclosure requirements set out in:

- FRS2 *Accounting for subsidiary undertakings*;
- FRS6 *Acquisitions and mergers*; and
- FRS7 *Fair values in acquisition accounting*;

and, as they apply in respect of consolidated financial statements:

- FRS5 *Reflecting the substance of transactions*;
- FRS9 *Associates and joint ventures*;
- FRS10 *Goodwill and intangible assets*; and
- FRS11 *Impairment of fixed assets and goodwill.*

8.18 It would be interesting to see a real set of consolidated financial statements prepared using the FRSSE and complying with the above accounting regulations. The prospect of excessive detail in some areas and a relative absence in others must make for an interesting set of financial statements. However, research efforts to date have not found such an example. The best advice to someone wishing to prepare consolidated financial statements for small companies is probably to do so as non-statutory financial statements.

Cash flow information

8.19 As Chapter 1 notes, there has been controversy over whether the FRSSE should require the disclosure of cash flow information. The ASB exempted small companies from preparing a cash flow statement when it issued its first FRS in 1991. The exemption has proved popular. But in both the December 1995 consultation exercise and in the 1996 Exposure Draft from the ASB, the question of whether cash flow information should be required was asked. On both occasions, the majority of commentators said no. The ASB therefore recognised that there was insufficient support for a mandatory cash flow statement. Its compromise has been to include Part D in the FRSSE headed *Voluntary disclosures*. Companies are encouraged to provide a cash flow statement prepared using the indirect method which is the method adopted in FRS1 *Cash flow statements*. An example of a cash flow statement is provided in Appendix III to the FRSSE. Research to date has not yet found a company volunteering such a statement.

Chapter nine

Implications for auditors

Introduction

9.1 Under s235 of the Companies Act 1985 a company's auditors are required to state, in a report accompanying the financial statements and addressed to the members of the company, their opinion as to whether or not the financial statements of the company (or group, if group financial statements are prepared):

(1) give a true and fair view of:
 (a) its state of affairs at the end of the financial year; and
 (b) its profit or loss for the financial year; and
(2) have been properly prepared in accordance with the Act.

9.2 In forming their opinion, the auditors will need to consider the disclosures which the company should make by reference to the disclosure requirements of the Act and the relevant accounting standards or the FRSSE. In this chapter, it is presumed that the FRSSE is being used. Both sources of disclosure need to be considered since, subject to the override discussed below, financial statements cannot be true and fair or prepared in accordance with the Act if they have not complied with the accounting requirements of the Act or relevant accounting standards.

9.3 Where the directors believe a departure from an accounting standard or a requirement of the Act is necessary to give a true and fair view then an 'override' can be applied. In such cases the Act and paragraph 2.9 of the FRSSE (which follows FRS18 and the *Foreword to Accounting Standards*) require the financial statements to provide full disclosure of the departure, the reason for it and its effect. Where the auditors disagree with the departure they will need to qualify their auditors' report.

9.4 Where a small company takes advantage of the entitlement to adopt Schedule 8 and the FRSSE the auditors will therefore need to consider whether:

(1) the company qualifies as small;

Implications for auditors

(2) the financial statements comply with the requirements of Schedule 8 and the FRSSE; and
(3) the financial statements give a true and fair view.

Accordingly, this chapter examines these considerations affecting auditors.

Assessing whether the company is entitled to the exemptions

9.5 A key issue for directors and auditors alike will be to determine whether or not the company is entitled to take advantage of the exemptions afforded by Schedule 8 and the FRSSE. To do this they will need to consider carefully the criteria outlined in Chapter 3 relating to small companies and to assess whether the various conditions have been met for the year under review.

9.6 In the case of both modified financial statements and abbreviated accounts the directors are required to include on the balance sheet in a prominent position above the signature, a statement that the accounts have been prepared in accordance with the special provisions of Part VII of the Act relating to small companies – s246(8). This should focus the attention of the directors on whether or not the company is entitled to the exemptions. If the conclusions were found to be invalid, the accounts sent for filing are likely to be rejected by the Registrar and potentially the directors could be liable to a fine and for the costs incurred in rectifying the situation.

9.7 Where the company's financial statements are subject to audit and the auditors do not believe that the company is entitled to the exemptions then they would need to communicate this fact to their client as soon as practicable. In the unlikely event that the directors persevere with preparing financial statements which are drawn up either under the FRSSE or Schedule 8 where the company is not entitled to do so then the auditors would need to qualify their report – s237(4A).

9.8 In the annual reports published by the Registrar of Companies the point is frequently made that a number of companies have been found to be taking advantage of the exemptions in Schedule 8 although they were not entitled to do so. One of the most common reasons is that the company was part of an ineligible group - see Chapter 3. Auditors who fail to draw attention to this and who have issued an unqualified report will routinely be reported by the Registrar to the ICAEW, ICAS or other relevant accountancy body for disciplinary action to be considered.

Can modified financial statements be true and fair?

9.9 Where the company's financial statements are not subject to audit, because the company has taken advantage of the exemptions in s249A (discussed in Chapter 4) the onus placed on the directors to ensure that the relevant conditions for qualifying as a small company are met is all the greater. The directors would again potentially be liable to fines and for the cost of rectifying the situation were their conclusions as to eligibility proven to be invalid. Any chartered accountant involved in the preparation of the financial statements would potentially be liable to disciplinary action by his or her accountancy body.

Compliance with the Companies Act and the FRSSE

9.10 The next issue to address is whether the financial statements comply with Schedule 8 (or Schedule 4) and the FRSSE. The restructuring of Schedule 8, so that the Act now indicates what should be disclosed, rather than what can be omitted, has helped enormously in assessing whether a company's financial statements comply with the Act.

9.11 By the same token, the omission from the FRSSE of a number of disclosure items in accounting standards has meant that disclosure checklists used by preparers of financial statements and firms of auditors have been reduced considerably. Ensuring compliance, in terms of providing the required disclosures, is now a far simpler, relatively mechanical, process.

Can modified financial statements be true and fair?

9.12 Assuming that it is valid for the financial statements to have been drawn up to take advantage of the various disclosure exemptions, the preparation of financial statements which are abridged in some way then raises the issue of the form which the auditors' report should take and in particular whether the auditors (or indeed the directors) can conclude that such financial statements:

(1) are still capable of giving a true and fair view; and
(2) have been prepared in accordance with the Act.

9.13 To be true and fair, financial statements must comply with accounting standards:

> '*Accounting standards are authoritative statements of how particular types of transaction and other events should be reflected in financial statements and accordingly compliance with accounting standards will*

Implications for auditors

normally be necessary for financial statements to give a true and fair view' (Foreword to Accounting Standards, paragraph 16).

9.14 However, it has long been established that the need for compliance with accounting standards should not be taken to override specific exemptions given by the Act:

'Where accounting standards prescribe information to be contained in financial statements, such requirements do not override exemptions from disclosure given by law to, and utilised by, certain types of entity' (Foreword to Accounting Standards, paragraph 15).

9.15 The application of this rule is clear where the disclosure requirement from which the exemption is granted is identical with that in an accounting standard. The position has always been less clear where the requirements are similar or related but not identical. Fortunately, this problem largely becomes irrelevant when a company uses the FRSSE.

9.16 In setting out its status at the beginning of the FRSSE, the Accounting Standards Board has indicated that reporting entities which have applied the FRSSE are exempt from complying with other accounting standards or UITF Abstracts, unless preparing consolidated financial statements (in which case certain other standards will apply). The adoption of the FRSSE in place of existing accounting standards may therefore mean that not all of the disclosures which a company might otherwise need to make to reflect adequately its financial position or economic performance will be given.

9.17 Financial statements drawn up by small companies in compliance with the FRSSE are still intended to present a true and fair view of the results for the period and the state of affairs of the company at the end of the period. However, whilst the measurement bases in the FRSSE are the same as, or a simplification of, those in the accounting standards comprising Big GAAP, the FRSSE in many cases reduces to a minimum the disclosure requirements of those standards.

9.18 Where additional information is required for the financial statements to give a true and fair view then the FRSSE requires that information to be given (as does s226(4) of the Act). In this context, the FRSSE comments that to achieve a true and fair view regard should be had to the substance of any arrangement or transaction entered into and that:

'Where there is doubt whether applying provisions of the FRSSE would be sufficient to give a true and fair view, adequate explanation should be given in the notes to the accounts of the transaction or arrangement

Additional guidance to auditors

concerned and the treatment adopted.' (FRSSE, paragraph 2.2).

9.19 For transactions or events not dealt with by the FRSSE the preparer of the financial statements (and therefore the auditor) should also have regard to other accounting standards and UITF Abstracts, not as mandatory documents, but as a means of establishing current practice. Of course it may be that there is no accounting standard or UITF Abstract dealing with a particular transaction or series of transactions which the company has entered into in the period. In such cases the preparer will need to fall back on the underlying principles within the FRSSE, namely by assessing the substance of transactions and giving adequate disclosure to enable a true and fair view to be given. However, in the vast majority of cases it is anticipated that no disclosures outside those stipulated in the FRSSE (and the Act) need be given.

9.20 Provided any such additional disclosures of 'non-routine' transactions are made, a company can therefore adopt the FRSSE and produce financial statements which can be reported on by the auditors as being true and fair and in accordance with the Act.

Additional guidance to auditors

9.21 In July 1997 the APB issued Practice Note 13 *The Audit of Small Businesses*. Rather than establish a separate auditing standard for smaller entities (i.e., an auditing equivalent of the FRSSE), the Practice Note sets out the considerations relevant to the application of existing auditing standards to the audit of smaller entities. It is outside the scope of this book to consider the various practical issues faced by the auditors of smaller entities.

9.22 In December 1997 the APB issued Bulletin 1997/3 *The FRSSE: Guidance for auditors*. The Bulletin dealt with the following four specific questions arising directly from the FRSSE.

(1) In considering whether financial statements prepared using the FRSSE give a true and fair view, do auditors need to refer to Statements of Standard Accounting Practice, Financial Reporting Standards, and UITF Abstracts?

This has already been mentioned above in the context of whether modified financial statements can give a true and fair view. The APB Bulletin draws attention to the requirement in the FRSSE that for transactions or events not dealt with in the FRSSE, smaller entities should have regard to other accounting standards and UITF Abstracts, not as mandatory documents,

Implications for auditors

but as a means of establishing current practice. It adds that where guidance relevant to a particular matter is available in other pronouncements, auditors will normally expect it to be followed, subject to any modifications judged reasonable in its application to a smaller entity in the context of the particular circumstances.

(2) What responsibilities do auditors have with regard to additional voluntary disclosures made in financial statements prepared using the FRSSE?

The APB confirms that the auditors' responsibilities extend to all information included within the financial statements (and therefore within the scope of the auditors' report), whether required by the FRSSE or disclosed on a voluntary basis. So if a small company includes a cash flow statement on a voluntary basis as part of the financial statements, the statement will have to be audited.

If a cash flow statement or other additional information is included in the annual report but outside the financial statements, auditors' responsibilities are set out in SAS 160 *Other information in documents containing audited financial statements*. SAS 160 requires auditors to 'read' such information and seek to resolve any apparent misstatements or material inconsistencies with the audited financial statements.

(3) Are there any special considerations for auditors in applying particular Statements of Auditing Standards to the audit of financial statements prepared using the FRSSE?

SAS 460 *Related parties* has a particularly direct relationship with FRS8 *Related party disclosures*. The requirements of the FRSSE in relation to related party disclosures are similar to, but not identical with, those in FRS8. In particular, FRS8 requires the materiality of certain related party transactions to be assessed both in relation to the reporting entity and to the other party whereas the FRSSE only requires materiality to be judged in terms of significance to the reporting entity. The APB guidance confirms that the section of paragraph 7 of SAS 460 which deals with the assessment of materiality from the viewpoint of the other party will not be relevant to auditors, where the FRSSE has been adopted.

(4) What effect does the FRSSE have on the auditors' report on the financial statements?

This is dealt with in the next section below.

Reporting on modified financial statements

9.23 It is a requirement of the Act that modified financial statements include a statement that they have been prepared in accordance with the special provisions relating to small companies – s246(8). It is similarly a requirement of the FRSSE (paragraph 2.3) that financial statements disclose the fact that they have been prepared in accordance with it. This level of disclosure is appropriate given that there are two significantly different reporting regimes and users should be able to understand easily which of those is being followed.

9.24 An example of such a statement is as follows:

'These financial statements have been prepared in accordance with the special provisions relating to small companies within Part VII of the Companies Act 1985 and with the Financial Reporting Standard for Smaller Entities (effective June 2002).'

9.25 Before 1997 it was common practice for auditors' reports on modified financial statements to draw attention to the use of the small company exemptions by concluding the opinion paragraph with 'properly prepared in accordance with the provisions of the Companies Act 1985 applicable to small companies'. To some extent these words owe their origin to the small company regime prior to SI 1997/220 when auditors were permitted to report that the modified financial statements had been 'properly prepared', omitting reference to a true and fair view. However, it continues to be common practice to include the expanded wording.

9.26 APB Bulletin 1997/3 went further than this and stated that in view of the relevance of the use of the FRSSE to an appreciation of the financial statements, auditors are encouraged to refer to it in the introductory paragraph of their report. An example of such a statement is as follows:

'We have audited the financial statements of [company name] for the year ended [date] set out on pages [ ] to [ ]. These financial statements have been prepared in accordance with the Financial Reporting Standard for Smaller Entities (effective June 2002) and under the accounting policies set out therein.'

9.27 A complete example auditors' report on the financial statements of a small company taking advantage of the exemptions permitted by Schedule 8 and the FRSSE is included in the example financial statements in Appendix 1.

Implications for auditors
Reporting on abbreviated accounts

9.28 Small and medium-sized companies are entitled to file abbreviated accounts with the Registrar of Companies. Where this is proposed the auditors will need to consider whether in their opinion the requirements for exemption are satisfied – s247B. If the auditors are satisfied they are required to provide the directors of the company with a special report (for delivery to the Registrar with the abbreviated accounts), stating that in their opinion:

(1) the company is entitled to deliver abbreviated accounts; and
(2) the abbreviated accounts to be delivered are properly prepared in accordance with the relevant provisions.

9.29 The auditors should date the special report when they sign it in manuscript and this cannot happen until the directors have approved and signed the abbreviated accounts. The special report should be dated on, or as soon as possible after, the date of the report on the full financial statements. The impression should not be given that this report updates the auditors' report on the full financial statements in any way.

9.30 Where there is to be a change of auditors, it is advisable that the abbreviated accounts are reported upon by the retiring auditors who expressed an opinion on the full financial statements for the year in question – APB Bulletin 1997/1.

9.31 If the auditors are not satisfied that the requirements for exemption have been met or do not consider the abbreviated accounts to have been properly prepared in accordance with the Act they should discuss this with the directors. The Act makes no provision for a qualified report and it would appear that the directors would be in breach of the Act if abbreviated accounts were delivered to the Registrar with a qualified report.

9.32 The fact that the auditors' report on the full financial statements was qualified (or contained reference to a fundamental uncertainty) does not prevent the abbreviated accounts being properly prepared in accordance with the Act. However, in the circumstances APB Bulletin 1997/1 advises that the auditors should consider whether the maximum effect of the matter giving rise to the qualification or uncertainty could affect the company's eligibility to file abbreviated accounts.

9.33 Until the 1997 revisions to Schedule 8 the special report, addressed to the directors, was required to reproduce the text of the auditors' report on the full financial statements. Now, the special report under s247B requires the audit report on the full financial statements to be set out in full only if that report was:

Reporting on abbreviated accounts

(1) qualified, in which case any further material necessary to understand the qualification should also be included; or
(2) contained a statement under:
   (a) s237(2) – accounts, records or returns inadequate or accounts not agreeing with the records and returns; or
   (b) s237(3) – failure to obtain necessary information and explanations.

9.34 It is recommended that this is done after the opinion paragraph of the special report and introduced by the following words:

Other information

On [date] we reported, as auditors of [company name], to the members on the full financial statements prepared under s226 of the Companies Act 1985 for the year ended [date] and our report was as follows:

9.35 Where the auditors' report is reproduced and the abbreviated accounts do not contain the information or the note to which it makes reference then such information should be included immediately after the report.

9.36 In addition, APB Bulletin 1997/1, *The Special Auditors' Report on Abbreviated Accounts in Great Britain*, recommended that where the audit report on the full financial statements included an explanatory paragraph relating to a fundamental uncertainty (e.g., concerning the applicability of the going concern basis) then the paragraph, together with any further material necessary to understand it, should be included in the auditors' report. It is not necessary to reproduce the whole report on the full financial statements. The paragraph of the report dealing with the fundamental uncertainty could be introduced as follows:

Other information

On [date] we reported, as auditors of [company name], to the members on the full financial statements prepared under s226 of the Companies Act 1985 for the year ended [date] and our report included the following paragraph:

Going concern

In forming our opinion, we have considered the adequacy of the disclosures made in note 1 of the financial statements concerning the uncertainty as to the continuation and renewal of the company's bank

Implications for auditors

> overdraft facility. In view of the significance of this uncertainty we consider that it should be drawn to your attention but our opinion is not qualified in this respect.
>
> Extract from note 1 to the full financial statements
>
> [Reproduce text from note 1.]

9.37 An example special auditors' report on abbreviated accounts is included in Appendix 2. In respect of medium-sized companies, the references in the auditors' report are replaced as follows: s246 becomes s246A; s246(5) and (6) become s246A(3) in the second and fourth paragraphs; and 'those provisions' becomes 'that provision'.

Group financial statements exemption

9.38 As described in Chapter 3, a parent company need not prepare group financial statements if the group headed by that company qualifies as a small or medium-sized group. The Act previously provided that where the directors elected to take advantage of this exemption they were required to obtain a report from the auditors confirming that they were able to take advantage of the exemption. This requirement was repealed in 1996 but auditors are still required by law to consider whether or not the directors are entitled to take advantage of the exemption.

9.39 The auditors are now required by s237(4A) to report only where they form the opinion that the directors are not entitled to the exemption (i.e., reporting by exception). In such circumstances the auditors should discuss the matter with the directors. If the matter cannot be resolved in this way the auditors would qualify their report on the individual financial statements for their failure to include group financial statements as required by s227 (subject to the company not being able to take advantage of any of the other exemptions from preparing group financial statements). An example of such a report is as follows:

> Extract from auditors' report
>
> 'Qualified opinion arising from disagreement about the failure to prepare group financial statements
>
> In preparing the financial statements the directors have relied on the exemption conferred by section 248 of the Companies Act 1985 not to prepare group financial statements on the grounds that the group headed by the company is a [small / medium]-sized group. In our opinion the

Group financial statements exemption

directors are not able to take advantage of the exemption because [reasons]. Consequently, the company has failed to prepare the group financial statements required by section 227 of the Companies Act 1985 and [Financial Reporting Standard 2 Accounting for subsidiary undertakings / *the Financial Reporting Standard for Smaller Entities (effective June 2002)].*

Except for the failure to prepare group financial statements, in our opinion the financial statements give a true and fair view...'

Appendix 1

Example financial statements

Smallco Limited

Financial statements 31 December 2002
together with directors' and auditors' reports

Registered number: _____

These financial statements illustrate some of the more common disclosures made by small companies. For information on the more detailed requirements please refer to the disclosure checklist in Appendix 4.

Example financial statements

Directors' report
For the year ended 31 December 2002

Financial statements
The directors present their report and financial statements for the year ended 31 December 2002.

Directors' responsibilities
Company law requires the directors to prepare financial statements for each financial year which give a true and fair view of the state of affairs of the company and of the profit or loss of the company for that period. In preparing those financial statements, the directors are required to:

- select suitable accounting policies and then apply them consistently;
- make judgements and estimates that are reasonable and prudent; and
- prepare the financial statements on the going concern basis unless it is inappropriate to presume that the company will continue in business.

The directors are responsible for keeping proper accounting records which disclose with reasonable accuracy at any time the financial position of the company and to enable them to ensure that the financial statements comply with the Companies Act 1985. They are also responsible for safeguarding the assets of the company and hence for taking reasonable steps for the prevention and detection of fraud and other irregularities.

Principal activity
The principal activity of the company in the year under review was the [manufacture and distribution of art and design equipment including software packages]. The principal activity of the company's subsidiary, Subsid Limited was the [provision of promotional services].

* Results and dividends
The profit for the year after taxation amounted to £* (2001: £*). The directors recommend a dividend of £* for the year (2001: £*) which leaves a profit of £* to be retained.

* Review of the business
Turnover increased by 15% during the year and the directors believe that the trend will continue as export sales in Eire have increased by 25% and now comprise 15% of total turnover.

* Future developments
The directors intend to take advantage of the single European market and open up further export markets in Europe and have opened negotiations with various European agencies to this end.

(* Company Law does not strictly require this information to be included in the directors' report although inclusion of such information is customary.)

Appendix 1
Directors' report (continued)

Directors and their interests
The directors, all of whom served throughout the year, had the following interests in the £1 ordinary shares of the company at the beginning and the end of the financial year.

	31 December 2002	1 January 2002
Mr M. Clarke		
Mrs F. Mullen		
Miss J. Bennett		
Miss T. Green		

Political and charitable contributions
During the year the company made charitable donations of £* , principally to local charities serving the community in which the company operates.

Political donations were made to [name of political organisation] amounting to £* and political contributions to non-EU political organisations amounting to £* were made during the year. [*Where a company incurs any EU political expenditure or makes donations to any registered party or any other EU political organisations which exceed £5,000 in a 12-month period, an approval resolution must be passed by the company in general meeting before the donation is made or expenditure incurred.*]

Auditors
In accordance with section 385 of the Companies Act 1985, a resolution proposing that [Firm] be reappointed auditors will be put to the Annual General Meeting.

This report has been prepared in accordance with the special provisions relating to small companies within Part VII of the Companies Act 1985.

[Address of registered office]   By order of the Board,

J. Bennett
Secretary

[Date]

Example financial statements

Independent auditors' report

To the Shareholders of Smallco Limited:
We have audited the financial statements of Smallco Limited for the year ended 31 December 2002 set out on pages [4 to 15]. These financial statements have been prepared in accordance with the Financial Reporting Standard for Smaller Entities (effective June 2002) and under the accounting policies set out therein.

Respective responsibilities of directors and auditors
The directors' responsibilities for preparing the financial statements in accordance with applicable law and United Kingdom Accounting Standards are set out in the statement of directors' responsibilities. Our responsibility is to audit the financial statements in accordance with relevant legal and regulatory requirements and United Kingdom Auditing Standards.

We report to you our opinion as to whether the financial statements give a true and fair view and are properly prepared in accordance with the Companies Act 1985. We also report to you if, in our opinion, the Directors' report is not consistent with the financial statements, if the company has not kept proper accounting records or if we have not received all the information and explanations we require for our audit.

We read the Directors' report and consider the implications for our report if we become aware of any apparent misstatements within it.

Basis of opinion
We conducted our audit in accordance with United Kingdom Auditing Standards issued by the Auditing Practices Board. An audit includes examination, on a test basis, of evidence relevant to the amounts and disclosures in the financial statements. It also includes an assessment of the significant estimates and judgements made by the directors in the preparation of the financial statements and of whether the accounting policies are appropriate to the company's circumstances, consistently applied and adequately disclosed.

We planned and performed our audit so as to obtain all the information and explanations which we considered necessary in order to provide us with sufficient evidence to give reasonable assurance that the financial statements are free from material misstatement, whether caused by fraud or other irregularity or error. In forming our opinion we also evaluated the overall adequacy of the presentation of information in the financial statements.

Appendix 1
Independent auditors' report (continued)

Opinion
In our opinion the financial statements give a true and fair view of the state of the company's affairs as at 31 December 2002 and of its profit for the year then ended and are properly prepared in accordance with the provisions of the Companies Act 1985 applicable to small companies.

Chartered Accountants and Registered Auditors
[Name]

[Address]

[Date]

Example financial statements

Profit and loss account

For the year ended 31 December 2002

	Notes	2002 £	2001 £
Turnover	1	****	****
Cost of sales		****	***
Gross profit		***	**
Distribution costs		**	*
Administrative expenses		**	*
Operating profit	2	**	*
Income from participating interest		*	*
Profit on disposal of fixed assets		*	*
Interest receivable and similar income		**	**
Interest payable and similar charges		**	*
Profit on ordinary activities before taxation		**	*
Tax on profit on ordinary activities	3	*	*
Profit for the financial year		**	*
Dividends paid and proposed	4	**	*
Retained profit for the financial year		**	*
Retained profit (loss) at the beginning of the year		***	**
Retained profit carried forward		***	***

Appendix 1
Statement of total recognised gains and losses

For the year ended 31 December 2002

	2002 £	2001 £
Statement of total recognised gains and losses		
Profit for the financial year	**	**
Unrealised surplus on revaluation of properties	**	**
Total recognised gains and losses	**	**

Example financial statements

Balance sheet
31 December 2002

	Notes	2002 £	2001 £
Fixed assets			
Intangible assets	5	**	**
Tangible assets	6	**	**
Investments	7	**	**
		***	***
Current assets			
Stocks		**	**
Debtors	8	**	**
Cash at bank and in hand		**	**
		***	***
Creditors: Amounts falling due within one year	9	**	*
Net current assets		**	**
Total assets less current liabilities		***	***
Creditors: Amounts falling due after more than one year	10	*	*
Provisions for liabilities and charges	11	*	*
Net assets		****	****
Capital and reserves			
Called up share capital	12	**	**
Share premium account		**	**
Revaluation reserve		**	**
Profit and loss account		***	***
Shareholders' funds		****	****

These financial statements have been prepared in accordance with the special provisions relating to small companies within Part VII of the Companies Act 1985 and with the Financial Reporting Standard for Smaller Entities (effective June 2002).

[See Appendix 3 for substitute wording required where the company has taken advantage of the exemption from audit.]

Signed on behalf of the Board

[Name]   Director

[Date]

Appendix 1
Statement of accounting policies

31 December 2002

[Note the FRSSE requires the disclosure of each material accounting policy followed – FRSSE paragraph 2.7. The following accounting policies have been included for illustrative purposes but clearly the policies for any particular reporting entity would need to be tailored to reflect its individual circumstances.]

The financial statements have been prepared in accordance with the Financial Reporting Standard for Smaller Entities (effective June 2002) under the historical cost convention, modified by the revaluation of certain fixed assets.

(a) Consolidation
The company and its subsidiary undertaking form a small group as defined by statute and therefore the company has taken advantage of the exemption under section 248 of the Companies Act 1985 not to prepare group financial statements.

(b) Goodwill
Goodwill arising on acquisitions since 1 January 1999 is capitalised and amortised over its estimated useful economic life, subject to a maximum of 20 years. Goodwill written off to reserves under the company's previous accounting policy has not been reinstated and will be charged or credited to the profit and loss account on subsequent disposal of the business to which it relates.

(c) Turnover
Turnover consists of invoiced sales net of returns, trade discounts and value added tax.

(d) Depreciation
Depreciation has been provided at the following rates in order to write off the assets over their estimated useful lives.

Freehold and long-leasehold buildings	– 2% on cost or revalued amounts
Plant and machinery	– 10% straight-line
Fixtures and fittings	– 10% straight-line
Motor vehicles	– 25% straight-line
Intangible assets	– 10% straight-line
Goodwill	– 5% straight-line

Statement of accounting policies (continued)

(e) Revaluation of properties
As permitted by the transitional provisions of the Financial Reporting Standard for Smaller Entities (effective June 2002) the company has elected not to adopt a policy of revaluation of tangible fixed assets. The company will retain the book value of land and buildings, previously revalued at [date], and will not update that valuation.

(f) Investments
Fixed asset investments are shown at cost less provision for impairment. Current asset investments are stated at the lower of cost and net realisable value.

(g) Leases
Assets held under finance leases, which confer rights and obligations similar to those attached to owned assets, are capitalised as tangible fixed assets and are depreciated over the shorter of the lease terms and their useful lives. The capital elements of future lease obligations are recorded as liabilities, while the interest elements are charged to the profit and loss account over the period of the leases to produce a constant rate of charge on the balance of capital repayments outstanding. Hire purchase transactions are dealt with similarly, except that assets are depreciated over their useful lives.

Rentals under operating leases are charged on a straight-line basis over the lease term, even if the payments are not made on such a basis. Benefits received and receivable as an incentive to sign an operating lease are similarly spread on a straight-line basis over the lease term, except where the period to the review date on which the rent is first expected to be adjusted to the prevailing market rate is shorter than the full lease term, in which case the shorter period is used.

(h) Stocks and work in progress
Stocks and work in progress have been valued at the lower of cost and net realisable value.

(i) Current taxation
Corporation tax payable is provided on taxable profits at the current rate.

(j) Deferred taxation
Deferred tax is recognised in respect of all timing differences that have originated but not reversed at the balance sheet date. Timing differences are differences between the taxable profits and the results as stated in the financial statements that arise from the inclusion of gains and losses in tax assessments in periods different from those in which they are recognised in the financial statements.

Appendix 1
Statement of accounting policies (continued)

A net deferred tax asset is regarded as recoverable and therefore recognised only when it can be regarded as more likely than not that there will be suitable taxable profits from which the future reversal of underlying timing differences can be deducted.

Deferred tax is not recognised when fixed assets are revalued unless by the balance sheet date there is a binding agreement to sell the revalued assets and the asset has been revalued to selling price. Neither is deferred tax recognised when fixed assets are sold and it is more likely than not that the taxable gain will be rolled over, being charged to tax only if and when the replacement assets are sold.

Deferred tax is measured at the average tax rates that are expected to apply in the periods in which the timing differences are expected to reverse, based on tax rates and laws that have been enacted by the balance sheet date. Deferred tax is measured on a non-discounted basis.

(k) Pension costs and other post-retirement benefits
The company operates a defined contribution scheme. The amount charged to the profit and loss account in respect of pension costs and other post-retirement benefits is the contributions payable in the year. Differences between contributions payable in the year and contributions actually paid are shown as either accruals or prepayments in the balance sheet.

[See Appendix 3 for illustrative disclosures where the company operates a defined benefit scheme.]

(l) Foreign currencies
Transactions in foreign currencies are recorded at the rate of exchange at the date of the transaction or, if hedged, at the forward contract rate. Monetary assets and liabilities denominated in foreign currencies at the balance sheet date are reported at the rates of exchange prevailing at that date or, if appropriate, at the forward contract rate. Any gain or loss arising from a change in exchange rates subsequent to the date of the transaction is included as an exchange gain or loss in the profit and loss account.

(m) Research and development
Research expenditure is written off as incurred. Development expenditure is also written off, except where the directors are satisfied as to the technical, commercial and financial viability of individual projects. In such cases, the identifiable expenditure is deferred and amortised over the period during which the group is expected to benefit.

Statement of accounting policies (continued)

(n) Government grants

Government grants relating to tangible fixed assets are treated as deferred income and released to the profit and loss account over the expected useful lives of the assets concerned. Other grants are credited to the profit and loss account as the related expenditure is incurred.

Appendix 1
Notes to financial statements

31 December 2002

1 Turnover
Turnover attributable to geographical markets outside the United Kingdom amounted to 15% (2001 – 14%).

2 Operating profit
Operating profit is stated after charging:

	2002 £	2001 £
Depreciation	*	*
Pension contribution	*	*
Auditors' remuneration	*	*
Directors' remuneration	**	**

Directors remuneration includes emoluments and company contributions made to money purchase pension schemes. Three (2001– *) of the directors are members of money purchase pension schemes.

3 Taxation
The tax charge for the year has been calculated at *% (2001 – *%). The tax charge comprises:

	2002 £	2001 £
Current tax		
UK corporation tax	*	*
Deferred tax		
Origination and reversal of timing differences	*	*
Effect of increase in tax rate on opening liability	*	*
Total deferred tax (see note 11)	**	**
Total tax on profit on ordinary activities	**	**

No deferred tax has been provided by the company in respect of the revaluation of tangible fixed assets. Had the revalued assets been sold at the year end at their carrying values a tax liability of £* (2001 – £*) would have arisen.

Example financial statements

Notes to financial statements (continued)

4 Dividends

	2002 £	2001 £
Proposed dividend on Ordinary shares	*	*
Dividend paid on 7% Preference shares	*	*

5 Intangible fixed assets

	Goodwill £	Other intangible assets £	Total £
Cost			
1 January 2002	**	**	***
Additions	*	*	*
Disposals	*	*	*
31 December 2002	**	**	***
Amortisation			
1 January 2002	*	*	*
Disposals	*	*	*
Charge for the year	*	*	*
31 December 2002	*	*	*
Net book value			
31 December 2002	**	**	**
31 December 2001	**	**	**

Other intangible assets comprise development expenditure which has been capitalised in accordance with generally accepted accounting practice and is therefore not treated, for dividend purposes, as a realised loss.

Appendix 1
Notes to financial statements (continued)

6 Tangible fixed assets

	Land and buildings £	Plant and machinery £	Total £
Cost or valuation			
1 January 2002	***	***	***
Additions	**	**	**
Disposals	*	*	*
31 December 2002	***	***	***
Depreciation			
1 January 2002	**	**	**
Disposals	*	*	*
Charge for the year	**	**	**
31 December 2002	**	**	**
Net book value			
31 December 2002	***	***	***
31 December 2001	***	***	***

Land and buildings were revalued at [date] by A Surveyor, FRICS, on an existing use basis.

The historical cost of land and buildings included at a valuation of £* (2001 – £*) was £* (2001 – £*) and aggregate depreciation thereon would have been £* (2001 – £*).

7 Investments

	Subsidiary undertaking £	Listed investments £	Total £
Cost			
1 January 2002	***	***	***
Additions	**	**	**
31 December 2002	***	***	***

Example financial statements

Notes to financial statements (continued)

Subsidiary undertaking
The company's investment in its subsidiary company represents the whole of the issued share capital of Subsid Limited, which provides promotional services.

At 30 September 2002 the aggregate share capital and reserves of Subsid Limited were £* (2001 – £*) and the profit for the year to that date was £* (2001 – £*).

Listed investments
Listed investments comprise investments which are listed on The London Stock Exchange. The market value of these investments was £* at 31 December 2002 (2001 – £*).

8 Debtors

	2002 £	2001 £
Trade debtors	***	***
Amounts owed by subsidiary undertaking	**	**
Other debtors	**	**
	****	****

Debtors include an amount of £* (2001 – £*) falling due after more than one year.

9 Creditors: Amounts falling due within one year

	2002 £	2001 £
Bank loans and overdrafts (secured)	**	**
Trade creditors	**	**
Amounts owed by subsidiary undertaking	**	**
Other creditors	**	**
Taxation and social security costs	**	**
	***	**

The bank loans and overdrafts are secured on the freehold property.

Appendix 1
Notes to financial statements (continued)

10 Creditors: Amounts falling due after more than one year

	2002 £	2001 £
Amounts owed by subsidiary undertaking	**	**
Other creditors	**	**
	**	**

Included within other creditors is an amount of £* (2001 – £*) due in more than five years.

11 Provisions for liabilities and charges

	Deferred taxation £
At 1 January 2002	**
Charged/credited to profit and loss account	**
At 31 December 2002	**

Deferred tax is provided as follows:

	2002 £	2001 £
Accelerated capital allowances	**	**
Other timing differences	**	**
Tax losses available	**	**
Other	**	**
Provision for deferred tax	**	**

12 Called up share capital

	2002 £	2001 £
Authorised		
** Ordinary shares of £1 each	****	****
** 7% Cumulative Preference shares of £1 each	***	***
	****	****

Example financial statements

Notes to financial statements (continued)

Allotted, called up and fully paid
**	Ordinary shares of £1 each	***	***
**	7% Cumulative Preference shares of £1 each	***	***
		****	****

The 7% Cumulative Preference shares are redeemable at par at the option of the company on 1 January 2005 and on each anniversary of that date.

13 Related party transactions

During the year Mr Churchill supplied goods, to the value of £* (2001 – £*), to the company in the ordinary course of business. Mr Churchill is the father-in-law of Mrs Mullen, a director. Amounts owed to Mr Churchill amounted to £* (2001 – £*) at 31 December 2002.

14 Controlling party

Mr Clarke, a director, and members of his close family control the company as a result of controlling directly or indirectly *% of the issued Ordinary share capital.

Appendix 2

Example abbreviated accounts

Smallco Limited

Abbreviated accounts 31 December 2002

Registered number: _____

> Abbreviated accounts are required to contain, as a minimum, an abbreviated balance sheet, notes to the accounts, a directors' statement and, if appointed, a special report by the auditors. These accounts illustrate some of the more common disclosures made by small companies. For information on the more detailed requirements, please refer to the disclosure checklist in Appendix 4.

Example abbreviated accounts

Independent auditors' report

To Smallco Limited under section 247B of the Companies Act 1985:
We have examined the abbreviated accounts of Smallco Limited for the year ended 31 December 2002 set out on pages [2 to 8] together with the financial statements of the company prepared under section 226 of the Companies Act 1985.

Respective responsibilities of directors and auditors
The directors are responsible for preparing the abbreviated accounts in accordance with United Kingdom law under section 246 of the Companies Act 1985. It is our responsibility as established by relevant legal and regulatory requirements and United Kingdom Auditing Standards to form an opinion as to whether the company is entitled to deliver abbreviated accounts prepared in accordance with sections 246 (5) and (6) of the Act to the Registrar of Companies and whether the abbreviated accounts to be delivered are properly prepared in accordance with those relevant provisions and to report our opinion to you.

Basis of opinion
We have carried out the procedures we consider necessary to confirm, by reference to the financial statements, that the company is entitled to deliver abbreviated accounts and that the abbreviated accounts to be delivered are properly prepared. [The scope of our work for the purpose of this report did not include examining or dealing with events after the date of our report on the financial statements.]

Opinion
In our opinion the company is entitled to deliver abbreviated accounts prepared in accordance with sections 246 (5) and (6) of the Companies Act 1985 in respect of the year ended 31 December 2002 and the abbreviated accounts on pages [2 to 8] are properly prepared in accordance with those provisions.

Chartered Accountants and Registered Auditors

[Name]
[Address]

[Date]

Appendix 2
Balance sheet
31 December 2002

	Notes	2002 £	2001 £
Fixed assets			
Intangible assets	1	**	**
Tangible assets	2	**	**
Investments	3	**	**
		***	***
Current assets			
Stocks		**	**
Debtors	4	**	**
Cash at bank and in hand		**	**
		***	***
Creditors: Amounts falling due within one year	5	**	*
Net current assets		**	**
Total assets less current liabilities		***	***
Creditors: Amounts falling due after more than one year	6	*	*
Provisions for liabilities and charges		*	*
Net assets		****	****
Capital and reserves			
Called up share capital	7	**	**
Share premium account		**	**
Revaluation reserve		**	**
Profit and loss account		***	***
Shareholders' funds		****	****

The abbreviated accounts have been prepared in accordance with the special provisions relating to small companies within Part VII of the Companies Act 1985.

[See Appendix 3 for substitute wording required where the company has taken advantage of the exemption from audit.]

Signed on behalf of the Board
[Name]   Director

[Date]

Example abbreviated accounts

Statement of accounting policies

31 December 2002

The full financial statements, from which these abbreviated accounts have been extracted, have been prepared in accordance with the Financial Reporting Standard for Smaller Entities (effective June 2002) under the historical cost convention, modified by the revaluation of certain fixed assets.

[The policies to be listed here should be identical with those in the full financial statements.]

(a) Consolidation
The company and its subsidiary undertaking form a small group as defined by statute and therefore the company has taken advantage of the exemption under section 248 of the Companies Act 1985 not to prepare group financial statements.

(b) Goodwill
Goodwill arising on acquisitions since 1 January 1999 is capitalised and amortised over its estimated useful economic life, subject to a maximum of 20 years. Goodwill written off to reserves under the company's previous accounting policy has not been reinstated and will be charged or credited to the profit and loss account on subsequent disposal of the business to which it relates.

(c) Turnover
Turnover consists of invoiced sales net of returns, trade discounts and value added tax.

(d) Depreciation
Depreciation has been provided at the following rates in order to write off the assets over their estimated useful lives.

Freehold and long-leasehold buildings	– 2% on cost or revalued amounts
Plant and machinery	– 10% straight-line
Fixtures and fittings	– 10% straight-line
Motor vehicles	– 25% straight-line
Intangible assets	– 10% straight-line
Goodwill	– 5% straight-line

(e) Revaluation of properties
As permitted by the transitional provisions of the Financial Reporting Standard for Smaller Entities (effective June 2002) the company has elected not to adopt a policy of revaluation of tangible fixed assets. The company will retain the book value of land and buildings, previously revalued at [date], and will not update that valuation.

Appendix 2
Statement of accounting policies (continued)

(f) Investments
Fixed asset investments are shown at cost less provision for impairment. Current asset investments are stated at the lower of cost and net realisable value.

(g) Leases
Assets held under finance leases, which confer rights and obligations similar to those attached to owned assets, are capitalised as tangible fixed assets and are depreciated over the shorter of the lease terms and their useful lives. The capital elements of future lease obligations are recorded as liabilities, while the interest elements are charged to the profit and loss account over the period of the leases to produce a constant rate of charge on the balance of capital repayments outstanding. Hire purchase transactions are dealt with similarly, except that assets are depreciated over their useful lives.

Rentals under operating leases are charged on a straight-line basis over the lease term, even if the payments are not made on such a basis. Benefits received and receivable as an incentive to sign an operating lease are similarly spread on a straight-line basis over the lease term, except where the period to the review date on which the rent is first expected to be adjusted to the prevailing market rate is shorter than the full lease term, in which case the shorter period is used.

(h) Stocks and work in progress
Stocks and work in progress have been valued at the lower of cost and net realisable value.

(i) Current taxation
Corporation tax payable is provided on taxable profits at the current rate.

(j) Deferred taxation
Deferred tax is recognised in respect of all timing differences that have originated but not reversed at the balance sheet date. Timing differences are differences between the taxable profits and the results as stated in the financial statements that arise from the inclusion of gains and losses in tax assessments in periods different from those in which they are recognised in the financial statements.

A net deferred tax asset is regarded as recoverable and therefore recognised only when it can be regarded as more likely than not that there will be suitable taxable profits from which the future reversal of underlying timing differences can be deducted.

Example abbreviated accounts

Statement of accounting policies (continued)

Deferred tax is not recognised when fixed assets are revalued unless by the balance sheet date there is a binding agreement to sell the revalued assets and the asset has been revalued to selling price. Neither is deferred tax recognised when fixed assets are sold and it is more likely than not that the taxable gain will be rolled over, being charged to tax only if and when the replacement assets are sold.

Deferred tax is measured at the average tax rates that are expected to apply in the periods in which the timing differences are expected to reverse, based on tax rates and laws that have been enacted by the balance sheet date. Deferred tax is measured on a non-discounted basis.

(k) Pension costs and other post retirement benefits
The company operates a defined contribution scheme. The amount charged to the profit and loss account in respect of pension costs and other post-retirement benefits is the contributions payable in the year. Differences between contributions payable in the year and contributions actually paid are shown as either accruals or prepayments in the balance sheet.

[See Appendix 3 for illustrative disclosures where the company operates a defined benefit scheme.]

(l) Foreign currencies
Transactions in foreign currencies are recorded at the rate of exchange at the date of the transaction or, if hedged, at the forward contract rate. Monetary assets and liabilities denominated in foreign currencies at the balance sheet date are reported at the rates of exchange prevailing at that date or, if appropriate, at the forward contract rate. Any gain or loss arising from a change in exchange rates subsequent to the date of the transaction is included as an exchange gain or loss in the profit and loss account.

(m) Research and development
Research expenditure is written off as incurred. Development expenditure is also written off, except where the directors are satisfied as to the technical, commercial and financial viability of individual projects. In such cases, the identifiable expenditure is deferred and amortised over the period during which the group is expected to benefit.

(n) Government grants
Government grants relating to tangible fixed assets are treated as deferred income and released to the profit and loss account over the expected useful lives of the assets concerned. Other grants are credited to the profit and loss account as the related expenditure is incurred.

Appendix 2
Notes to accounts
31 December 2002
1 Intangible fixed assets

	Total £
Cost	
1 January 2002	***
Additions	*
Disposals	*
31 December 2002	***
Amortisation	
1 January 2002	*
Disposals	*
Charge for the year	*
31 December 2002	*
Net book value	
31 December 2002	**
31 December 2001	**

2 Tangible fixed assets

	Total £
Cost or valuation	
1 January 2002	***
Additions	**
Disposals	*
31 December 2002	***
Depreciation	
1 January 2002	**
Disposals	*
Charge for the year	**
31 December 2002	**
Net book value	
31 December 2002	***
31 December 2001	***

Example abbreviated accounts

Notes to accounts (continued)

3 Investments

	Total £
Cost	
1 January 2002	***
Additions	*
31 December 2002	***

Subsidiary undertaking

The company's investment in its subsidiary company represents the acquisition of the whole of the share capital of Subsid Limited, a company registered in England and Wales, which provides promotional services.

At 30 September 2002 the aggregate share capital and reserves of Subsid Limited were £* (2001 – £*) and the profit for the year to that date was £* (2001 – £*).

4 Debtors

Debtors include an amount of £* (2001 – £*) falling due after more than one year.

5 Creditors: Amounts falling due within one year

The company's bank loans and overdrafts of £* (2001 – £*) are secured on the freehold property.

6 Creditors: Amounts falling due after more than one year

Included within other creditors is an amount of £* (2001 – £*) due in more than five years.

Appendix 2
Notes to accounts (continued)

7 Called up share capital

	2002 £	2001 £
Authorised		
** Ordinary shares of £1 each	****	****
** 7% Cumulative Preference shares of £1 each	***	***
	****	****
Allotted, called up and fully paid		
** Ordinary shares of £1 each	***	***
** 7% Cumulative Preference shares of £1 each	***	***
	****	****

The 7% Cumulative Preference shares are redeemable at par at the option of the company on 1 January 2005 and on each anniversary of that date.

Appendix 3

Illustrative wordings

Audit exemption wording

Where the company has made use of the exemption not to have an audit of the financial statements, the following words should be included on the balance sheet immediately above the signature approving the financial statements on behalf of the board, as required by section 233 of the Companies Act 1985. However, if the company has taken advantage of the small company exemptions for the preparation of its financial statements, this statement should appear above the statement required by section 246 (8).

The additional wording, as set out below, is required on the balance sheet of both the modified financial statements circulated to shareholders and the abbreviated accounts filed with the Registrar of Companies.

Modified financial statements
In preparing these unaudited financial statements advantage has been taken of the exemption under section 249A (1) of the Companies Act 1985. Members have not required the company to obtain an audit under section 249B (2).

Company law requires the directors to prepare financial statements for each financial year which give a true and fair view of the state of affairs of the company and of the profit or loss of the company for that period and which comply with the provisions of the Companies Act 1985. The directors are responsible for keeping proper accounting records which disclose with reasonable accuracy at any time the financial position of the company and enable them to ensure that the financial statements comply with the Companies Act. They are also responsible for safeguarding the assets of the company and hence taking reasonable steps for the prevention and detection of fraud and other irregularities.

These financial statements have been prepared in accordance with the special provisions relating to small companies within Part VII of the

Appendix 3

Companies Act 1985 and with the Financial Reporting Standard for Smaller Entities (effective June 2002).

Abbreviated accounts

These abbreviated accounts are derived from unaudited financial statements. In preparing the unaudited financial statements advantage has been taken of the exemption under section 249A (1) of the Companies Act 1985. Members have not required the company to obtain an audit under section 249B (2).

Company law requires the directors to prepare financial statements for each financial year which give a true and fair view of the state of affairs of the company and of the profit or loss of the company for that period and which comply with the provisions of the Companies Act 1985. The directors are responsible for keeping proper accounting records which disclose with reasonable accuracy at any time the financial position of the company and enable them to ensure that the financial statements comply with the Companies Act. They are also responsible for safeguarding the assets of the company and hence taking reasonable steps for the prevention and detection of fraud and other irregularities.

The abbreviated accounts have been prepared in accordance with the special provisions relating to small companies within Part VII of the Companies Act 1985.

Illustrative wordings

Defined benefit scheme wording

The example financial statements in Appendix 1 contain the disclosures required for companies which operate defined contribution schemes. More extensive disclosures are required in financial statements of companies which operate defined benefit schemes. The FRSSE has different requirements in respect of financial statements relating to periods ending on or after 22 June 2002, 2003 and 2004. Recognition of the amounts disclosed is not required until periods ending on or after 22 June 2004. However, the information disclosed over the preceding two years will form the basis for calculating the prior year adjustment when the accounting treatment under paragraph 2 of Appendix II (required for accounting periods ending on or after 22 June 2004) is adopted. Illustrative disclosures for each of these periods is shown below.

Example 1: For periods ending between 22 June 2002 and 21 June 2003

Accounting policy note / Pension costs:
For defined benefit schemes the amounts charged to operating profit are the current service costs and gains and losses on settlements and curtailments. They are included as part of staff costs. Past service costs are recognised immediately in the profit and loss account if the benefits have vested. If the benefits have not vested immediately, the costs are recognised over the period until vesting occurs. The interest cost and the expected return on assets are shown as a net amount of other finance costs or credits adjacent to interest. Actuarial gains and losses are recognised immediately in the statement of total recognised gains and losses.

Defined benefit schemes are funded, with the assets of the scheme held separately from those of the group, in separate trustee administered funds. Pension scheme assets are measured at fair value and liabilities are measured on an actuarial basis using the projected unit method and discounted at a rate equivalent to the current rate of return on a high quality corporate bond of equivalent currency and term to the scheme liabilities. The actuarial valuations are obtained at least triennially and are updated at each balance sheet date. The resulting defined benefit asset or liability, net of the related deferred tax, is presented separately after other net assets on the face of the balance sheet.

Pension note to the financial statements:
The company provides pension arrangements to the majority of full-time employees through a defined benefit scheme. The scheme is funded, with the assets of the scheme held separately from those of the company [in separate trustee administered funds / being invested with insurance companies]. The

Appendix 3

contributions to the scheme are assessed in accordance with the advice of professionally qualified actuaries. Differences between amounts charged to the profit and loss account and amounts funded are shown as either provisions or prepayments in the balance sheet.

The pension cost charge for the year for the defined benefit scheme was £_____ (20YY – £_____).

[*Details of the most recent actuarial valuation of the scheme should be provided. The FRSSE provides no further details of what should be provided. The following content is included in SSAP 24 and may be regarded as 'best practice':*

- *date of actuarial valuation;*
- *actuarial method used and description of the main assumptions;*
- *percentage level of funding; and*
- *comments on material actuarial surplus or deficit.*]

For periods ending on or after 22 June 2004 a new method of accounting for defined benefit schemes is required by the Financial Reporting Standard for Smaller Entities (effective June 2002). The following transitional disclosures are required in the current period to ensure ease of implementation of the new requirements. The actuarial valuation described above has been updated at [*balance sheet date*] by a qualified actuary using revised assumptions that are consistent with these new requirements. Investments have been valued, for this purpose, at fair value. [*A new valuation may have to be obtained if the valuation previously used was not the projected unit method. This paragraph will have to be revised accordingly.*]

The fair value of the assets in the scheme and the present value of the liabilities in the scheme at the balance sheet date were:

	20XX £
Fair value of assets	***
Present value of scheme liabilities	**
[Surplus / deficit] in the scheme	***
Related deferred tax [liability / asset]	**
Net pension [asset / liability]	****

[The deficit on the scheme should be eliminated by [*date*] at the current employer's contribution rate of __% of pensionable earnings. / The surplus

Illustrative wordings

on the scheme should be eliminated by [*date*] as a result of [lower contributions/a pension contribution holiday].]

[*Where the asset or liability that would be recorded in the balance sheet would differ from the surplus or deficit in the scheme, an explanation of the difference should be given without comparative disclosure.*]

Example 2: For periods ending between 22 June 2003 and 21 June 2004

The company provides pension arrangements to the majority of full-time employees through a defined benefit scheme. The scheme is funded with the assets of the scheme held separately from those of the company [in separate trustee administered funds / being invested with insurance companies]. The contributions to the scheme are assessed in accordance with the advice of professionally qualified actuaries. Differences between amounts charged to the profit and loss account and amounts funded are shown as either provisions or prepayments in the balance sheet.

The pension cost charge for the year for the defined benefit scheme was £_____ (20YY – £_____).

[*Details of the most recent actuarial valuation of the scheme should be provided. The FRSSE provides no further details of what should be provided. The following content is included in SSAP 24 and may be regarded as 'best practice':*

- *date of actuarial valuation;*
- *actuarial method used and description of the main assumptions;*
- *percentage level of funding; and*
- *comments on material actuarial surplus or deficit.*]

For periods ending on or after 22 June 2004 a new method of accounting for defined benefit schemes is required by the Financial Reporting Standard for Smaller Entities (effective June 2002). The following transitional disclosures are required in the current period to ensure ease of implementation of the new requirements. The actuarial valuation described above has been updated at [*balance sheet date*] by a qualified actuary using revised assumptions that are consistent with these new requirements. Investments have been valued, for this purpose, at fair value. [*A new valuation may have to be obtained if the valuation previously used was not the projected unit method. This paragraph will have to be revised accordingly.*]

The fair value of the assets in the scheme and the present value of the liabilities in the scheme at the balance sheet date were:

Appendix 3

	20XX	20YY
	£	£
Fair value of assets	***	***
Present value of scheme liabilities	**	**
[Surplus / deficit] in the scheme	***	***
Related deferred tax [liability / asset]	**	**
Net pension [asset / liability]	****	****

[*Where the asset or liability that would be recorded in the balance sheet would differ from the surplus or deficit in the scheme, an explanation of the difference should be given with comparative information.*]

Movement in scheme surplus during the year

	20XX
	£
At 1 January 20XX	****
Current service cost	**
Contributions	**
Past service costs	*
Net finance income	*
Actuarial gain	**
At 31 December 20XX	****

Illustrative wordings

Example 3: For periods ending after 22 June 2004

Extract from balance sheet

	Notes	20XX £	20YY £
Net current assets		**	**
Creditors: Amounts falling due after more than one year	*	*	*
Net assets excluding pension [asset / liability]		****	****
Pension [asset / liability]	*	****	****
Net assets including pension [asset / liability]		****	****
Capital and reserves			
Called up share capital	*	**	**
Profit and loss account		***	***
Shareholders' funds		****	****

Disclosure notes

The group operates a defined benefit pension scheme in the UK. A full actuarial valuation was carried out at 31 December 20YY and updated to 31 December 20XX by a qualified actuary. [*Disclose if actuary is an employee or officer of the reporting entity or the group to which it belongs.*]

The fair value of the assets in the scheme and the present value of the liabilities in the scheme at each balance sheet date were:

	20XX £	20YY £
Fair value of assets	***	***
Present value of scheme liabilities	**	**
[Surplus / deficit] in the scheme	***	***
Related deferred tax [liability / asset]	**	**
Net pension [asset / liability]	****	****

[*Where the asset or liability that would be recorded in the balance sheet would differ from the surplus or deficit in the scheme, an explanation of the difference should be given with comparative information.*]

Appendix 3

The contribution rate for 20XX was __% of pensionable earnings and the agreed contribution rates for the next [*number of years*] years is __% of pensionable earnings.

[*Where the scheme is closed or those in which the age profile of the active membership is rising significantly.* The [scheme is a closed scheme / scheme's active membership has an age profile that is rising significantly] and therefore under the projected unit method the current service cost would be expected to increase as the members of the scheme approach retirement.]

Movement in scheme surplus during the year

	20XX £	20YY £
At 1 January 20XX	****	****
Current service cost	**	**
Contributions	**	**
Past service costs	*	*
Net finance income	*	*
Actuarial gain	**	**
At 31 December 20XX	****	****

[*The components of the change, except for contributions paid, in the defined benefit asset or liability should be disclosed separately. Separate analysis in the notes to the financial statements would normally be the most appropriate method of disclosure.*]

Appendix 4

Small companies' disclosure checklist

This checklist is suitable for use in reviewing the form and content of the financial statements of small companies that are entitled to the exemptions available in s246 Companies Act 1985 and have chosen to prepare their financial statements in accordance with the Financial Reporting Standard for Smaller Entities (FRSSE). This checklist is not appropriate for companies which are charities.

Such companies are exempt from the requirement to prepare group financial statements when they have subsidiaries. This checklist is not suitable for use when group financial statements have been prepared by choice.

The checklist is based on company law as at 1 March 2002 and FRSSE 2002, which is effective for accounting periods ending on or after 22 June 2002 (although earlier adoption is encouraged).

The checklist is a summary. While the intention has been to provide explanation and guidance where helpful, reference should be made to the specific provisions of the legislation and the FRSSE where necessary. The checklist is concerned with disclosure requirements only and does not attempt to deal with other requirements of the FRSSE.

Principal sections	Questions
General	1–12
Directors' report	13–24
Independent auditor's report	25–30
Profit and loss account	31–46
Statement of total recognised gains and losses	47–48
Balance sheet	49–94

Appendix 4

Additional notes to the financial statements	95–148
Abbreviated accounts	149–165

References in the checklist are to the FRSSE and Company Law requirements. Unless otherwise indicated the number in the FRSSE column relates to the relevant paragraph, and s or Sch in the Reference column refer to the section or Schedule number of the Companies Act 1985.

Small companies' disclosure checklist

Disclosure Checklist

Client:
Year end:
Completed by: Reviewed by:

No.	Disclosure Item	Reference	FRSSE reference	Complies?	Comments
General					
1	The financial statements should present a true and fair view of the results for the period and of the state of affairs at the end of the period. To achieve this, the financial statements should in normal circumstances comply with generally accepted accounting principles. Accounting policies and estimation techniques should be consistent with the requirements of the FRSSE and of companies legislation. Where this permits a choice, an entity should select the policies and techniques most appropriate to its particular circumstances for the purpose of giving a true and fair view, taking account of the objectives of relevance, reliability, comparability and understandability.	s226	2.1 2.4		
2	To achieve a true and fair view, regard should be had to the substance of any arrangement or transaction, or series of such, into which the entity has entered. To determine the substance of a transaction it is necessary to identify whether the transaction has given rise to new, or changes to existing, assets or liabilities. Where there is any doubt as to whether applying any provisions of the FRSSE would be sufficient to give a true and fair view, adequate explanation should be given in the notes to the financial statements of	s226(4)	2.1 2.2		

Appendix 4

No.	Disclosure Item	Reference	FRSSE reference	Complies?	Comments
	the transaction or arrangement concerned and the treatment adopted. There should be adequate disclosure of additional information necessary to show a true and fair view.				
3	Where it is necessary to depart from the Companies Act 1985 requirements in order to provide a true and fair view, the following should be given:	s226(4) s226(5)	2.9 2.10		
	(1) a statement of the treatment that would normally be required in the circumstances and a description of the treatment actually adopted;				
	(2) a statement explaining why the treatment provided would not give a true and fair view; and				
	(3) a description of how the position shown in the financial statements is different as a result of the departure, normally with quantification, except (i) where quantification is already evident in the financial statements themselves, or (ii) whenever the effect cannot be reasonably quantified, in which case the circumstances should be explained.				
	Note: Where a departure continues in subsequent financial statements, the disclosures should be made in all subsequent statements and should include corresponding amounts for the previous period.				
4	When preparing financial statements, directors should assess whether there are any significant doubts about the entity's ability to continue as a going concern. Any material uncertainties, of which the directors are aware in making their assessment, should be disclosed.		2.6		

Small companies' disclosure checklist

No.	Disclosure Item	Reference	FRSSE reference	Complies?	Comments
	Where the period considered in making this assessment has been limited to a period of less than one year from the date of approval of the financial statements, that fact should be stated.				
5	Corresponding amounts for the previous year should be disclosed for each item in the profit and loss account, balance sheet and notes to the financial statements (exceptions to this rule are noted, where appropriate, in this checklist).	Sch8:4(1) Sch8:51(2)			
6	Assets or income should not be set off against liabilities or expenditure respectively (debit and credit balances should be aggregated into a single net item only where they do not constitute separate assets and liabilities).	Sch8:5			
7	The financial statements should be approved by the board of directors and signed on the company balance sheet on behalf of the board by a director of the company.	s233(1) s233(2)			
8	Disclose the date on which the financial statements are approved by the board of directors.		14.6		
9	Disclose the name of the director signing the balance sheet.	s233(3)			
10	The copy of the financial statements delivered to the Registrar must state in a prominent position the registered number of the company, be signed by, and state the name of, the directors and registered auditors as appropriate and comply with the requirements prescribed by regulations to enable clear copies to be made. Note: This applies equally to abbreviated accounts delivered to the Registrar. The copy of the directors' report which is delivered to the Registrar shall be signed on behalf of the board by a director or the secretary of the company.	s233(4) s234A(3) s236(3) s246(7) s706			

Appendix 4

No.	Disclosure Item	Reference	FRSSE reference	Complies?	Comments
11	The directors' report and balance sheet should each contain, in a prominent position above the signature, a statement that they have been prepared in accordance with the special provisions in Part VII of the Companies Act 1985 relating to small companies. Note: These requirements do not apply where the company is dormant and exempt from the requirement to appoint auditors by virtue of s249AA. The statement on the balance sheet may be combined with the statement that the financial statements have been prepared in accordance with the FRSSE (see Q95), for example as follows: 'The financial statements have been prepared in accordance with the special provisions relating to small companies within Part VII of the Companies Act 1985 and the Financial Reporting Standard for Smaller Entities (effective June 2002).'	s246(8) s246(9)			
12	If the company has taken advantage of the exemption from audit under s249A, a statement is required above the signatures on the balance sheet. This must state that: (1) in the year in question, the company was entitled to the exemption under subsections (1) or (2) of s249A; (2) no member or members have deposited a notice in the specified manner requesting an audit; and (3) the directors acknowledge their responsibility for ensuring the company keeps accounting records which comply with s221 and for preparing financial statements which give	s249B(4)			

Small companies' disclosure checklist

No.	Disclosure Item	Reference	FRSSE reference	Complies?	Comments
	a true and fair view of the state of the company's affairs as at the end of the financial year and of its profit or loss in that financial year, in accordance with s226 and which otherwise comply with the Act in relation to financial statements. For example, as follows: 'In preparing these unaudited financial statements advantage has been taken of the exemption under section 249A(1) of the Companies Act 1985. Members have not required the company to obtain an audit under section 249B(2). Company law requires the directors to prepare financial statements for each financial year which give a true and fair view of the state of affairs of the company and of the profit or loss of the company for that period and which comply with the provisions of the Companies Act 1985. The directors are responsible for keeping proper accounting records which disclose with reasonable accuracy at any time the financial position of the company and to enable them to ensure that the financial statements comply with the Companies Act. They are also responsible for safeguarding the assets of the company and hence taking reasonable steps for the prevention and detection of fraud and other irregularities.'				
	Directors' report				
13	Indicate the principal activities of the company (and of its subsidiary undertakings) during the period and any significant changes in those activities.	s234(2)			
14	Disclose the names of all of the persons who were directors during the period. Note: Although there is no statutory requirement to do so, it is conventional to disclose the names of	s234(2)			

Appendix 4

No.	Disclosure Item	Reference	FRSSE reference	Complies?	Comments
	directors who have been appointed or who have retired after the year end and also the names of the directors due for reappointment at the AGM.				

15	Disclose in respect of each director in office at the year end, his or her interest in the shares or debentures of the company or other body corporate in the same group (as recorded in the Register of Directors' Interests and including those of spouse and children under 18).
	
	 (1) If an interest arises give the:
	     (a) name of company;
	     (b) number of shares and amount of debentures; and
	     (c) a comparative figure at the beginning of the year or date of appointment if later.
	 (2) Provide a negative statement if no such interests exist.
	
	 Note: This information may alternatively be given in the notes to the financial statements.
	
	 Exemptions:
	 The following interests do not have to be notified to the company for inclusion in the Register:
	   (i) directors' nominee shareholdings in wholly owned subsidiaries of a body corporate;
	   (ii) interests of the directors of wholly owned subsidiaries of companies incorporated in Great Britain where the directors are also directors of the holding company, to the subsidiaries themselves;
		s324(6) Sch7:2 Sch7:2A SI 1985/ 802			

Small companies' disclosure checklist

No.	Disclosure Item	Reference	FRSSE reference	Complies?	Comments
	(iii) interests of the directors of wholly owned subsidiaries of companies incorporated outside Great Britain in companies incorporated outside Great Britain; (iv) directors' holdings as trustees of trusts over which the Public Trustee is also a trustee; (v) directors' holdings as trustees or beneficiaries of a pension fund or scheme; and (vi) interests in shares which arise solely on account of a limitation in the right to dispose of a share imposed by the memorandum or articles of association.				
16	Disclose in respect of each director in office at the year end, in respect of each group company, the number of shares and amount of debentures for which rights (e.g. options) to subscribe were granted to or exercised by the director or his immediate family in the financial year. Note: (i) Exemptions in Q15 above also apply. (ii) This information may alternatively be given in the notes to the financial statements.	Sch7:2 Sch7:2B			
17	If charitable donations made by a company and its subsidiaries between them in a financial period exceed £200 in amount, the directors' report should include a statement of the amount given for each purpose. Note: (i) The above disclosures are not required for	Sch7:5			

143

Appendix 4

No.	Disclosure Item	Reference	FRSSE reference	Complies?	Comments
	wholly owned subsidiaries of companies incorporated in Great Britain. (ii) Money given for charitable purposes to a person who, when it was given, was ordinarily resident outside the UK should not be included. (iii) Prior to the 'relevant date' (i.e. the earlier of the company's first AGM to be held between 16 February 2001 – 15 February 2002 and 16 February 2002), this disclosure need only be made if the aggregate of charitable and political donations exceeds £200.				
18	(1) If, in the financial year, the company and its subsidiaries have made any donation to any registered party or to any other EU political organisation or incurred any EU political expenditure which together exceed £200, the directors' report for the year should disclose: (a) the name of each registered party or other organisation to whom any such donation has been made; (b) the total amount given to that party or organisation; and (c) the total amount of any EU political expenditure incurred. (2) If, in the financial year, the company and its subsidiaries have made any contribution to any non-EU political party, the directors' report should disclose the total amount of the contributions.	Sch7:3,4			

Small companies' disclosure checklist

No.	Disclosure Item	Reference	FRSSE reference	Complies?	Comments
	Note: (i) The above disclosures are not required for wholly owned subsidiaries of companies incorporated in Great Britain. (ii) Prior to the 'relevant date' (i.e. the earlier of the company's first AGM to be held between 16 February 2001 – 15 February 2002 and 16 February 2002), disclosure is only required of the total UK political contributions together with, in respect of any amount over £200, a statement of the amount and the name of the political party or person paid. This disclosure is not required for wholly owned subsidiaries of companies incorporated in Great Britain or if aggregate charitable and political contributions are not more than £200.				
19	In respect of any acquisition by the company of its own shares disclose the: (1) number and nominal value of shares purchased, aggregate consideration paid by the company and the reasons for the purchase; (2) number and nominal value of shares acquired or charged during the financial year; (3) maximum number and nominal value of such shares held during the year; and (4) number and nominal value of such shares disposed of or cancelled during the year and, where applicable, the amount	Sch7:7 Sch7:8			

Appendix 4

No.	Disclosure Item	Reference	FRSSE reference	Complies?	Comments
	or value of the consideration in each case.				
	In each case above, state the percentage of the called-up share capital which they represent and, in each case where shares have been charged, the amount of the charge.				
	Note: These disclosure requirements apply where own shares are: (i) purchased by the company or acquired by the company by forfeiture or surrender in lieu of forfeiture; (ii) acquired by the company otherwise than for valuable consideration; (iii) acquired by a nominee of the company without financial assistance from the company, or by any person with financial assistance from the company and, in either case, the company has a beneficial interest in the shares; or (iv) made subject to a lien or charge under s150 or s6(3) of the Companies Consolidation (Consequential Provisions) Act 1985.				
20	Where a UK partner or employee of the firm of auditors acts as a trustee of a trust, or trusts, which hold securities in the company, disclose details of the investment unless the aggregate of all relevant trustee shareholdings is less than one per cent of the issued capital of the company. Note: This disclosure may alternatively be made in the notes to the financial statements or the audit report.	ICAEW Members' Handbook 1.201 Para 4.42–4.47			

Small companies' disclosure checklist

No.	Disclosure Item	Reference	FRSSE reference	Complies?	Comments
21	The directors' report should refer to the resolution to reappoint the auditors at the AGM or to the fact that there is an elective resolution in force under s386 and the auditors are deemed to be reappointed. *Note: This is not a statutory requirement, but disclosure is customary.*				
22	A statement of directors' responsibilities, complying with the minimum requirements of SAS600, should be set out in the directors' report or elsewhere in the annual report. *For example, as follows:* 'Company law requires the directors to prepare financial statements for each financial year which give a true and fair view of the state of affairs of the company and of the profit or loss of the company for that period. In preparing those financial statements, the directors are required to: - select suitable accounting policies and then apply them consistently; - make judgements and estimates that are reasonable and prudent; and - prepare the financial statements on the going concern basis unless it is inappropriate to presume that the company will continue in business. The directors are responsible for keeping proper accounting records which disclose with reasonable accuracy at any time the financial position of the company and to enable them to ensure that the financial statements comply with the Companies Act 1985. They are also responsible for safeguarding the assets of the company and hence for taking reasonable steps for the prevention and detection of fraud and other irregularities.'	SAS600 (20–23)			

Appendix 4

No.	Disclosure Item	Reference	FRSSE reference	Complies?	Comments
23	Where the average number of employees exceeds 250 the directors' report should include a statement describing the policy which the company has adopted for: (1) giving full and fair consideration to applications for employment by disabled persons, taking account of their aptitudes and abilities; (2) continuing employment and training of employees becoming disabled during the year; and (3) otherwise for the training, career development and promotion of disabled persons employed by the company.	Sch7:9			
24	The directors' report should be approved by the board of directors and signed by a director or the company secretary on its behalf. The name of the director or company secretary so signing should be stated.	s234A			
	Independent auditors' report				
25	The auditors' report should state: (1) whether the annual financial statements have been properly prepared in accordance with the Companies Act 1985; and (2) whether the financial statements give a true and fair view. Where any of the following circumstances arise, the auditors should state that fact in their report: (1) the directors' report is not consistent with the financial statements; (2) proper accounting records have not been kept by the company; (3) proper returns adequate for the audit have not been received from branches not visited; (4) the financial statements are not in agreement with the accounting records and returns; or (5) the auditors fail to obtain all	s235(2) s235(3) s237(1) s237(2) s237(3)			

Small companies' disclosure checklist

No.	Disclosure Item	Reference	FRSSE reference	Complies?	Comments
	the information and explanations which to the best of their knowledge and belief are necessary for the purposes or their audit. *Note:* *The abbreviated accounts delivered to the Registrar need not reproduce this report except under those circumstances noted in Q165.*				
26	If the financial statements do not contain adequate disclosure of the emoluments and other benefits of directors, the auditors should include a statement giving the required particulars in their report, so far as they are reasonably able to do so.	s237(4)			
27	If the period to which the directors have paid particular attention in assessing going concern is less than one year from the date of approval of the financial statements, and this has not been disclosed by the directors elsewhere in the financial statements, the auditors should do so within the section of their audit report. The disclosure should set out the basis of their opinion, unless the fact is clear from any other references in their report. *Note:* *Auditors should not qualify their opinion on the financial statements on these grounds alone.*	SAS130.7			
28	The audit report should comply with the requirements of SAS600.	SAS600			
29	The independent auditors' report must state the name of the auditors and be signed by them. The copy delivered to the Registrar must state the names of the auditors and have an original signature. *Note:* *(i)* *Every copy of the auditors' report which is laid before the company in general*	s236			

Appendix 4

No.	Disclosure Item	Reference	FRSSE reference	Complies?	Comments
	meeting, or which is otherwise circulated, published or issued must state the name of the auditors. (ii) Where the office of auditor is held by a body corporate or partnership, the signature must be in the name of the body corporate or partnership by a person authorised to sign on its behalf.				
30	Where a qualified audit report has been given, a written statement from the auditors as to whether the qualification is material for determining whether a proposed distribution is permitted under s270 of the Act must be laid before the company in general meeting.	s271(4)			
	Profit and loss account				
31	The format of the profit and loss account should comply with one of the formats set out in Sch 8 (although greater detail may be given). The same format should be used for subsequent years unless in the directors' opinion there are special reasons for a change to another format. Where a change from one of the formats prescribed in Sch 8 to another is adopted, disclose details and reasons in a note to the first financial statements in which the new format is adopted. All items listed in the prescribed formats must be shown in a company's financial statements unless there is no amount for that item for both the current year and the immediately preceding year. Profit and loss items may be combined on the face of the profit and loss account if they are not material or if the combination facilitates the assessment of the company's state of affairs but,	Sch8:1 Sch8:2(1) Sch8:2(2) Sch8:3(1) Sch8:3(3) Sch8:3(4) Sch8:3(5) Sch8:4(3)			

Small companies' disclosure checklist

No.	Disclosure Item	Reference	FRSSE reference	Complies?	Comments
	in this latter case, the individual amounts must be disclosed in a note.				
	The order, arrangement and headings of the profit and loss account items should be adapted where the special nature of the company's business requires such adaptation.				
32	Where any amount relating to any preceding financial year is included in any item in the profit and loss account, state the effect.	Sch8:50(1)			
33	The following exceptional items, including provisions in respect of such items, should be shown separately on the face of the profit and loss account after operating profit and before interest: (1) profits or losses on the sale or termination of an operation; (2) costs of a fundamental reorganisation or restructuring having a material effect on the nature and focus of the reporting entity's operations; and (3) profits or losses on the disposal of fixed assets. *Note: The profit or loss on disposal of an asset should be accounted for in the profit and loss account of the period in which the disposal occurs as the difference between the net sale proceeds and the net carrying amount, whether carried at historical cost (less any provisions made) or at valuation.* *Profit or loss on disposal of a previously acquired business should include the attributable amount of purchased goodwill where it has previously been eliminated against reserves as a matter of accounting policy and has not previously been charged in the profit and loss account.*		3.3 3.4		

Appendix 4

No.	Disclosure Item	Reference	FRSSE reference	Complies?	Comments
34	All exceptional items other than those listed in Q33 (i.e. except FRSSE paragraph 3.3 items) should be: (1) credited or charged in arriving at the profit or loss on ordinary activities; (2) included under the statutory format headings to which they relate; (3) shown individually or as an aggregate of items of a similar type; (4) disclosed by way of note or on the face of the profit and loss account if necessary in order to give a true and fair view; and (5) described adequately to enable their nature to be understood.	Sch8:50(3)	3.2		
35	The amount of the profit or loss on ordinary activities before taxation should be shown on the face of the profit and loss account.	Sch8:3(6)			
36	Dividends (1) All dividends should be reported as appropriations of profit in the profit and loss account. (2) The aggregate amount of dividends paid and proposed should be shown separately on the face of the profit and loss account. *Note: Dividends should include any withholding tax but exclude other taxes, such as attributable tax credits.*	Sch8:3 (7)(b)	9.12, 12.5		
37	Any profit or loss arising from extraordinary items (which are extremely rare) should be shown separately on the face of the profit and loss account after profit or loss on ordinary activities after tax but before appropriations.	Sch8:50(2)	3.5		
38	The euro Costs involved with the introduction of the euro should be written off to the profit and loss account, except where they meet the conditions to be capitalised.		3.6		

Small companies' disclosure checklist

No.	Disclosure Item	Reference	FRSSE reference	Complies?	Comments
	If material, the costs written off to the profit and loss account are exceptional items and should be disclosed as such.				
39	Transfers to or from reserves (i.e. from or to the profit and loss account) should be shown on the face of the profit and loss account.	Sch8:3 (7)(a)			
40	The amount of any provisions for depreciation and impairment of tangible and intangible fixed assets should be shown in a note to the financial statements if not otherwise disclosed as a statutory format item in the profit and loss account. *Note: 'Depreciation and other amounts written off tangible and intangible fixed assets' is a format heading when format 2 or format 4 is used.*	Sch8:8 (Note 14)			
41	Disclose auditors' remuneration for audit work, including expenses and benefits in kind (stating the nature and estimated money value of benefits in kind). *Note: (i) This disclosure is not required in abbreviated accounts.* *(ii) Disclosure of auditors' remuneration for non-audit fees is not required for companies which qualify as small or medium-sized under s247.*	s246(6)(d) s390A SI 1991/ 2128			
42	Show separately any income or interest derived from group undertakings which is included in income from other fixed asset investments or other interest receivable and similar income. *Note: Group undertakings include parent undertakings, subsidiary undertakings and fellow subsidiary undertakings.*	s259(5) Sch8:8 (Note 12)			

153

Appendix 4

No.	Disclosure Item	Reference	FRSSE reference	Complies?	Comments
43	Show separately the amount of interest and similar charges payable to group companies (i.e. holding companies, subsidiaries and fellow subsidiaries).	Sch8:8 (Note 13)			
44	Taxation (1) Current and deferred tax should be recognised in the profit and loss account, except to the extent that it is attributable to a gain or loss that is or has been recognised directly in the statement of total recognised gains and losses (in which case the tax should also be recognised directly in that statement). (2) The material components of the (current and deferred) tax charge (or credit) for the period should be disclosed separately. (3) Any special circumstances that affect the overall tax charge or credit for the period, or may affect those of future periods, should be disclosed by way of note to the profit and loss account and their individual effects quantified. (4) The effects of a fundamental change in the basis of taxation should be included in the tax charge or credit for the period and separately disclosed on the face of the profit and loss account.		9.1A 9.1B 9.2		
45	Prior year adjustments (1) Prior period adjustments should be accounted for by restating the comparative figures for the preceding period in the primary statements and notes and adjusting the opening reserves for the cumulative effect. (2) The effect of prior period adjustments on the results for the preceding period should be disclosed where practicable.		2.8		
46	Disclose geographical analysis of turnover (this may be limited to a statement of the percentage of	Sch8:49			

Small companies' disclosure checklist

No.	Disclosure Item	Reference	FRSSE reference	Complies?	Comments
	turnover attributable to markets outside the UK).				
Statement of total recognised gains and losses					
47	A primary statement (having the same prominence as the profit and loss account) should be presented showing the total of recognised gains and losses and its components. *Note: (i) The components should be the gains and losses that are recognised in the period insofar as they are attributable to shareholders (but excluding transactions with shareholders).* *(ii) Where the only recognised gains and losses are the results included in the profit and loss account, no separate statement to that effect need be made.*		4.1		
48	The cumulative effect of prior year adjustments should be noted at the foot of the statement of total recognised gains and losses.		2.8		
Balance sheet					
49	The format of the balance sheet should comply with one of the formats set out in Sch 8 (although more detail may be given). The format selected should be adopted in subsequent years unless in the directors' opinion there are special reasons for changing the format. Where a change from one of the formats prescribed in Sch 8 to another is adopted, disclose details and reasons in a note to the first financial statements in which the new format is adopted. All items listed in the prescribed formats must be shown in a company's financial statements unless there is no amount for that item for both the current year and	Sch8:1 Sch8:2(1) Sch8:2(2) Sch8:3(1) Sch8:3(3) Sch8:3(4) Sch8:3(5) Sch8:4(3)			

Appendix 4

No.	Disclosure Item	Reference	FRSSE reference	Complies?	Comments
	the immediately preceding year.				
	Balance sheet items to which Arabic numbers are assigned in the formats may be combined on the face of the balance sheet if they are not material or if the combination facilitates the assessment of the company's state of affairs but, in this latter case, the individual amounts must be disclosed in a note.				
	The order, arrangement and headings of the balance sheet items should be adapted where the special nature of the company's business requires such adaptation.				

50	Where the company departs from any of the historical cost accounting rules state:
	
	(1) the items affected and the basis of valuation adopted for each such item; and
	(2) for each balance sheet item (except stocks) affected either:
	  (a) the comparable amounts determined according to the historical cost accounting rules; or
	  (b) the differences between those amounts and the corresponding amounts actually shown in the balance sheet in respect of that item.
	
	Note: Applies to both fixed and current assets.
		Sch8:33(2)
		Sch8:33(3)			

51	Asset valuations
	
	(1) Where the amount of any fixed asset (other than listed investments) is arrived at on the basis of any of the alternative accounting rules the following should be disclosed:
	  (a) the years (so far as they are known to the directors) in which the assets were severally valued and the several values;
	  (b) where assets have been valued during the year, the
		Sch8:31(3)
		Sch8:41
			5.39		

Small companies' disclosure checklist

No.	Disclosure Item	Reference	FRSSE reference	Complies?	Comments
	names of the valuers or particulars of their qualifications for so doing, and (whichever is stated) the bases of valuation used; and (c) for investment properties, if the valuer is an employee or officer of the company or group. (2) Where, under the alternative accounting rules, the amount of any fixed asset investment is determined on any basis (other than at market value) which appears to the directors to be appropriate in the circumstances of the company, disclose in a note, particulars of the method of valuation adopted and the reasons for adopting it.				
52	Fixed or current assets – disclosure where original cost unknown Give particulars where the purchase price or production cost is unknown and for the first time is taken as being the value ascribed to it by the earliest available record of the company.	Sch8:28 Sch8:47			
53	In respect of investments and other fixed assets, show separately: (1) provisions for temporary diminution in value; (2) provisions for permanent diminution in value (impairment); and (3) the reversal of any such provisions.	Sch8:19			
54	Revaluation gains and losses Revaluations gains should be recognised in the statement of total recognised gains and losses (STRGL). However, where the gain reverses a loss previously reported in the profit and loss account, it should be recognised in the profit and loss account.		5.23 5.24		

Appendix 4

No.	Disclosure Item	Reference	FRSSE reference	Complies?	Comments
	Revaluation losses should be recognised in the profit and loss account. However, losses caused by changing market prices should instead be recognised in the STRGL until the carrying amount of the asset reaches depreciated historical cost. *Note: The amount of the gain recognised in the profit and loss account is that after adjusting for subsequent depreciation. This is to achieve the same overall effect had the original downward revaluation not taken place.*				
55	Consideration of fixed asset values for distribution rules Where, for the purpose of the Act's distribution rules, fixed assets are not revalued in the balance sheet but their value is 'considered' by the directors, state that: (1) the directors have considered the value of fixed assets without revaluing them; (2) the directors are satisfied that the aggregate value of those assets at the time in question is or was not less than the aggregate amount at which they are or were for the time being stated in the company's financial statements; and (3) that the assets affected are accordingly stated in the financial statements on the basis that a revaluation of the company's fixed assets, which by virtue of ss275(4) and (5) included the assets in question, took place at that time.	s275(6)			
Intangible fixed assets					
56	For each item under intangible fixed assets state (comparatives not required): (1) the cost at the beginning and end of the year;	Sch8:40 Sch8:51(3)	5.14 9.14		

Small companies' disclosure checklist

No.	Disclosure Item	Reference	FRSSE reference	Complies?	Comments

	(2) the effect of any:
	  (a) acquisitions during the year;
	  (b) disposals during the year; and
	  (c) transfers during the year; and
	(3) in respect of provisions for depreciation or diminution in value:
	  (a) the cumulative amount of such provisions as at the beginning and end of the year;
	  (b) the amount provided during the year;
	  (c) the amount of any adjustments on disposal; and
	  (d) the amount of any other adjustments (e.g. exchange differences).
	
	Note: (i) *The cost of intangible fixed assets and other items disclosed should include irrecoverable VAT (where practicable and material).*
	  (ii) *Goodwill and intangible assets should not be revalued.*				

57	For deferred development costs disclose: (1) the amount carried forward at the beginning and end of the year under intangible fixed assets in the balance sheet or in the notes thereto; (2) the period over which amounts capitalised are being written off, and the reasons for capitalisation; and (3) any special reasons for not regarding unamortised amounts as reducing the company's distributable profits. Note: (i) *Development costs may only be shown in a company's balance sheet in special*	s269 Sch8:20(2)	5.6 5.8		

Appendix 4

No.	Disclosure Item	Reference	FRSSE reference	Complies?	Comments
	circumstances (Sch 8:20). Compliance with the conditions in the FRSSE (paragraphs 5.3 and 5.4) will usually be sufficient to meet this requirement. (ii) If development costs are deferred to future periods, they should be amortised. (iii) Development costs must be treated as a realised loss in the calculation of distributable profits unless there are such 'special circumstances' and the disclosure at (3) above is made.				
58	Amounts in respect of concessions, patents, licences, trade marks and similar rights and assets shall only be included in a company's balance sheet if either: (1) the assets were acquired for valuable consideration and are not required to be shown under goodwill; or (2) the assets in question were created by the company itself. Note: Internally generated intangible assets should not be capitalised.	Sch8:8 (Note 3)	5.9		
59	Goodwill Where goodwill is shown as an asset state the period selected for amortising the goodwill and the reason for choosing that period. Capitalised goodwill should be depreciated on a straight-line (or more appropriate) basis over its useful economic life, which shall not exceed 20 years. Note: The residual value assigned to goodwill should be zero.	Sch8:8 (Note 2) Sch8:21(4)	5.9 5.10 5.11 5.12		
60	Negative goodwill The amount of negative goodwill		5.15		

Small companies' disclosure checklist

No.	Disclosure Item	Reference	FRSSE reference	Complies?	Comments
	on the balance sheet and the period(s) in which it is being written back should be disclosed.				
Tangible fixed assets					

61	For each item under tangible fixed assets disclose:
	
	(1) the cost or valuation at the beginning and end of the year;
	(2) the effect of any:
	  (a) revaluation made during the year;
	  (b) acquisitions during the year;
	  (c) disposals during the year; and
	  (d) transfers during the year; and
	(3) in respect of provisions for depreciation or diminution in value:
	  (a) the cumulative amount of such provisions as at the beginning and end of the year;
	  (b) the amount provided during the year;
	  (c) the amount of any adjustments on disposal; and
	  (d) the amount of any other adjustments (e.g. exchange differences).
	
	Note:
	  (i) Comparatives are not required.
	  (ii) Cost of tangible fixed assets and other items disclosed should include irrecoverable VAT (where practicable and material).
		Sch8:40
		Sch8:51(3)
			5.17
			5.18
			9.14		

62	Where, under the transitional provisions of the FRSSE, the company has retained previously revalued assets at their book amounts without adopting a policy of revaluation, disclose: (1) the fact that the transitional provisions of the FRSSE are being followed;		17.3		

Appendix 4

No.	Disclosure Item	Reference	FRSSE reference	Complies?	Comments
	(2) that the valuation has not been updated; and
(3) the date of the last revaluation.				
63	Investment Properties
(1) The carrying value of investment properties (open market value) should be displayed prominently either on the face of the balance sheet or in the notes.
(2) Changes in the value of investment properties should be taken to the statement of total recognised gains and losses (being a movement on an investment revaluation reserve) unless a deficit (or its reversal) on an individual investment property is expected to be permanent, in which case it should be charged (or credited) in the profit and loss account.
Note: *In accordance with paragraph 5.37 investment properties (except leaseholds with an unexpired term of 20 years or less) will not be depreciated. This is a departure from the statutory accounting provisions and it will be necessary to disclose particulars of the departure, the reasons for it and its effect as required by s226 Companies Act 1985 unless the amount involved is not material (in which case this fact should be stated). In giving the disclosures required by law regard should be had to paragraph 2.9 of the FRSSE – see Q3 above.*		5.37
5.38
5.40		
64	Where the entity is a lessee, disclose either:
(1) the gross amount of assets held under finance leases and HP contracts together with the related accumulated		6.16(a)		

Small companies' disclosure checklist

No.	Disclosure Item	Reference	FRSSE reference	Complies?	Comments
	depreciation, analysed between land and buildings and other assets; or (2) the information in (1) integrated with owned assets, with separate disclosure of the net amount of assets held under finance leases and HP contracts and the amount of depreciation allocated for the period to such assets.				
65	Where the entity is a lessor the following should be disclosed: (1) the cost of assets acquired (whether by purchase or finance lease), held for the purpose of letting under finance leases; and (2) the gross amounts of assets held for use in operating leases, and the related accumulated depreciation charges.		6.18(a) 6.18(b)		
Investments					

66	For each item under fixed asset investments state:
	(1) the cost or valuation at the beginning and end of the year;
	(2) the effect as a result of any:
	  (a) revaluation made during the year;
	  (b) acquisitions during the year;
	  (c) disposals during the year; and
	  (d) transfers during the year; and
	(3) in respect of provisions for depreciation or diminution in value:
	  (a) the cumulative amount of such provisions as at the beginning and end of the year;
	  (b) the amount provided during the year;
	  (c) the amount of any adjustments on disposal; and
	  (d) the amount of any other adjustment (e.g. exchange differences).
		Sch8:40
		Sch8:51(3)			

Appendix 4

No.	Disclosure Item	Reference	FRSSE reference	Complies?	Comments
	Note: Comparatives are not required.				
67	Where the company has at the end of the financial year a significant shareholding in an undertaking (which is not a subsidiary) which represents:	s231 Sch5:7–9 Sch8:51(3)			
	(1) 20 per cent or more of the nominal value of the allotted shares of any class of the undertaking's equity share capital; or (2) more than 20 per cent of the book value of the investing company's total assets;				
	state in relation to that other body:				
	(1) its name; (2) its country of incorporation, if not incorporated in Great Britain; (3) the identity and proportion of the nominal value of each class of shares held (comparatives not required); (4) if it is unincorporated, the address of its principal place of business; (5) the aggregate amount of its capital and reserves at the end of its most recent financial year ending with or before that of the investing company; and (6) its profit or loss for that period.				
	Notes: (i) Where the disclosures required would result in a statement of excessive length, they may be limited to the principal investments provided that it is indicated that it is so limited. Full details must be attached to the company's next annual return. (ii) Information need not be disclosed with respect to an undertaking which is established under the law of a country				

Small companies' disclosure checklist

No.	Disclosure Item	Reference	FRSSE reference	Complies?	Comments
	outside the UK or carries on business outside the UK, if in the opinion of the directors of the company the disclosure would be seriously prejudicial to the business of that undertaking, or to the business of the company or any of its subsidiary undertakings, and the DTI agrees that the information need not be disclosed. The fact that advantage has been taken of the exemption must be stated.				
	(iii) The information required by (5) and (6) (aggregate capital and reserves and profit or loss) need not be given if:				
	(a) the undertaking is not required by the Act (either as a company incorporated in Great Britain or as an overseas company) to file its financial statements with the Registrar of Companies, and does not otherwise publish its financial statements in Great Britain or elsewhere; and the investing company or group holds less than one half in nominal value of its allotted share capital;				
	(b) it is not material; or				

Appendix 4

No.	Disclosure Item	Reference	FRSSE reference	Complies?	Comments
	(c) the company is exempt from preparing group financial statements by virtue of s228 (parent company included in the financial statements of a larger group); and the investment of the company in all undertakings in which it has such a holding is shown, in aggregate, in the notes to the financial statements by way of the equity method. (iv) Comparatives are not required.				
68	Listed investments (1) The aggregate amount of listed investments included under each item of investments should be shown under fixed assets. (2) For each item which includes listed investments disclose: (a) the aggregate market value of the listed investments where it differs from their balance sheet amount; and (b) both the market value and stock exchange value where the market value is taken as being higher than the stock exchange value.	Sch8:42			
69	Show separately the nominal value of own shares held. Note: Own shares that are purchased or redeemed should be cancelled immediately.	s160(4) s162 Sch8:8 (Note 4)			
70	State cumulative amount of interest included in determining the production cost of any fixed asset, indicating the balance sheet item affected.	Sch8:26 (3)(b)			

Small companies' disclosure checklist

No.	Disclosure Item	Reference	FRSSE reference	Complies?	Comments
Current assets: stocks					
71	Stock held subject to reservation of title Consider disclosure if a material proportion of stock is held subject to reservation of title by the supplier, including whether, and the extent to which, the liability to the supplier is secured, and the nature of the security given.	ICAEW Members Handbook 2.404			
72	Consignment stock Where consignment stock is in substance an asset of the company, the stock should be recognised as such on the company's balance sheet, together with a corresponding liability to the manufacturer. Any deposit should be deducted from the liability and the excess classified as a trade creditor. Where stock is not in substance an asset of the company, the stock should not be included on the company's balance sheet until the transfer of title has crystallised. Any deposit should be included under 'other debtors'.		8.5		
73	Long-term contracts (1) Show separately by way of note under the heading 'long-term contract balances' (within stocks) costs incurred net of amounts transferred to cost of sales, less foreseeable losses and payments on account not matched with turnover. (2) The balance sheet note should disclose separately the balances of: (a) net cost less foreseeable losses; and (b) applicable payments on account.		8.4(c)		
74	State cumulative amount of interest included in determining the production cost of any current asset, indicating the balance sheet item affected.	Sch8:26 (3)(b)			

Appendix 4

No.	Disclosure Item	Reference	FRSSE reference	Complies?	Comments
	Current assets: debtors				
75	Factored debts (1) Where the entity has retained significant benefits and risks relating to factored debts and the conditions for a linked presentation are met (as set out in the FRSSE paragraph 8.7) show the non-returnable proceeds deducted from the factored debts on the face of the balance sheet and disclose in a note if the company is not required to support bad debts in respect of factored debts and that the factors have stated in writing that they will not seek recourse other than out of factored debts. (2) Where separate presentation is required disclose the gross amount of factored debts outstanding at the balance sheet date and a corresponding liability in respect of the proceeds received from the factor.		8.7 8.8		
76	Show separately the amount falling due after more than one year either for each item under debtors unless the aggregate amount is disclosed in the notes to the financial statements.	Sch8:8 (Note 5)			
77	Where the entity acts as a lessor, separately disclose the net investment in (i) finance leases and (ii) hire purchase contracts as a debtor.		6.18(c)		
78	Long-term contracts State separately under the heading 'amounts recoverable on contracts' (within debtors) the excess of recorded turnover over payments received on account.		8.4(a)		
79	Disclose the following in respect of pension contributions: (1) prepaid pension contributions *(for a defined contribution scheme)*; and (2) *(for defined benefit schemes*		10.2(c) AII, 1(f) AII, 1(h)(v)		

Small companies' disclosure checklist

No.	Disclosure Item	Reference	FRSSE reference	Complies?	Comments
	with periods ending before 22 June 2004 only) prepayments arising from the excess of the amount funded over the pension cost charged (for a defined benefit scheme).				
Current assets: investments					
80	Aggregate the amount of listed investments under each item of investments shown under current assets and for each item which includes listed investments disclose: (1) the aggregate market value of the listed investments where it differs from their balance sheet amount; and (2) both the market value and stock exchange value where the market value is taken as being higher than the stock exchange value.	Sch8:42			
Creditors					
81	Convertible loans The amounts attributable to convertible debt, included within liabilities, should be disclosed separately from that of other liabilities.	Sch8:8 (Note 7)			
82	Long-term contracts Show separately as 'payments on account' (within creditors) the balance of payments on account in excess of amounts matched with turnover or offset against long-term contract balances.		8.4(b)		
83	The amounts of creditors falling due within one year and of creditors falling due after more than one year should be shown separately, either on the face of the balance sheet or in a note. Note: This requirement is automatically met by the Format 1 balance sheet but requires an additional disclosure when Format 2 is followed.	Sch8:8 (Note 10)			
84	For the aggregate of all items shown as creditors in the balance sheet	Sch8:44(1)			

Appendix 4

No.	Disclosure Item	Reference	FRSSE reference	Complies?	Comments
	state the aggregate of the amounts which fall due for payment more than five years after the balance sheet date.				
	If any such amounts are payable or repayable by instalments, disclose the amount of any instalments which fall due for payment after the end of the period.				
85	For each item shown under creditors in the balance sheet state the aggregate amount of liabilities included on which any security has been given by the company.	Sch8:44(2)			
86	Where the amount repayable on any debt owed by a small company is greater than the value of the consideration received in the transaction giving rise to the debt, the amount of difference may be treated as an asset.	Sch8:24			
	The unamortised amount must be shown separately, either on the face of the balance sheet or in a note to the financial statements.				
87	Obligations under finance leases and HP contracts		6.16(b)		
	The amount of obligations under finance leases and HP contracts (net of finance charges allocated to future periods) should be disclosed separately from other liabilities and obligations either on the face of the balance sheet or in the notes to the financial statements.				
88	In respect of pension cost creditors: (1) any amount of outstanding contributions should be disclosed as a creditor due within one year; and (2) *(for periods ending before 22 June 2004 only)* where the cumulative pension cost recognised in the profit and loss account has not been completely discharged by payments of contributions or directly paid pensions, the excess should be shown as a net pension provision.		10.2(c) AII, 1(f) AII, 1(h)(v) AII, 2(g)		

Small companies' disclosure checklist

No.	Disclosure Item	Reference	FRSSE reference	Complies?	Comments
89	Taxation/social security Show separately the amount included in respect of taxation and social security.	Sch8:8 (Note 7)			
90	Tax on dividends Outgoing dividends and similar amounts payable should be recognised at an amount that includes any withholding tax but excludes other taxes, such as attributable tax credits. Incoming dividends and similar income receivable should be recognised at an amount that includes any withholding tax but excludes other taxes, such as attributable tax credits. Any withholding tax suffered should be shown as part of the tax charge.		9.12 9.13		
91	Disclose the amount of any arrears of fixed cumulative dividends and the period for which each class is in arrears.	Sch8:45			
Provisions					
92	Movement on provisions Where there is any movement on provisions disclose: (1) the amount of the provision as at the beginning and end of the financial year; (2) the amount transferred to or from the provisions during the year; (3) the source and application of the amounts transferred; and (4) particulars of each material provision included under 'other provisions'. Note: (i) *Comparatives are not required;* (ii) *The above are not required where the movement consists of the application of a provision for the purpose for which it was established.*	Sch8:43 Sch8:51(3)			

Appendix 4

No.	Disclosure Item	Reference	FRSSE reference	Complies?	Comments
93	Long-term contracts Show the amount by which a provision for foreseeable losses exceeds the costs incurred (after transfers to cost of sales), as a provision for liabilities. Where appropriate the foreseeable losses may have been set up as an accrual, in which case this excess should be classified as accruals within creditors.		8.4(d)		
Pension asset / liability					
94	For defined benefit schemes with periods ending on or after 22 June 2004 only, disclose any defined benefit asset or liability, presented separately on the face of the balance sheet: (1) after item J Accruals and deferred income but before item K Capital and reserves for format 1 balance sheets; or (2) (a) after ASSETS item D Prepayments and accrued income in format 2 balance sheets for an asset; or (b) after LIABILITIES item D Accruals and deferred income in format 2 balance sheets for a liability.		AII, 2(g)		
	Additional notes to the financial statements				
Accounting policies					
95	The financial statements should state that they have been prepared in accordance with the Financial Reporting Standard for Smaller Entities (effective June 2002). *Note: This statement may be included with the accounting policies note or, for those entities taking advantage of the exemptions for small companies in companies legislation, in the statement required by companies legislation to be given on the balance sheet.* *If abbreviated accounts are also prepared, the*		2.3		

Small companies' disclosure checklist

No.	Disclosure Item	Reference	FRSSE reference	Complies?	Comments
	statement referring to the Financial Reporting Standard for Smaller Entities (effective June 2002) should be included with the note of accounting policies so that it is reproduced in the abbreviated accounts.				
96	A description of each material accounting policy adopted by the company in determining the amounts to be included in respect of items shown in the balance sheet and in determining the profit or loss of the company (including such policies with respect to the depreciation and diminution in value of assets) should be stated in the financial statements. The explanation should be clear, fair and as brief as possible.	Sch8:36	2.7(a)		

97	(1) Accounting policies should be reviewed regularly to ensure that they remain the most appropriate to the entity's particular circumstances for the purpose of giving a true and fair view.
	(2) In judging whether a new policy is more appropriate than the existing policy, due weight should be given to the impact on comparability.
	(3) Where a new policy is adopted, details of any changes to the accounting policies followed in the preceding period should be given. This should include:
	  (a) a brief explanation of why each new accounting policy is thought more appropriate; and
	  (b) the disclosures necessary for prior period adjustments (Q45).
	(4) Where practicable, an indication of the effect of the change on the results for the current period should be given.
	(5) The amounts for the current and corresponding periods
			2.5
			2.7(b)		

Appendix 4

No.	Disclosure Item	Reference	FRSSE reference	Complies?	Comments
	should be restated on the basis of the new policies.				
98	Where there has been a change in the depreciation method used, the effect, if material, should be disclosed in the period of change. The reason for the change should also be disclosed.		5.31		
99	Where corresponding amounts have been adjusted to make them comparable (for example because of a change in accounting policy), disclose details and reasons in a note.	Sch8:4(2) Sch8:51(2)	2.5		
100	Disclose details and effects of, and reasons for, departure from any of the five fundamental principles (going concern, consistency, prudence, accruals, separate valuation).	Sch8:15			
101	Where the effect of a change to an estimation technique is material, a description of the change should be given. Where practicable, the effect on the results for the current period arising from a change to an estimation technique should be given.		2.7(c)		
102	For (i) land and buildings and (ii) other tangible fixed assets in aggregate disclose: (1) the depreciation methods used; (2) the useful economic lives or depreciation rates used; and (3) where material, the financial effect of a change during the period in either the estimate of useful economic lives or the estimate of residual values.		5.30		
103	Foreign currency translation. Disclose the basis of translating foreign currencies for the profit and loss account and balance sheet.	Sch8:51(1)			
104	In respect of government grants disclose: (1) the effects of grants on the results for the period and/or the financial position of the		5.44		

Small companies' disclosure checklist

No.	Disclosure Item	Reference	FRSSE reference	Complies?	Comments
	enterprise; and (2) where the results are materially affected by government assistance other than grants, the nature and an estimate of the effect of that assistance (to the extent that they can be measured). Note: *In rare cases potential liabilities to repay grants may need to be disclosed as contingent liabilities but only to the extent that they exceed any unamortised deferred income relating to the same grants. They do not need to be disclosed if the possibility of repayment is remote.*				
Directors' emoluments					
105	(1) Disclose the total of the following in respect of qualifying services: (a) the aggregate amount of emoluments paid to or receivable by directors (including any amounts in respect of a person's accepting office as a director); (b) the aggregate amount of money paid to or receivable by directors under long-term incentive schemes and the net value of assets (other than shares and share options) received or receivable by directors under such schemes; and (c) the aggregate value of any company contributions paid, or treated as paid, to a money purchase pension scheme. (2) Also disclose the number of directors (if any) to whom retirement benefits are accruing in respect of qualifying services for: (a) money purchase schemes; and (b) defined benefit schemes.	s246(3)(a) s246(6) Sch6:1(1)(a) Sch6:1(1)(c) Sch6:1(1)(d) Sch6:1(1)(e)			

175

Appendix 4

No.	Disclosure Item	Reference	FRSSE reference	Complies?	Comments
	Note: These disclosures may be omitted from abbreviated accounts filed with the Registrar.				
106	In respect of directors (and past directors) of the company disclose aggregate compensation for loss of office received or receivable, including the estimated amount of benefits in kind and stating the nature of such benefits. Note: (i) This should include compensation received or receivable for loss of office as a director of the company, as director of any subsidiary undertaking or otherwise in connection with the management of the affairs of the company or any of its subsidiary companies. (ii) Compensation for loss of office includes retirement payments and payments for damages or in settlement of any claim for breach of contract. (iii) These disclosures may be omitted from abbreviated accounts filed with the Registrar.	s246(6) Sch6:8			
107	Disclose the aggregate amount of any consideration paid to, or receivable by, third parties for making available the services of any person: (1) as a director of the company; or (2) while a director of the company, as director of any subsidiary undertaking, or otherwise in connection with the management of the affairs of the company or any of its subsidiary undertakings.	s246(6) Sch6:9			

Small companies' disclosure checklist

No.	Disclosure Item	Reference	FRSSE reference	Complies?	Comments
	Note: (i) Third parties are persons other than: (a) the director himself or a person connected with him or body corporate controlled by him; and (b) the company or any of its subsidiary undertakings. Amounts paid to or receivable by a person connected with a director, or a body corporate controlled by a director, should be included instead within the disclosures set out at Q105 above. (ii) Include the estimated money value of benefits, the nature of which should be disclosed. (iii) These disclosures may be omitted from abbreviated accounts filed with the Registrar.				
In respect of subsidiary undertakings					
108	Where the company holds subsidiary undertakings at the end of the financial year but is not required to prepare group financial statements, there should be a statement giving the reason why the company is not required to prepare group financial statements. Note: If the reason is that all the subsidiary undertakings fall within the exclusions in s229, state with respect to each subsidiary which exclusions apply.	Sch5:1(4), (5)			
109	If the company has taken advantage of the exemption for small groups from the need to prepare group	s237(4A)			

Appendix 4

No.	Disclosure Item	Reference	FRSSE reference	Complies?	Comments
	financial statements and in the auditors opinion they were not entitled to do so, the auditors shall state this fact in their report.				

110	If the company has taken advantage of the exemption not to prepare group financial statements available to certain subsidiaries of an immediate parent undertaking established under the law of an EU member state:
	
	(1) the company should disclose in its individual financial statements that it is exempt from the obligation to prepare and deliver group financial statements; and
	(2) the company should state within its individual financial statements the name of the parent undertaking which draws up the group financial statements; and also
	  (a) if the parent is incorporated outside Great Britain, the country of incorporation; or
	  (b) if it is not incorporated, the address of the principal place of business.
		s228(2)			

111	In relation to each subsidiary undertaking, state:
	
	(1) the name of each subsidiary;
	(2) if incorporated outside Great Britain, the country of incorporation; and
	(3) if unincorporated, the address of its principal place of business.
	
	Note: Exemptions
	  (i) Where the disclosures required would result in a statement of excessive length, they may be limited to:
	    (a) principal subsidiaries; and
	    (b) those subsidiaries excluded from consolidation by virtue of s229(3) and (4);
		s231
		Sch5:1(1)			

Small companies' disclosure checklist

No.	Disclosure Item	Reference	FRSSE reference	Complies?	Comments
	provided that it is indicated that it is so limited, full details must be attached to company's next annual return. (ii) *If DTI approval is obtained, the disclosures required may be omitted in respect of an undertaking which is established outside the law of the UK or carries on business outside the UK where disclosure would be harmful. The fact of the omission should be stated.*				
112	State in relation to each class of share held by the company in subsidiary undertakings (comparatives not required): (1) the identity of the class; and (2) the proportion of the nominal value of the shares held. Note: (i) The exemptions in Q111 above apply. (ii) The shares held by, or on behalf of the company itself should be distinguished from those attributed to the company which are held on behalf of a subsidiary undertaking.	Sch5:2 Sch8:51(3)			
113	In respect of each subsidiary undertaking show: (1) the aggregate amount of capital and reserves at the end of its financial year; and (2) its profit or loss for the year. Note: (i) This information is not required to be given if the company is exempt by virtue of s228 from the requirement to prepare group	Sch5:3			

Appendix 4

No.	Disclosure Item	Reference	FRSSE reference	Complies?	Comments
	financial statements, if the subsidiary is not required under the Companies Act to deliver its balance sheet (and does not otherwise publish it) and the company's holding is less than 50 per cent of the nominal value of the shares in the undertaking or if the subsidiary is included in the company's financial statements by way of equity accounting. (ii) The exemptions in Q111 above apply.				
114	Qualifying partnerships Where the company is a member of a qualifying partnership, disclose either: (1) that a copy of the latest financial statements of the partnership has been or is to be appended to a copy of the company's financial statements sent to the Registrar in accordance with s242; or (2) that the name of at least one body corporate (which may be the company) in whose group financial statements the undertaking has been or is to be dealt with on a consolidated basis. This need not be disclosed if the company's financial statements disclose that advantage has been taken of the exemption in Regulation 7 of SI 1993/1820 (see note (ii) below). Note: (i) Each limited company which is a member of a qualifying partnership at the end of any financial year of the partnership must attach to the	Sch5:9A SI1993/ 1820			

Small companies' disclosure checklist

No.	Disclosure Item	Reference	FRSSE reference	Complies?	Comments
	copy of its annual financial statements which is next delivered to the Registrar a copy of the financial statements of the partnership for that year.				
	(ii) By virtue of Regulation 7 of SI 1993/1820 Partnerships and Unlimited Companies (Accounts) Regulations, members of a qualifying partnership which is dealt with by full consolidation, proportional consolidation or equity accounting in group financial statements are exempt from the requirement to prepare financial statements and to attach a copy of the partnership financial statements to their own individual filed financial statements, provided that the group financial statements:				
	(a) are prepared by a member of the partnership which is established under the law of a Member of State or a parent undertaking of such a member which is so established;				
	(b) are prepared and audited under the provisions of the Seventh Directive; and				

Appendix 4

No.	Disclosure Item	Reference	FRSSE reference	Complies?	Comments
	(c) disclose that advantage has been taken of this exemption.				
115	Qualifying undertakings Where at the end of its financial year the company is a member of a qualifying undertaking, disclose: (1) the name and legal form of the undertaking; and (2) the address of the undertaking's registered office or, if none, its head office. Note: *This information need not be given if it is not material.*	Sch5:9A			
Deferred taxation					
116	Deferred tax should only be recognised on timing differences relating to revaluation gains and losses if: (1) the timing difference has originated but not reversed by the balance sheet date; (2) the entity has entered into a binding agreement to sell the asset and has revalued the asset to the selling price; and (3) it is more likely than not that the gain will not be rolled over into a replacement asset. However, if assets have been revalued, or if their market values have been disclosed in a note, the amount of tax that would be payable or recoverable if the assets were sold at the values shown should be disclosed.		9.3 9.11		
117	In respect of deferred tax disclose: (1) the deferred tax balance and its material components; (2) the movement between the opening and closing net deferred tax balances, and the material components of this movement; and (3) where discounting is used, the unwinding of the discount shown as a component of the tax charge and disclosed separately.		9.8 9.9 9.10		

Small companies' disclosure checklist

No.	Disclosure Item	Reference	FRSSE reference	Complies?	Comments
	Note: The discounting of deferred tax assets and liabilities is not required. However, if a policy of discounting is adopted, all deferred tax balances that have been measured by reference to undiscounted cash flows and for which the impact of discounting is material should be discounted.				
Share capital					
118	In respect of authorised, issued and paid up share capital, disclose: (1) authorised share capital; (2) the amount of allotted share capital and amount of called up share capital which has been paid up; and (3) the number and aggregate nominal value of allotted shares of each class where more than one class of shares have been allotted.	Sch8:8 (Note 9) Sch8:38(1)			
119	In addition to the above, indicate in respect of redeemable shares: (1) the earliest and latest dates on which the company has power of redemption; (2) whether redemption is required in any event or at the option of the company or the shareholder; and (3) whether any (and if so, what) premium is payable on redemption.	Sch8:38(2)			
120	Where the company has allotted any shares during the financial year disclose: (1) the classes of shares allotted; and (2) for each class of shares, the number allotted, their aggregate nominal value and the consideration received by the company.	Sch8:39			
121	Disclose the number, description and amount of shares in the company held by or on behalf of its subsidiaries or their nominees.	s231(5), (6) s246(6)(b) Sch5:6			

Appendix 4

No.	Disclosure Item	Reference	FRSSE reference	Complies?	Comments
	Exemptions (i) Where the disclosures required would result in a statement of excessive length, they may be limited to: (a) principal subsidiaries; and (b) those subsidiaries excluded from consolidation by virtue of s229(3) and (4); provided that it is indicated that it is so limited. Full details must be attached to company's next annual return. (ii) If DTI approval is obtained, the disclosures required may be omitted in respect of an undertaking which is established outside the law of the UK or carries on business outside the UK where disclosure would be harmful. The fact of the omission should be stated. *Note:* This disclosure may be omitted in abbreviated accounts filed with the Registrar.				
Reserves					
122	Where there is any movement on reserves, disclose: (1) the amount of the reserves as at the beginning and end of the financial year; (2) any amount transferred to or from the reserves (e.g. exchange differences) during the year; and (3) the source and application respectively of any amounts transferred. *Note:* Comparatives are not required.	Sch8:43(1) Sch8:43(2) Sch8:51(3)	13.7		

Small companies' disclosure checklist

No.	Disclosure Item	Reference	FRSSE reference	Complies?	Comments
123	It is recommended that the analysis of reserves should distinguish between distributable and non-distributable reserves (where this is not evident from their description).	-			
124	The amount of any revaluation reserve should be shown in the balance sheet under a separate sub-heading in the position given in Sch 8 for the item 'revaluation reserve', although a different name is acceptable.	Sch 8: 34(2)			
125	State the treatment for taxation purposes of amounts debited or credited to the revaluation reserve.	Sch8:34(6)			
Commitments and contingencies					
126	Contingent liabilities Except where their existence is remote, disclose the following for contingent liabilities: (1) a brief description of the contingent item, including its legal nature; (2) where practicable, an estimate of its financial effect; and (3) whether, and if so what, valuable security has been provided by the company in respect thereof. *Note: (i) Contingent liabilities should not be recognised.* *(ii) Any commitments which are undertaken for or on behalf of or for the benefit of:* *(a) any holding company or fellow subsidiary of the company, or* *(b) any subsidiary of the company, should be stated separately from other commitments. Commitments within (a) should be stated separately from those within (b).*	Sch8:46(2) Sch8:46(6)	11.7		

Appendix 4

No.	Disclosure Item	Reference	FRSSE reference	Complies?	Comments
127	Contingent assets For contingent assets where an inflow of economic benefits is probable, disclose: (1) a brief description of the contingent item; and (2) where practicable, an estimate of its financial effect; *Note:* (i) *Contingent assets should not be recognised.* (ii) *Contingent assets should only be disclosed when an inflow of economic benefits is probable. It is important that disclosures for contingent assets avoid giving misleading indications of the likelihood of a profit arising.*		11.7		
128	Commitments Disclose the aggregate or estimated amounts of: (1) capital commitments not provided for; and (2) commitments in respect of finance leases and hire purchase contracts entered into but whose inception occurs after the balance sheet date. *Note:* (i) *Include irrecoverable VAT where practicable and material.* (ii) *Any commitments which are undertaken for, or on behalf of, or for the benefit of:* (a) *any holding company or fellow subsidiary of the company, or* (b) *any subsidiary of the company, should be stated separately from other*	Sch8:46(3) Sch8:46(6)	6.16(c) 9.14		

Small companies' disclosure checklist

No.	Disclosure Item	Reference	FRSSE reference	Complies?	Comments
	commitments. Commitments within (a) should be stated separately from those within (b).				
129	Operating lease commitments		6.17		
	Disclose the payments that the company is committed to make during the next year, analysed into:				
	(1) those in which the commitment expires within that year; (2) those expiring in the second to fifth years inclusive; and (3) those expiring over five years from the balance sheet date.				
130	Give particulars of any other financial commitments which:	Sch8:46(5) Sch8.46(6)			
	(1) have not been provided for; and (2) are relevant to assessing the company's state of affairs.				
	Note: Any commitments which are undertaken for or on behalf of or for the benefit of: *(a) any holding company or fellow subsidiary of the company, or* *(b) any subsidiary of the company,* *should be stated separately from other commitments. Commitments within (a) should be stated separately from those within (b).*				
131	Disclose particulars of any charge on the assets of the company to secure liabilities of another person and, where practicable, the amount secured.	Sch8:46(1) Sch8:46(6)			
	Note: Any commitments which are undertaken for, or on behalf of, or for the benefit of: *(a) any holding company or fellow subsidiary of the company, or* *(b) any subsidiary of the company,* *should be stated separately*				

Appendix 4

No.	Disclosure Item	Reference	FRSSE reference	Complies?	Comments
	from other commitments. Commitments within (a) should be stated separately from those within (b).				
Pension arrangements					
132	State the nature of the pension scheme (e.g. defined contribution or defined benefit).		10.2(a) AII, 1(h) AII, 2(j)		
133	*In respect of a defined benefit scheme for periods ending before 22 June 2004 only*, state: (1) whether the pension cost and provision (or asset) are based on advice from a professionally qualified actuary and, if so, the date of the most recent formal actuarial valuation or later formal review used for this purpose; (2) the amount of any deficiency on a current funding level basis indicating the action being taken to deal with it in current and future accounting periods; (3) outline of the most recent formal actuarial valuation or later formal review of the scheme on an ongoing basis. (*SSAP 24 stipulates the following content for such an outline. This is not reproduced in the FRSSE but may be regarded as 'best practice'*: • *actuarial method used and description of the main assumptions;* • *market value of scheme assets;* • *percentage level of funding; and* • *comments on material actuarial surplus or deficiency);* (4) any commitment to make additional payments over a limited number of years; (5) details of expected effects on future costs of any material changes in the group's and/or company's pension arrangements;		AII, 1(g) AII, 1(h)		

Small companies' disclosure checklist

No.	Disclosure Item	Reference	FRSSE reference	Complies?	Comments
	(6) whether the scheme is funded or unfunded; and (7) the pension cost charge for the period. The following transitional disclosures, which are based on FRS 17, are also required: (8) the fair value of the scheme assets, the present value of the scheme liabilities and the resulting surplus or deficit, determined in accordance with the requirement of paragraph 2, FRSSE Appendix II; and (9) an explanation where the asset or liability that would be recognised in the balance sheet under the requirements of paragraph 2, FRSSE Appendix II differs from the surplus or deficit in the scheme. *Note: If the entity is a subsidiary that is a member of a group scheme, it would be exempt from disclosure of information required in (2) and (3) if the holding company is registered in UK or Republic of Ireland and the name of holding company in whose financial statements particulars of the actuarial valuation are contained is disclosed.* *Comparatives are not required for items (8) and (9) above for periods ending before 22 June 2003.*				
134	*In respect of defined benefits schemes, for periods ending before 22 June 2004 only,* a company which is a subsidiary and a member of a group pension scheme should disclose: (1) that it is a member of a group scheme; and (2) where appropriate that contributions are based on pension costs across the group as a whole.		AII, 1(g)		

Appendix 4

No.	Disclosure Item	Reference	FRSSE reference	Complies?	Comments
135	In respect of defined benefit schemes, for periods ending on or after 22 June 2003, but before 22 June 2004, an analysis of movements during the period in the surplus or deficit in the defined benefit should also be given (without comparatives for the previous period).		AII, 1(i)		
136	In respect of defined benefit schemes, for periods ending on or after 22 June 2004 only: The components of the charge in the defined benefit asset or liability (other than those arising from contributions to the scheme) should be presented separately in the performance statements as follows: (1) the current service cost should be included within operating profit in the profit and loss account; (2) the net of interest cost and expected return on assets should be included as other finance costs (or income) adjacent to interest; (3) actuarial gains and losses should be recognised in the statement of total recognised gains and losses; (4) past service costs should be recognised in the profit and loss account in the period in which the increases in benefit vest; and (5) losses arising on a settlement or curtailment should be recognised in the profit and loss account when the employer becomes demonstrably committed to the transaction. Note: Gains on a settlement or curtailment should be recognised only once all parties whose consent is required are irrevocably committed.		AII, 2(i)		
137	In respect of a defined benefit scheme, for periods ending on or after 22 June 2004: (1) Disclose:		AII, 2(j) AII, 2(k)		

Small companies' disclosure checklist

No.	Disclosure Item	Reference	FRSSE reference	Complies?	Comments
	(a) the date of the most recent full actuarial valuation on which the amounts in the financial statements are based; (b) that the actuary is an employee or officer of the reporting entity, or of the group of which it is a member, if this is the case; (c) the contributions made in respect of the accounting period and any agreed contribution rates for future years; and (d) for closed schemes and those in which the age profile of the active membership is rising significantly, the fact that under the projected unit method the current service cost will increase as the members of the scheme approach retirement. (2) The fair value of the scheme assets, the present value of the scheme liabilities based on the accounting assumptions and the resulting surplus or deficit should be disclosed in a note to the financial statements. (3) Where the asset or liability in the balance sheet differs from the surplus or deficit in the scheme, an explanation of the difference should be given. (4) An analysis of the movements during the period in the surplus or deficit in the scheme should be given.				
138	Defined contribution schemes The cost of a defined contribution scheme is equal to the contribution payable to the scheme for the accounting period. The cost should be recognised within operating profit in the profit and loss account and the cost for the period should be separately disclosed.		10.1 10.2(b)		

Appendix 4

No.	Disclosure Item	Reference	FRSSE reference	Complies?	Comments

139	Pension commitments
	
	(1) Disclose particulars of:
	  (a) any pension commitments included under any provision shown in the company's balance sheet; and
	  (b) any such commitments for which no provision has been made.
	(2) Where any such commitment relates wholly or partly to pensions payable to past directors of the company, separate particulars of that commitment should be disclosed, so far as it relates to such pensions.
	
	Note: Any commitments which are undertaken for or on behalf of or for the benefit of:
	  (a) any holding company or fellow subsidiary of the company, or
	  (b) any subsidiary of the company,
	should be stated separately from other commitments. Commitments within (a) should be stated separately from those within (b).
		Sch8:46(4)
		Sch8:46(6)			

	Post balance sheet events				
140	A material post balance sheet event should be disclosed where: (1) it is a non-adjusting event of such materiality that its non-disclosure would affect the ability of the users of financial statements to reach a proper understanding of the financial position; or (2) it is the reversal or maturity after the year end of a transaction entered into before the year end, the substance of which was primarily to alter the appearance of the balance sheet. In respect of each post balance sheet event that is required to be		14.3 14.4 14.5		

Small companies' disclosure checklist

No.	Disclosure Item	Reference	FRSSE reference	Complies?	Comments
	disclosed, the following information should be stated: (1) the nature of the event; (2) an estimate of its pre-tax financial effect (or statement that estimation is not practicable); and (3) an explanation of the taxation implications, where necessary for proper understanding of the financial position.				
	Related parties and transactions involving directors				

141	(1) With respect to the company (if any) regarded by the directors as being the company's ultimate holding company state:
	  (a) the name of that company; and
	  (b) its country of incorporation if outside Great Britain.
	(2) When the reporting entity is controlled by another party disclose:
	  (a) the related party relationship;
	  (b) the name of that party; and if different
	  (c) the name of the ultimate controlling party.
	If these parties are not known disclose that fact.
	
	Note: (i) 'Company' includes any body corporate.
	(ii) This related party relationship should be disclosed irrespective of whether any transactions have taken place between the controlling parties and the reporting entity.
	(iii) These disclosures may be omitted if DTI approval is obtained, for an undertaking which is established outside the law of the UK or carries on business outside the UK where disclosure
		s231
		Sch5:12
			15.5		

Appendix 4

No.	Disclosure Item	Reference	FRSSE reference	Complies?	Comments
	would be harmful. The fact of the omission should be stated.				
142	Subsidiary within a larger group Where the company is a subsidiary undertaking, and one or more of its parent undertakings is preparing group financial statements, for each of (a) the largest group of which it is a member for which group financial statements are drawn up, and (b) the smallest such group, state with respect to the parent undertaking of that group: (1) the name of the parent undertaking; (2) the country of incorporation, if outside Great Britain; (3) if unincorporated, address of its principal place of business; and (4) if copies of either of the group financial statements referred to in (a) or (b) above are available to the public, the address from which they may be obtained. *Note: Information need not be disclosed with respect to an undertaking which is established under the law of a country outside the UK or carries on business outside the UK, if in the opinion of the directors of the company the disclosure would be seriously prejudicial to the business of that undertaking, or to the business of the company or any of its subsidiary undertakings, and the DTI agrees that the information need not be disclosed. The fact that advantage has been taken of the exemption must be stated.*	s231 Sch5:11			
143	Transactions with directors (including shadow directors)	Sch6:15–24 Sch8:51(3)			

Small companies' disclosure checklist

No.	Disclosure Item	Reference	FRSSE reference	Complies?	Comments
	The following requirements apply in respect of:				
	(a) any loans, quasi-loans, credit transactions made to directors or connected persons and any guarantee or security in connection therewith;				
	(b) any agreement (by the company or a subsidiary) to enter into any such transaction;				
	(c) any assignment to the company or an assumption by it of rights, obligations or liabilities under such transaction which, had it been entered into by the company would have contravened with the Act; or				
	(d) any arrangement by the company whereby another party enters into any such transaction which if entered into by the company would have contravened the Act and whereby that other party obtains any benefit from the company or other group company.				
	(1) Disclose separately for each transaction, arrangement or agreement (comparatives not required):				
	(a) a statement that it was made or subsisted during the period;				
	(b) the name of the director and, where applicable, the connected person; and				
	(c) its principal terms.				
	(2) For a loan or agreement for a loan or an arrangement under (c) or (d) above in relation to a loan, disclose:				
	(a) amount of the liability (principal and interest) at the beginning and end of the financial year;				
	(b) the maximum amount of the liability at any time during the period;				
	(c) amount of interest due but unpaid; and				
	(d) any provision in the				

Appendix 4

No.	Disclosure Item	Reference	FRSSE reference	Complies?	Comments
	financial statements for non-recovery of all or part of the loan or any interest thereon.				
	(3) For a guarantee or security or an arrangement under (c) above in relation to a guarantee or security disclose:				
	(a) amount of the liability of the company (or subsidiary) at the beginning and end of the financial year;				
	(b) the maximum amount for which company (or subsidiary) may become liable; and				
	(c) any amount paid or liability incurred by the company (or a subsidiary) in fulfilling a guarantee or in discharging any security.				
	(4) For any other transaction (i.e. including quasi-loans and credit transactions), disclose the value of the transaction or arrangement.				
	Note: (i) *The disclosure requirements are for directors at any time in the financial year, whether or not they were directors at the time the transaction or arrangement was made.*				
	(ii) *These requirements do not apply to:*				
	(a) transactions, arrangements or agreements between two companies where the director is interested in the second company only by virtue of being director in the first; and				
	(b) contracts of service between a company and one of its (or its				

Small companies' disclosure checklist

No.	Disclosure Item	Reference	FRSSE reference	Complies?	Comments
	holding company) directors or between a director of a company and any of its subsidiaries. (iii) *The requirements of (2)–(4) above do not apply to loans or quasi loans made by a company to certain group companies if disclosure is required only because the company is associated with a director at any time during the relevant period.*				
144	For any transaction or arrangement (other than those detailed in Q143) in which a director (including a shadow director) or connected person had directly or indirectly a material interest, disclose: (1) a statement that it was made or subsisted during the period; (2) its principal terms; (3) the name of the person for whom it was made (i.e. the other parties to the transactions) and where that person is connected with a director, the name of the director; (4) the name of the director with the material interest and the nature of the interest; and (5) the value of the transaction or arrangement. *Note:* (i) *Comparatives are not required.* (ii) *The disclosure requirements are for directors at any time in the financial year, whether or not they were directors at the time the transaction or arrangement was made.* (iii) *The above disclosure*	Sch6:15–27 Sch8:51(3)			

Appendix 4

No.	Disclosure Item	Reference	FRSSE reference	Complies?	Comments
	need not be applied where: (a) each party which is a member of the same group entered into the transaction in the ordinary course of business and the terms are not less favourable to any party than if the interest had not existed; or (b) the company is a wholly-owned subsidiary of a group and the material interest of the director would not have arisen if he had not been associated with the company at any time during the relevant period.				
145	In respect of transactions, arrangements and agreements by the company and, for holding companies, by their subsidiaries, for persons who at any time during the financial year were officers of the company (but not directors), under each of: (1) loans, (2) quasi-loans, or (3) credit transactions, in each case including related guarantees, security, arrangements for assignment or assumption, and indirect arrangements, disclose for each category: (1) the aggregate amounts outstanding at the end of the financial year; and (2) the number of officers for whom they were made. *Note: (i) Comparatives are not required.*	Sch6.28 Sch6:29 Sch8:51(3)			

Small companies' disclosure checklist

No.	Disclosure Item	Reference	FRSSE reference	Complies?	Comments
146	For material transactions with related parties (regardless of whether a price is charged) disclose: (1) the names of the transacting parties; (2) a description of the relationship between the parties; (3) a description of the transactions; (4) the amounts involved; and (5) any other elements of the transactions necessary for an understanding of the financial statements. Note: (i) Materiality of a related party transaction should be judged only in terms of significance to the reporting entity. (ii) Disclosure is not required of pension contributions paid to a pension fund, emoluments in respect of services as an employee of the reporting entity and transactions with the following parties, simply as a result of their role as: (a) providers of finance in the course of their business; (b) utility companies; (c) government departments and their sponsored bodies; or (d) a customer, supplier, franchiser, distributor or general agent. (iii) Disclosure may be on an aggregated basis (similar transactions by type of related party) unless disclosure of individual		15.1(i-v) 15.1 footnote 15.3 15.4		

Appendix 4

No.	Disclosure Item	Reference	FRSSE reference	Complies?	Comments
	transactions is necessary for an understanding of the impact of the transactions or is required by law.				
147	Disclose personal guarantees given by the directors in respect of the reporting entity's borrowings.		15.2		
148	In respect of amounts due to and from related parties disclose: (1) amounts at the balance sheet date; (2) provisions for doubtful debts at that date; and (3) amounts written off in the period. *Note: Disclosure may be on an aggregated basis (similar transactions by type of related party) unless disclosure of individual transactions is necessary for an understanding of the impact or is required by law.*		15.1(vi) 15.1(vii)		
Abbreviated accounts					
149	The balance sheet should accord with one of the prescribed formats.	Sch8A:1			
150	A directors' report and profit and loss account are not required for small company abbreviated accounts.	s246(5)			
151	State the accounting policies adopted by the company in determining the amounts to be included in respect of items shown in the balance sheet and in determining the profit or loss of the company (including such policies with respect to the depreciation and diminution in value of assets and including basis of conversion of foreign currency amounts into sterling).	Sch8A:4 Sch8A:9			
152	The abbreviated accounts should make clear that they have been derived from financial statements prepared in accordance with FRSSE 2002.		2.3 (footnote)		

Small companies' disclosure checklist

No.	Disclosure Item	Reference	FRSSE reference	Complies?	Comments
	This statement will normally be included with the accounting policies note. An example of such a statement is as follows: *'The full financial statements, from which these abbreviated accounts have been extracted, have been prepared in accordance with the Financial Reporting Standard for Smaller Entities (effective June 2002) under the historical cost convention.'*				

153	Intangible fixed assets
	Gross amounts, movements and depreciation:
	for each item under intangible fixed assets that does not have an Arabic numeral, i.e. for the aggregate of intangible fixed assets only, state (comparatives not required):
	(1) the cost at the beginning and end of the year;
	(2) the effect on any:
	  (a) acquisitions during the year;
	  (b) disposals during the year; and
	  (c) transfers during the year; and
	(3) in respect of provisions for depreciation or diminution in value:
	  (a) the cumulative amount of such provisions as at the beginning and end of the year;
	  (b) the amount provided during the year;
	  (c) the amount of any adjustments on disposal; and
	  (d) the amount of any other adjustments (e.g. exchange differences).
		Sch8A:7
		Sch8A: 9(3)(d)			

154	Tangible fixed assets Gross amounts, movements and depreciation: for each item under tangible fixed assets that does not have an Arabic numeral, i.e. for the aggregate of tangible fixed assets only, state (comparatives not required):	Sch8A:7 Sch8A: 9(3)(d)			

Appendix 4

No.	Disclosure Item	Reference	FRSSE reference	Complies?	Comments

	(1) the cost or valuation at the beginning and end of year;
	(2) the effect on any amount shown in the balance sheet in respect of each fixed asset item as a result of any:
	  (a) revaluation made during the year;
	  (b) acquisitions during the year;
	  (c) disposals during the year; and
	  (d) transfers during the year; and
	(3) in respect of provisions for depreciation or diminution in value:
	  (a) the cumulative amount of such provisions as at the beginning and end of the year;
	  (b) the amount provided during the year;
	  (c) the amount of any adjustments on disposals; and
	  (d) the amount of any other adjustments (e.g. exchange differences).				

155	Fixed asset investments
	
	Gross amounts, movements and depreciation:
	
	for each item under fixed asset investments that does not have an Arabic numeral, i.e. for the aggregate of fixed asset investments only, state (comparatives not required):
	
	(1) the cost or valuation at the beginning and end of the year;
	(2) the effect on any amount shown in the balance sheet in respect of each fixed asset item as a result of any:
	  (a) revaluation made during the year;
	  (b) acquisitions during the year;
	  (c) disposals during the year; and
	  (d) transfers during the year;
		Sch8A:7
		Sch8A: 9(3)(d)			

Small companies' disclosure checklist

No.	Disclosure Item	Reference	FRSSE reference	Complies?	Comments
	and (3) in respect of provisions for depreciation or diminution in value: (a) the cumulative amount of such provisions as at the beginning and end of the year; (b) the amount provided during the year; (c) the amount of any adjustments on disposals; and (d) the amount of any other adjustments (e.g. exchange differences).				
156	Disclose details of debtors falling due after more than one year, either on the face of the balance sheet or in a note.	Sch8A:2 (Note 1)			
157	The aggregate amount of creditors falling due within one year and of creditors falling due after more than one year shall be shown separately, either on the face of the balance sheet or in a note. Note: This requirement is automatically met by the Format 1 balance sheet but requires an additional disclosure when Format 2 is followed.	Sch8A:2 (Note 2)			
158	For creditors where: (1) security has been given, provide details of amounts; (2) there are amounts payable other than by instalments, and fall due for payment or repayment after five years, provide details of aggregate amounts; and (3) if paid by instalments, and any instalments fall due after five years, show total due.	Sch8A:8			
159	Authorised, issued and paid up capital Disclose: (1) authorised share capital; and (2) number and aggregate nominal value of allotted shares of each	Sch8A:5			

203

Appendix 4

No.	Disclosure Item	Reference	FRSSE reference	Complies?	Comments
	class where more than one class of shares have been allotted. For redeemable shares indicate: (1) earliest and latest dates on which the company has power of redemption; (2) whether redemption is required in any event or at option of company or shareholder; and (3) whether any (and if so what) premium is payable on redemption.				
160	Where the company has allotted any shares during the financial year disclose: (1) the classes of shares allotted; and (2) for each class of shares, the number allotted, their aggregate nominal value and the consideration received by the company.	Sch8A:6			
161	Give all of the Schedule 5 (i.e. related undertakings) information required to be disclosed by a small company (refer to checklist for full financial statements), except for financial years of subsidiary undertakings (paragraph 4) and shares and debentures held by subsidiaries (paragraph 6).	s246			
162	Disclose the information required by Part II and Part III of Schedule 6, (refer to checklist for full financial statements) i.e. transactions involving directors, connected persons and officers of the company.	s246			
163	The company's balance sheet should contain in a prominent position above the signature, a statement that the accounts are prepared in accordance with the special provisions relating to small companies within Part VII of the Companies Act 1985. *For example, as follows:* *'The abbreviated accounts have been prepared in accordance with*	s246(8) s246(9)			

204

Small companies' disclosure checklist

No.	Disclosure Item	Reference	FRSSE reference	Complies?	Comments
	the special provisions relating to small companies within Part VII of the Companies Act 1985.' Note: Does not apply where the company is exempt by virtue of s249AA (dormant companies) from the obligation to appoint auditors).				
164	If the company has taken advantage of the exemption from audit under s249A, a statement is required above the signatures on the balance sheet complying with the requirements described at Q12 above. For example, as follows: 'These abbreviated accounts are derived from unaudited financial statements. In preparing the unaudited financial statements advantage has been taken of the exemption under section 249A(1) of the Companies Act 1985. Members have not required the company to obtain an audit under section 249B(2). Company law requires the directors to prepare financial statements for each financial year which give a true and fair view of the state of affairs of the company and of the profit or loss of the company for that period and which comply with the provisions of the Companies Act 1985. The directors are responsible for keeping proper accounting records which disclose with reasonable accuracy at any time the financial position of the company and to enable them to ensure that the financial statements comply with the Companies Act. They are also responsible for safeguarding the assets of the company and hence taking reasonable steps for the prevention and detection of fraud and other irregularities.'	s249B			

Appendix 4

No.	Disclosure Item	Reference	FRSSE reference	Complies?	Comments

165	Independent auditors' report for abbreviated accounts
	
	(1) The accounts to be delivered should be accompanied by a special report of the auditors stating that in their opinion:
	  (a) the company is entitled to deliver abbreviated accounts prepared in accordance with s246(5) and/or s246(6); and
	  (b) the accounts to be delivered are properly prepared in accordance with that (those) provisions.
	(2) The auditors' report on the abbreviated accounts should reproduce the report on the full financial statements if it contained a qualification. Any further material necessary to understand the qualification must also be given.
	(3) Where statements were made under s237(2) (accounts, records or returns inadequate or accounts not agreeing with returns and records) or s237(3) (failure to obtain necessary information and explanations) these should be set out in full in the auditors' report on the abbreviated accounts.
	(4) The auditors' report should also include any explanatory paragraph relating to a fundamental uncertainty (together with any further material necessary for an understanding of this) where such a statement was included in the auditors' report on the full financial statements.
	
	Note: (i) The above does not apply where the company is dormant and is exempt by virtue of s249AA from the obligation to appoint auditors or where the directors have taken advantage
		s247B
		APB Bulletin 1997/1			

Small companies' disclosure checklist

No.	Disclosure Item	Reference	FRSSE reference	Complies?	Comments
	of the exemption from audit conferred by s249A. (ii) The special report on the abbreviated accounts should be dated on, or as soon as possible after, the date of the report on the full financial statements.				

Appendix 5

- 6 **Leases**
    - Hire purchase and leasing
    - Accounting by lessees
    - Accounting by lessors
    - Manufacturer/dealer lessor
    - Sale and leaseback transactions – accounting by the seller/lessee
    - Sale and leaseback transactions – accounting by the buyer/lessor
    - Disclosure by lessees
    - Disclosure by lessors
- 7 [Section withdrawn]
- 8 **Current assets**
    - Stocks and long-term contracts
    - Consignment stock
    - Debt factoring
    - Start-up costs
- 9 **Taxation**
    - General
    - Deferred tax
    - Tax on dividends
    - Value added tax (VAT)
- 10 **Retirement benefits**
- 11 **Provisions, contingent liabilities and contingent assets**
    - Provisions
    - Contingent liabilities and contingent assets
- 12 **Capital instruments**
- 13 **Foreign currency translation**
    - Transactions in foreign currencies
    - Incorporating accounts of foreign entities
- 14 **Post balance sheet events**
- 15 **Related party disclosures**
- 16 **Consolidated financial statements**
- 17 **Date from which effective and transitional arrangements**
    - Transitional arrangements—goodwill
    - Transitional arrangements—tangible fixed assets
- 18 **Withdrawal of the FRSSE (effective March 2000)**

C **DEFINITIONS**

D **VOLUNTARY DISCLOSURES**

Cash flow information

Appendix 5

Financial Reporting Standard for Smaller Entities (effective June 2002)

Contents

Status of the FRSSE

Financial Reporting Standard for Smaller Entities
(Effective June 2002)

A   OBJECTIVE

B   STATEMENT OF STANDARD ACCOUNTING PRACTICE

    1   Scope
    2   General
          True and fair view
          Accounting policies
          Prior period adjustments
          True and fair view override disclosures
    3   Profit and loss account
          General
          Exceptional items
          Profit or loss on disposal
          Extraordinary items
          The euro
    4   Statement of total recognised gains and losses
    5   Fixed assets and goodwill
          Research and development
          Other intangible assets and goodwill
          Tangible fixed assets
          Depreciation
          Write-downs to recoverable amount
          Investment properties
          Government grants

ADOPTION OF THE FRSSE (EFFECTIVE JUNE 2002) BY THE BOARD

APPENDICES

I   NOTE ON LEGAL REQUIREMENTS

II   ACCOUNTING FOR RETIREMENT BENEFITS: DEFINED BENEFIT SCHEMES

III ILLUSTRATIVE EXAMPLES AND PRACTICAL CONSIDERATIONS

        Statement of total recognised gains and losses
        Disclosure – defined contribution pension scheme
        Disclosure – defined benefit pension scheme
        Stocks and long-term contracts
        Consignment stock
        Debt factoring
        Cash flow statement
        Discounting when making a provision

IV THE DEVELOPMENT OF THE FRSSE

V   DERIVATION TABLES

VI SIMPLIFICATIONS IN THE FRSSE

VII AMENDMENT TO THE FRSSE (EFFECTIVE MARCH 2000)

Appendix 5
Status of the FRSSE

General

The Financial Reporting Standard for Smaller Entities (effective June 2002) – the FRSSE – prescribes the basis, for those entities within its scope that have chosen to adopt it, for preparing and presenting their financial statements. The definitions and accounting treatments are consistent with the requirements of companies legislation and, for the generality of small entities, are the same as those required by other accounting standards or a simplified version of those requirements. The disclosure requirements exclude a number of those stipulated in other accounting standards.

Reporting entities that apply the FRSSE are exempt from complying with other accounting standards (Statements of Standard Accounting Practice and Financial Reporting Standards) and Urgent Issues Task Force (UITF) Abstracts, unless preparing consolidated financial statements, in which case certain other accounting standards apply, as set out in paragraph 16.1.

Financial statements will generally be prepared using accepted practice and, accordingly, for transactions or events not dealt with in the FRSSE, smaller entities should have regard to other accounting standards and UITF Abstracts, not as mandatory documents, but as a means of establishing current practice.

Criteria

When considering the application of accounting standards and UITF Abstracts to smaller entities, the Accounting Standards Board has had, and will continue to have, regard to the following criteria:[1]

(a) The standard or requirement is likely to be regarded as having general application and as an essential element of generally accepted accounting practice for all entities.
(b) The standard or requirement is likely to lead to a transaction being treated in a way that would be readily recognised by the proprietor or manager of the business as corresponding to his or her understanding of the transaction.
(c) The standard or requirement is likely to meet the information needs and legitimate expectations of a user of a small entity's accounts.
(d) The standard or requirement results in disclosures that are likely to be

---

[1] *Legal advice has been obtained that in accounting standards smaller entities may properly be allowed exemptions or differing treatments provided that there are rational grounds for doing so: see Appendix I.*

Financial Reporting Standard for Smaller Entities

meaningful and comprehensive to such a user. Where disclosures are aimed at a particular group of users, that group would be likely to receive the information, given that they may have access only to abbreviated accounts.

(e) The requirements of the standard significantly augment the treatment prescribed by legislation.
(f) The treatment prescribed by the standard or requirement is compatible with that already used, or expected to be used, by the Inland Revenue in computing taxable profits.
(g) The standard or requirement provides the least cumbersome method of achieving the desired accounting treatment and/or disclosure for an entity that is not complex.
(h) The standard provides guidance that is expected to be widely relevant to the transactions of small entities and is written in terms that can be understood by such businesses.
(i) The measurement methods prescribed in the standard are likely to be reasonably practical for small entities.

The satisfaction of a majority of the above criteria would suggest that the standard or requirement under consideration may also be appropriate for application to smaller entities, whereas failure to satisfy a majority of the above criteria would suggest that exemption, or differing treatment, from the standard, or a specific requirement within that standard, may be more appropriate.

Scope

The FRSSE may be applied to all financial statements intended to give a true and fair view of the financial position and profit or loss (or income and expenditure) of all entities[2] that are:

(a) small companies or groups as defined in companies legislation;[3] or
(b) entities that would also qualify under (a) if they had been incorporated under companies legislation, with the exception of building societies.

---

[2] *Some older accounting standards are drafted in terms of application to companies. References to companies and associated terms, such as board of directors and shareholders, in the FRSSE should therefore be taken to apply also to unincorporated entities.*

[3] *The legal definitions of small companies and small groups are set out in Appendix I. Small groups are not defined in Republic of Ireland legislation. However, in the Republic of Ireland, for the purposes of the FRSSE, small groups should meet, on a consolidated basis, the same legal conditions as are required for small companies. If a group does not qualify as small, then the parent undertaking of that group, even if it qualifies as a small company under Republic of Ireland legislation, is not entitled to adopt the FRSSE.*

Appendix 5

Accordingly, the FRSSE does not apply to:

(i) large or medium-sized companies, groups and other entities;
(ii) public companies;
(iii) banks, building societies or insurance companies;
(iv) authorised persons under the Financial Services Act 1986 (in the UK) or the Investment Intermediaries Act 1995 (in the Republic of Ireland); or
(v) members of groups that contain companies falling under (ii)–(iv) above.

Reporting entities that are entitled to adopt the FRSSE, but choose not to do so, should apply Statements of Standard Accounting Practice (SSAPS), other Financial Reporting Standards (FRSS) and UITF Abstracts when preparing financial statements intended to give a true and fair view of the financial position and profit or loss of the entity.

Statements of Recommended Practice (SORPS) and other equivalent guidance developed or revised after the FRSSE was first issued (in November 1997) may specify the circumstances, if any, in which entities in the industry or sector addressed in the SORP or equivalent guidance may adopt the current version of the FRSSE. Financial statements that purport to comply with existing SORPs that are drafted on the basis that the financial statements comply with the requirements of SSAPS, FRSS (other than the FRSSE) and UITF Abstracts, should also observe those requirements, rather than adopt the FRSSE.

Financial Reporting Standard for Smaller Entities (Effective June 2002)

A – Objective

The objective of the FRSSE is to ensure that reporting entities falling within its scope provide in their financial statements information about the financial position, performance and financial adaptability of the entity that is useful to users in assessing the stewardship of management and for making economic decisions, recognising that the balance between users' needs in respect of stewardship and economic decision-making for smaller entities is different from that for other reporting entities.

Appendix 5

B – Statement of Standard Accounting Practice

1 Scope

1.1 The FRSSE may be applied to all financial statements intended to give a true and fair view of the financial position and profit or loss (or income and expenditure) of all entities that are:

(a) companies incorporated under **companies legislation**[4] and entitled to the exemptions available in the legislation for small companies when filing accounts with the Registrar of Companies;[5] or
(b) entities that would have come into category (a) above had they been companies incorporated under **companies legislation**, excluding building societies. Such entities should have regard to the accounting principles, presentation and disclosure requirements in **companies legislation** (or other equivalent legislation) that, taking into account the FRSSE, are necessary to present a true and fair view.

2 General

True and fair view

2.1 The financial statements should present a true and fair view of the results for the period and of the state of affairs at the end of the period. To achieve such a view, regard should be had to the substance of any arrangement or transaction, or series of such, into which the entity has entered. To determine the substance of a transaction it is necessary to identify whether the transaction has given rise to new **assets** or **liabilities** for the reporting entity and whether it has changed the entity's existing **assets** or **liabilities**.

2.2 Where there is doubt whether applying provisions of the FRSSE would be sufficient to give a true and fair view, adequate explanation should be given in the notes to the accounts of the transaction or arrangement concerned and the treatment adopted.

---

[4] *Terms appearing in* **bold** *in the text are explained in the Definitions set out in Part C.*

[5] *In the Republic of Ireland, small companies that are also parent undertakings of groups which do not meet, on a consolidated basis, the same legal conditions as are required for small companies, are excluded from the scope of the FRSSE. In the UK this effect is achieved through companies legislation. The legal definition of a small company is set out in Appendix I.*

Financial Reporting Standard for Smaller Entities

Accounting policies

2.3[6] The financial statements should state that they have been prepared in accordance with the Financial Reporting Standard for Smaller Entities (effective June 2002).[7]

2.4 Accounting policies and **estimation techniques** should be consistent with the requirements of the FRSSE and of **companies legislation** (or other equivalent legislation). Where this permits a choice, an entity should select the policies and techniques most appropriate to its particular circumstances for the purpose of giving a true and fair view, taking account of the objectives of relevance, reliability, comparability and understandability.

2.5 Accounting policies should be reviewed regularly to ensure that they remain the most appropriate to the entity's particular circumstances for the purpose of giving a true and fair view. However, in judging whether a new policy is more appropriate than the existing policy, due weight should be given to the impact on comparability. Following a change in **accounting policy**, the amounts for the current and corresponding periods should be restated on the basis of the new policies.

2.6 When preparing financial statements, **directors** should assess whether there are significant doubts about the entity's ability to continue as a going concern. Any material uncertainties, of which the **directors** are aware in making their assessment, should be disclosed. Where the period considered by the **directors** in making this assessment has been limited to a period of less than one year from the date of approval of the financial statements, that fact should be stated.

2.7 Financial statements should include:

(a) a description of each material **accounting policy** followed;
(b) details of any changes to the **accounting policies** followed in the

---

[6] *Paragraphs that have significantly changed or been added since the FRSSE (effective March 2000) – the previous version of the FRSSE, which this version supersedes – are sidelined.*

[7] *This statement may be included with the note of accounting policies or, for those entities taking advantage of the exemptions for small companies in companies legislation, in the statement required by companies legislation to be given on the balance sheet. For example, in Great Britain the combined statement could read as follows 'These accounts have been prepared in accordance with the special provisions relating to small companies within Part VII of the Companies Act 1985 and with the Financial Reporting Standard for Smaller Entities (effective June 2002).' If abbreviated accounts are also to be prepared, the statement referring to the Financial Reporting Standard for Smaller Entities (effective June 2002) should be included with the note of accounting policies so that it is reproduced in the abbreviated accounts.*

Appendix 5

preceding period including, in addition to the disclosures necessary for **prior period adjustments**, a brief explanation of why each new **accounting policy** is thought more appropriate and, where practicable, an indication of the effect of the change on the results for the current period; and

(c) where the effect of a change to an **estimation technique** is material, a description of the change and, where practicable, the effect on the results for the current period.

Prior period adjustments

2.8 **Prior period adjustments** should be accounted for by restating the comparative figures for the preceding period in the primary statements and notes and adjusting the opening balance of reserves for the cumulative effect. The cumulative effect of the adjustments should also be noted at the foot of the statement of **total recognised gains and losses** of the current period. The effect of **prior period adjustments** on the results for the preceding period should be disclosed where practicable.

True and fair view override disclosures

2.9 In cases where the true and fair view override[8] is being invoked this should be stated clearly and unambiguously. To this end the following should be given:

(a) a statement of the treatment that would normally be required in the circumstances and a description of the treatment actually adopted;
(b) a statement explaining why the treatment prescribed would not give a true and fair view; and
(c) a description of how the position shown in the financial statements is different as a result of the departure, normally with quantification, except (i) where quantification is already evident in the financial statements themselves or (ii) whenever the effect cannot be reasonably quantified, in which case the **directors** should explain the circumstances.

2.10 Where a departure continues in subsequent financial statements, the disclosures should be made in all subsequent statements and should include corresponding amounts for the previous period.

---

[8] *The true and fair view override is set out in companies legislation. References to the legal requirements are given in Appendix I.*

Financial Reporting Standard for Smaller Entities

3 Profit and loss account

General

3.1 All gains and losses **recognised** in the financial statements for the period should be included in the profit and loss account or the statement of **total recognised gains and losses**. Gains and losses may be excluded from the profit and loss account only if they are specifically permitted or required to be taken direct to reserves by this standard or by **companies legislation**.

Exceptional items

3.2 All **exceptional items**, other than those included in the items listed in the next paragraph, should be credited or charged in arriving at the profit or loss on **ordinary activities** by inclusion under the statutory format headings to which they relate. The amount of each **exceptional item**, either individually or as an aggregate of items of a similar type, should be disclosed separately by way of note, or on the face of the profit and loss account if that degree of prominence is necessary in order to give a true and fair view. An adequate description of each **exceptional item** should be given to enable its nature to be understood.

3.3 The following items, including **provisions** in respect of such items, should be shown separately on the face of the profit and loss account after operating profit (which is normally profit before income from shares in group undertakings) and before interest:

(a) profits or losses on the sale or termination of an operation;
(b) costs of a fundamental reorganisation or restructuring having a material effect on the nature and focus of the reporting entity's operations; and
(c) profits or losses on the disposal of fixed **assets**.

Profit or loss on disposal

3.4 The profit or loss on the disposal of an asset should be accounted for in the profit and loss account of the period in which the disposal occurs as the difference between the net sale proceeds and the net carrying amount, whether carried at historical cost (less any **provisions** made) or at a valuation. Profit or loss on disposal of a previously acquired business should include the attributable amount of **purchased goodwill** that has previously been eliminated against reserves as a matter of **accounting policy** and has not previously been charged in the profit and loss account.

Appendix 5

Extraordinary items

3.5 Any profit or loss arising from **extraordinary items**, which are extremely rare, should be shown separately on the face of the profit and loss account, after the profit or loss on **ordinary activities** after taxation but before deducting any appropriations such as dividends paid or payable.

The euro

3.6 Costs involved with the introduction of the euro should be written off to the profit and loss account, except where they meet the conditions to be capitalised as a fixed **asset**. Costs may be capitalised (a) where an entity already has an **accounting policy** to capitalise **assets** of the relevant type and (b) to the extent that the expenditure clearly enhances the **asset** beyond that originally assessed, rather than merely maintaining it. If material, the costs written off to the profit and loss account are **exceptional items** and should be disclosed as such.

4 Statement of total recognised gains and losses

4.1 A primary statement should be presented, with the same prominence as the profit and loss account, showing the **total** of **recognised gains and losses** and its components. The components should be the gains and losses that are **recognised** in the period insofar as they are attributable to shareholders, excluding transactions with shareholders.[9] Where the only **recognised** gains and losses are the results included in the profit and loss account no separate statement to this effect need be made.

5 Fixed assets and goodwill

Research and development

5.1 The cost of fixed **assets** acquired or constructed in order to provide facilities for **research and development** activities over a number of accounting periods should be capitalised and written off over their useful lives through the profit and loss account.

5.2 Expenditure on **pure** and **applied research** should be written off in the period of expenditure through the profit and loss account.

5.3 **Development** expenditure should be written off in the period of expenditure except in the following circumstances when it may be deferred to future periods:

---

[9] *An illustration of a statement of total recognised gains and losses is given in Appendix III.*

Financial Reporting Standard for Smaller Entities

(a) there is a clearly defined project; and
(b) the related expenditure is separately identifiable; and
(c) the outcome of such a project has been assessed with reasonable certainty as to:
    (i) its technical feasibility; and
    (ii) its ultimate commercial viability considered in the light of factors such as likely market conditions (including competing products), public opinion, consumer and environmental legislation; and
(d) the aggregate of the deferred **development** costs, any further **development** costs, and related production, selling and administration costs is reasonably expected to be exceeded by related future sales or other revenues; and
(e) adequate resources exist, or are reasonably expected to be available, to enable the project to be completed and to provide any consequential increases in working capital.

5.4 In the foregoing circumstances **development** expenditure may be deferred to the extent that its recovery can be reasonably regarded as assured.

5.5 If an **accounting policy** of deferral of **development** expenditure is adopted, it should be applied to all **development** projects that meet the criteria in paragraph 5.3.

5.6 If **development** costs are deferred to future periods, they should be amortised. The amortisation should commence with the commercial production or application of the product, service, process or system and should be allocated on a systematic basis to each accounting period, by reference to either the sale or use of the product, service, process or system or the period over which these are expected to be sold or used.

5.7 Deferred **development** expenditure for each product should be reviewed at the end of each accounting period and where the circumstances that justified the deferral of expenditure no longer apply, or are considered doubtful, the expenditure, to the extent to which it is considered to be irrecoverable, should be written off immediately project by project.

5.8 The amount of deferred **development** expenditure carried forward at the beginning and end of the period should be disclosed under **intangible assets** in the balance sheet or in the notes to the balance sheet.

Other intangible assets and goodwill

5.9 Positive **purchased goodwill** and purchased **intangible assets** should be capitalised. Internally generated **goodwill** and **intangible assets** should not be capitalised.

Appendix 5

5.10 An **intangible asset** purchased with a business should be **recognised** separately from the **purchased goodwill** if its value can be measured reliably.

5.11 Capitalised **goodwill** and **intangible assets** should be **depreciated** on a straight-line (or more appropriate) basis over their **useful economic lives**, which should not exceed 20 years.

5.12 The **residual value** assigned to **goodwill** should be zero. A higher **residual value** may be assigned to an **intangible asset** only when this value can be established reliably, for example when it has been agreed contractually.

5.13 **Useful economic lives** should be reviewed at the end of each reporting period and revised if necessary, subject to the constraint that the revised life should not exceed 20 years from the date of acquisition. The carrying amount at the date of revision should be **depreciated** over the revised estimate of remaining **useful economic life**.

5.14 **Goodwill** and **intangible assets** should not be revalued.

5.15 If an acquisition appears to give rise to negative **goodwill**, **fair values** should be checked to ensure that those of the acquired **assets** have not been overstated and those of the acquired **liabilities** have not been under-stated. Once this has been done, remaining negative **goodwill** up to the **fair values** of the non-monetary **assets** acquired should be released in the profit and loss account over the lives of those **assets**. Any additional negative **goodwill** should be **recognised** in the profit and loss account over the period expected to benefit from it. The amount of negative **goodwill** on the balance sheet and the period(s) in which it is being written back should be disclosed.

Tangible fixed assets

5.16 Paragraphs 5.17–5.24 apply to all **tangible fixed assets** other than **investment properties**.

5.17 A **tangible fixed asset** should initially be measured at its cost, then written down to its **recoverable amount** if necessary. The initial carrying amount of a **tangible fixed asset** received as a gift or donation by a charity should be its current value, i.e. the lower of replacement cost and **recoverable amount**, at the date it is received.[10]

---

[10] *Generally, where issues of practicality or of cost-benefit arise, these will be addressed in the relevant sector-specific guidance and Statements of Recommended Practice (SORPs).*

Financial Reporting Standard for Smaller Entities

5.18 Costs that are directly attributable to bringing the **tangible fixed asset** into working condition for its intended use should be included in its measurement. Other costs should not be included. An entity may adopt an **accounting policy** of capitalising finance costs (such as interest). Where such a policy is adopted, **finance costs** that are directly attributable to the construction of **tangible fixed assets** should be capitalised as part of the cost of those **assets**. The total amount of finance costs capitalised during a period should not exceed the total amount of **finance costs** incurred during that period.

5.19 Capitalisation of directly attributable costs, including **finance costs**, should be suspended during extended periods in which active development is interrupted. Capitalisation should cease when substantially all the activities that are necessary to get the **tangible fixed asset** ready for use are complete, even if the asset has not yet been brought into use.

5.20 Subsequent expenditure should be capitalised only if:

(a) it enhances the economic benefits of a **tangible fixed asset** in excess of the previously assessed standard of performance (i.e. if it is an 'improvement'); or
(b) it replaces or restores a component that has been separately depreciated over its **useful economic life**.

Otherwise it should be **recognised** in the profit and loss account as it is incurred.

5.21 Where an entity adopts an **accounting policy** of revaluation in respect of a **tangible fixed asset**, its carrying amount should be its market value (or the best estimate thereof) as at the balance sheet date. Where the **directors** believe that market value is not an appropriate basis, current value (i.e. the lower of replacement cost and **recoverable amount**) may be used instead. Where a **tangible fixed asset** is revalued all **tangible fixed assets** of the same class (i.e. having a similar nature, function or use in the business) should be revalued, but a policy of revaluation need not be applied to all classes of **tangible fixed assets**.

5.22 It may be possible to establish with reasonable reliability the values of certain **tangible fixed assets**, other than properties, by reference to active second-hand markets or appropriate publicly available indices. For other **tangible fixed assets**, including properties, a valuation should be performed by an experienced valuer (i.e. one who has recognised and relevant recent professional experience, and sufficient knowledge of the state of the market, in the location and category of the **tangible fixed asset** being valued) at least every five years. It should be updated by an experienced valuer in the

Appendix 5

intervening years where it is likely that there has been a material change in value.[11]

5.23 Revaluation losses caused only by changing market prices should be **recognised** in the statement of **total recognised gains and losses** until the carrying amount of the **asset** reaches its depreciated historical cost. Other revaluation losses should be **recognised** in the profit and loss account.

5.24 Revaluation gains should be **recognised** in the statement of **total recognised gains and losses**, except to the extent (after adjusting for subsequent **depreciation**) that they reverse revaluation losses on the same asset that were previously **recognised** in the profit and loss account. To that extent they should be **recognised** in the profit and loss account. The adjustment for subsequent **depreciation** is to achieve the same overall effect that would have been reached had the original downward revaluation reflected in the profit and loss account not occurred.

Depreciation

5.25 Paragraphs 5.26–5.31 apply to all **tangible fixed assets** other than **investment properties**.

5.26 The cost (or revalued amount) less estimated **residual value** of a **tangible fixed asset** should be depreciated on a systematic basis over its **useful economic life**. The **depreciation** method used should reflect as fairly as possible the pattern in which the **asset's** economic benefits are consumed by the entity. The **depreciation** charge for each period should be **recognised** as an expense in the profit and loss account unless it is permitted to be included in the carrying amount of another **asset**.

5.27 Where a **tangible fixed asset** comprises two or more major components with substantially different **useful economic lives**, each component should be accounted for separately for **depreciation** purposes and depreciated over its individual **useful economic life**. With certain exceptions, such as sites used for extractive purposes or landfill, land has an unlimited life and therefore is not depreciated.

5.28 The **useful economic lives** and **residual values** of **tangible fixed assets** should be reviewed regularly and, when necessary, revised. On revision, the carrying amount of the **tangible fixed asset** at the date of revision less the

---

[11] *Where, for cost/benefit reasons, alternative approaches are set out in relevant sector-specific guidance and SORPs, these may be adopted instead of the approach in paragraph 5.22.*

Financial Reporting Standard for Smaller Entities

revised **residual value** should be depreciated over the revised remaining **useful economic life**.

5.29 A change from one method of providing **depreciation** to another is permissible only on the grounds that the new method will give a fairer presentation of the results and of the financial position. Such a change does not, however, constitute a change of **accounting policy**; the carrying amount of the **tangible fixed asset** is depreciated using the revised method over the remaining **useful economic life**, beginning in the period in which the change is made.

5.30 The following should be disclosed in the financial statements for (1) land and buildings and (2) other **tangible fixed assets** in aggregate:

(a) the **depreciation** methods used;
(b) the **useful economic lives** or the **depreciation** rates used; and
(c) where material, the financial effect of a change during the period in either the estimate of **useful economic lives** or the estimate of **residual values**.

5.31 Where there has been a change in the **depreciation** method used, the effect, if material, should be disclosed in the period of change. The reason for the change should also be disclosed.

Write-downs to recoverable amount

5.32 Paragraphs 5.33–5.36 apply to capitalised **goodwill** and all fixed assets (i.e. **tangible fixed assets, intangible assets** and investments) except **investment properties** and financial instruments (other than investments in subsidiaries, associates and joint ventures).

5.33 Fixed **assets** and **goodwill** should be carried in the balance sheet at no more than **recoverable amount**. If the net book amount of a fixed **asset** or **goodwill** is considered not to be recoverable in full at the balance sheet date (perhaps as a result of obsolescence or a fall in demand for a product), the net book amount should be written down to the estimated **recoverable amount**, which should then be written off over the remaining **useful economic life** of the **asset**.

5.34 If the **recoverable amount** of a **tangible fixed asset** or investment subsequently increases as a result of a change in economic conditions or in the expected use of the **asset**, the net book amount should be written back to the lower of **recoverable amount** and the amount at which the **asset** would have been recorded had the original write-down not been made.

Appendix 5

5.35 If the **recoverable amount** of an **intangible asset** or capitalised **goodwill** subsequently increases, the net book amount should be written back only if an external event caused the original write-down and subsequent external events clearly and demonstrably reverse the effects of that event in a way that was not foreseen when the original write-down was calculated.

5.36 Write-downs (and any reversals) to **recoverable amount** should be charged (or credited) in the profit and loss account for the period. However, write-downs of revalued **tangible fixed assets** that reverse previous revaluation gains simply as a result of changing market prices should instead be **recognised** in the statement of **total recognised gains and losses**, to the extent that the carrying amount of the **asset** is greater than its depreciated historical cost.

Investment properties

5.37 **Investment properties** should not be subject to periodic charges for **depreciation** except for properties held on lease, which should be **depreciated** at least over the period when the unexpired term is 20 years or less.

5.38 **Investment properties** should be included in the balance sheet at their open market value and the carrying value should be displayed prominently either on the face of the balance sheet or in the notes.

5.39 The names of the persons making the valuation, or particulars of their qualifications, should be disclosed together with the bases of valuation used by them. If a person making a valuation is an employee or officer of the company or group that owns the property this fact should be disclosed.

5.40 Changes in the market value of **investment properties** should not be taken to the profit and loss account but should be taken to the statement of **total recognised gains and losses** (being a movement on an investment revaluation reserve), unless a deficit (or its reversal) on an individual **investment property** is expected to be permanent, in which case it should be charged (or credited) in the profit and loss account of the period.

Government grants[12]

5.41 Subject to paragraph 5.42, **government grants** should be **recognised** in the profit and loss account so as to match them with the expenditure

---

[12] Notes on the legal requirements for the Republic of Ireland are included in Appendix I.

Financial Reporting Standard for Smaller Entities

towards which they are intended to contribute. To the extent that the grant is made as a contribution towards expenditure on a fixed **asset**, in principle it may be deducted from the purchase price or production cost of that **asset**. However, the option to deduct **government grants** from the purchase price or production costs of fixed assets is not available to companies governed by the accounting and reporting requirements of UK **companies legislation**. In such cases, the amount so deferred should be treated as deferred income.

5.42 A **government grant** should not be **recognised** in the profit and loss account until the conditions for its receipt have been complied with and there is reasonable assurance that the grant will be received.

5.43 Potential **liabilities** to repay grants either in whole or in part in specified circumstances should be provided for only to the extent that repayment is probable. The repayment of a **government grant** should be accounted for by setting off the repayment against any unamortised deferred income relating to the grant. Any excess should be charged immediately to the profit and loss account.

5.44 The following information should be disclosed in the financial statements:

(a) the effects of **government grants** on the results for the period and/or the financial position of the entity; and
(b) where the results of the period are affected materially by the receipt of forms of **government** assistance other than grants, the nature of that assistance and, to the extent that the effects on the financial statements can be measured, an estimate of those effects.

6 Leases

Hire purchase and leasing

6.1 Those **hire purchase contracts** which are of a financing nature should be accounted for on a basis similar to that set out below for **finance leases**. Conversely, other **hire purchase contracts** should be accounted for on a basis similar to that set out below for **operating leases**.

Accounting by lessees

6.2 A **finance lease** should be recorded in the balance sheet of a lessee as an **asset** and as an **obligation** to pay future rentals. At the **inception** of the lease the sum to be recorded both as an **asset** and as a **liability** should normally be the **fair value** of the **asset**.

6.3 In those cases where the **fair value** of the **asset** does not give a realistic

Appendix 5

estimate of the cost to the lessee of the **asset** and of the **obligation** entered into, a better estimate should be used. In principle this should approximate to the present value of the **minimum lease payments,** derived by discounting them at the interest rate implicit in the lease. An example of where this might be used would be where the lessee has benefited from grants and capital allowances that enable the **minimum lease payments** under a **finance lease** to be adjusted to a total that is less than the **fair value** of the asset. A negative **finance charge** should not be shown.

6.4 The total **finance charge** under a **finance lease** should be allocated to accounting periods during the **lease term** so as to produce a constant periodic rate of charge on the remaining balance of the **obligation** for each accounting period, or a reasonable approximation thereto. The straight-line method may provide such a reasonable approximation.

6.5 The rental under an **operating lease** should be charged on a straight-line basis over the **lease term** even if the payments are not made on such a basis, unless another systematic and rational basis is more appropriate.

6.6 Incentives to sign a lease, in whatever form they may take, should be spread by the lessee on a straight-line basis over the **lease term** or, if shorter than the full **lease term,** over the period to the review date on which the rent is first expected to be adjusted to the prevailing market rate.

6.7 An **asset** leased under a **finance lease** should be depreciated over the shorter of the **lease term** or its useful life. However, in the case of a **hire purchase contract** that has the characteristics of a **finance lease** the **asset** should be **depreciated** over its useful life.

Accounting by lessors

6.8 The amount due from the lessee under a **finance lease** should be recorded in the balance sheet of a lessor as a debtor at the amount of the **net investment** in the lease after making **provisions** for items such as bad and doubtful rentals receivable.

6.9 The total **gross earnings** under **finance leases** should be **recognised** on a systematic and rational basis. This will normally be a constant periodic rate of return on the lessor's **net investment.**

6.10 Rental income from an **operating lease** should be **recognised** on a straight-line basis over the period of the lease, even if the payments are not made on such a basis, unless another systematic and rational basis is more representative of the time pattern in which the benefit from the leased **asset** is receivable.

Financial Reporting Standard for Smaller Entities

6.11 An **asset** held for use in **operating leases** by a lessor should be recorded as a fixed **asset** and **depreciated** over its useful life.

Manufacturer/dealer lessor

6.12 A manufacturer or dealer lessor should not **recognise** a selling profit under an **operating lease**. The selling profit under a **finance lease** should be restricted to the excess of the **fair value** of the **asset** over the manufacturer's or dealer's cost less any grants receivable by the manufacturer or dealer towards the purchase, construction or use of the **asset**.

Sale and leaseback transactions – accounting by the seller/lessee

6.13 In a sale and leaseback transaction that results in a **finance lease**, any apparent profit or loss (i.e. the difference between the sale price and the previous carrying value) should be deferred and amortised in the financial statements of the seller/lessee over the shorter of the **lease term** and the useful life of the **asset**.

6.14 If the leaseback is an **operating lease**:

(a) any profit or loss should be **recognised** immediately, provided it is clear that the transaction is established at **fair value**;
(b) if the sale price is below **fair value** any profit or loss should be **recognised** immediately, except that if the apparent loss is compensated for by future rentals at below market price it should to that extent be deferred and amortised over the remainder of the **lease term** (or, if shorter, the period during which the reduced rentals are chargeable);
(c) if the sale price is above **fair value**, the excess over **fair value** should be deferred and amortised over the shorter of the remainder of the **lease term** and the period to the next rent review (if any).

Sale and leaseback transactions – accounting by the buyer/lessor

6.15 A buyer/lessor should account for a sale and leaseback in the same way as other leases are accounted for, i.e. using the methods set out in paragraphs 6.8–6.12.

Disclosure by lessees

6.16 Disclosure should be made of:

(a) either:
   (i) the gross amounts of **assets** that are held under **finance leases** together with the related accumulated **depreciation** by (1) land and buildings and (2) other fixed **assets** in aggregate; or

Appendix 5

    (ii) alternatively to being shown separately from that in respect of owned fixed **assets**, the information in (i) above may be integrated with it, such that the totals of gross amount, accumulated **depreciation**, net amount and **depreciation** allocated for the period for (1) land and buildings and (2) other fixed **assets** in aggregate for assets held under **finance leases** are included with similar amounts for owned fixed **assets**. Where this alternative treatment is adopted, the net amount of **assets** held under **finance leases** and the amount of **depreciation** allocated for the period in respect of **assets** under **finance leases** included in the overall total should be disclosed separately.

(b) the amounts of **obligations** related to **finance leases** (net of **finance charges** allocated to future periods). These should be disclosed separately from other **obligations** and **liabilities**, either on the face of the balance sheet or in the notes to the accounts.

(c) the amount of any commitments existing at the balance sheet date in respect of **finance leases** that have been entered into but whose **inception** occurs after the year-end.

6.17 In respect of **operating leases**, the lessee should disclose the payments that it is committed to make during the next year, analysed into those in which the commitment expires within that year, those expiring in the second to fifth years inclusive, and those expiring over five years from the balance sheet date.

Disclosure by lessors

6.18 Disclosure should be made of:

(a) the gross amounts of **assets** held for use in **operating leases** and the related accumulated **depreciation** charges;

(b) the cost of **assets** acquired, whether by purchase or **finance lease**, for the purpose of letting under **finance leases**;

(c) the **net investment** in (i) **finance leases** and (ii) **hire purchase contracts** at each balance sheet date.

7 [Section withdrawn]

8 Current assets

Stocks and long-term contracts[13]

8.1 The amount at which stocks are stated in the financial statements

---

[13] *Guidance on the practical considerations of arriving at amounts at which stocks and long-term contracts are stated in financial statements is given in Appendix III.*

Financial Reporting Standard for Smaller Entities

should be the total of the lower of **cost** and **net realisable** value of the separate items of stock or of groups of similar items.

8.2 Long-term contracts should be assessed on a contract-by-contract basis and reflected in the profit and loss account by recording turnover and related costs as contract activity progresses. Turnover is ascertained in a manner appropriate to the stage of completion of the contract, the business and the industry in which it operates.

8.3 Where it is considered that the outcome of a **long-term contract** can be assessed with reasonable certainty before its conclusion, the prudently calculated **attributable profit** should be **recognised** in the profit and loss account as the difference between the reported turnover and related costs for that contract.

8.4 Long-term contracts should be disclosed in the balance sheet as follows:

(a) The amount by which recorded turnover is in excess of payments on account should be classified as 'amounts recoverable on contracts' and separately disclosed within debtors.
(b) The balance of payments on account (in excess of the amounts (i) matched with turnover and (ii) offset against **long-term contract** balances) should be classified as payments on account and separately disclosed within creditors.
(c) The amount of **long-term contracts**, at costs incurred, net of amounts transferred to cost of sales, after deducting **foreseeable losses** and payments on account not matched with turnover, should be classified as 'long-term contract balances' and separately disclosed within the balance sheet heading 'stocks'. The balance sheet note should disclose separately the balances of:
   (i) net cost less **foreseeable losses**; and
   (ii) applicable payments on account.
(d) The amount by which the **provision** or accrual for **foreseeable losses** exceeds the costs incurred (after transfers to cost of sales) should be included within either 'provisions for liabilities and charges' or 'creditors' as appropriate.

Consignment stock[14]

8.5 Where **consignment stock** is in substance an **asset** of the dealer, the stock should be **recognised** as such on the dealer's balance sheet, together

---

[14] A table illustrating the considerations affecting the treatment of consignment stock is given in Appendix III.

Appendix 5

with a corresponding **liability** to the manufacturer. Any deposit should be deducted from the **liability** and the excess classified as a trade creditor. Where stock is not in substance an **asset** of the dealer, the stock should not be included on the dealer's balance sheet until the transfer of title has crystallised. Any deposit should be included under 'other debtors'.

Debt factoring[15]

8.6 Where the entity has transferred to the factor all significant benefits (i.e. the future cash flows from payment by the debtors) and all significant risks (i.e. slow payment risk and the risk of bad debts) relating to the debts, and has no **obligation** to repay the factor, the debts should be removed from the entity's balance sheet and no **liability** should be shown in respect of the proceeds received from the factor. A profit or loss should be **recognised**, calculated as the difference between the carrying amount of the debts and the proceeds received.

8.7 Where the entity has retained significant benefits and risks relating to factored debts, and all the following conditions are met:

(a) there is absolutely no doubt that the entity's exposure to loss is limited to a fixed monetary amount (e.g. because there is no recourse or such recourse has a fixed monetary ceiling);
(b) amounts received from the factor are secured only on the debts factored;
(c) the debts factored are capable of separate identification;
(d) the debt factor has no recourse to other debts or **assets**;
(e) the entity has no right to reacquire the debts in the future;
(f) the factor has no right to return the debts even in the event of the cessation of the factoring agreement,

then the factored debts should be shown gross (after providing for bad debts, credit protection charges and any accrued interest) separately on the face of the balance sheet. Any amounts received from the factor in respect of those debts, to the extent that they are not returnable, should be shown as deductions therefrom on the face of the balance sheet (a 'linked presentation'). The financial statements should include a note stating that the entity is not required to support bad debts in respect of factored debts and that the factors have stated in writing that they will not seek recourse other than out of factored debts. The interest element of the factor's charges

---

[15] *Similar arrangements, such as invoice discounting, should be accounted for in the same way as debt factoring. A table illustrating the considerations affecting the treatment of debt factoring is given in Appendix III.*

Financial Reporting Standard for Smaller Entities

should be **recognised** as it accrues and included in the profit and loss account with other interest charges.

8.8 In all other cases a separate presentation should be adopted. A gross **asset** (equivalent in amount to the gross amount of the debts) should be shown on the balance sheet of the entity within **assets** and a corresponding **liability** in respect of the proceeds received from the factor should be shown within **liabilities**. The interest element of the factor's charges and other factoring costs should be recognised as they accrue and included in the profit and loss account with other interest charges.

Start-up costs

8.9 **Start-up costs** should be accounted for on a basis consistent with the accounting treatment of similar costs incurred as part of the entity's on-going activities. In cases where there are no such similar costs, **start-up costs** that do not meet the criteria for **recognition** as **assets** under another specific requirement of the FRSSE should be **recognised** as an expense when they are incurred. They should not be carried forward as an **asset**.

9 Taxation

General

9.1 Tax (**current** and **deferred**) should be **recognised** in the profit and loss account, except to the extent that it is attributable to a gain or loss that is or has been **recognised** directly in the statement of **total recognised gains and losses** (in which case the tax should also be **recognised** directly in that statement).

9.1A The material components of the (**current** and **deferred**) **tax** charge (or credit) for the period should be disclosed separately.

9.2 Any special circumstances that affect the overall tax charge or credit for the period, or may affect those of future periods, should be disclosed by way of note to the profit and loss account and their individual effects quantified. The effects of a fundamental change in the basis of taxation should be included in the tax charge or credit for the period and separately disclosed on the face of the profit and loss account.

Deferred tax

9.3 Deferred tax should be **recognised** in respect of all **timing differences** that have originated but not reversed by the balance sheet date; however, **deferred tax** should not be **recognised** on:

Appendix 5

  (a) revaluation gains and losses unless, by the balance sheet date, the entity has entered into a binding agreement to sell the **asset** and has revalued the **asset** to the selling price; or

  (b) taxable gains arising on revaluations or sales if it is more likely than not that the gain will be rolled over into a replacement **asset**.

9.4 Unrelieved tax losses and other **deferred tax assets** should be **recognised** only to the extent that it is more likely than not that they will be recovered against the reversal of **deferred tax liabilities** or other future taxable profits (the very existence of unrelieved tax losses is strong evidence that there may not be 'other future taxable profits' against which the losses will be relieved).

9.5 **Deferred tax** should be **recognised** when the tax allowances for the cost of a fixed **asset** are received before or after the **depreciation** of the fixed **asset** is **recognised** in the profit and loss account. However, if and when all conditions for retaining the tax allowances have been met, the **deferred tax** should be reversed.

9.6 **Deferred tax** should not be **recognised** on **permanent differences**.

9.7 **Deferred tax** should be measured at the average tax rates that would apply when the **timing differences** are expected to reverse, based on tax rates and laws that have been enacted by the balance sheet date.

9.8 The discounting of **deferred tax assets** and **liabilities** is not required. However, if an entity does adopt a policy of discounting, all **deferred tax** balances that have been measured by reference to undiscounted cash flows and for which the impact of discounting is material should be discounted. Where discounting is used, the unwinding of the discount should be shown as a component of the tax charge and disclosed separately.

9.9 The **deferred tax** balance and its material components should be disclosed.

9.10 The movement between the opening and closing net **deferred tax** balances, and the material components of this movement, should be disclosed.

9.11 If **assets** have been revalued, or if their market values have been disclosed in a note, the amount of tax that would be payable or recoverable if the **assets** were sold at the values shown should be disclosed.

Financial Reporting Standard for Smaller Entities

Tax on dividends

9.12 Outgoing dividends and similar amounts payable should be **recognised** at an amount that includes any **withholding tax** but excludes other taxes, such as attributable **tax credits**.

9.13 Incoming dividends and similar income receivable should be **recognised** at an amount that includes any **withholding tax** but excludes other taxes, such as attributable **tax credits**. Any **withholding tax** suffered should be shown as part of the tax charge.

Value added tax (VAT)

9.14 Turnover shown in the profit and loss account should exclude VAT on taxable outputs. Irrecoverable VAT allocable to fixed **assets** and to other items disclosed separately in the financial statements should be included in their cost where practicable and material.

10   Retirement benefits

10.1 The cost of a **defined contribution scheme** is equal to the contributions payable to the scheme for the accounting period. The cost should be **recognised** within operating profit in the profit and loss account.

10.2 The following disclosures should be made in respect of a **defined contribution scheme**:

(a)   the nature of the scheme (i.e. defined contribution);
(b)   the cost for the period; and
(c)   any outstanding or prepaid contributions at the balance sheet date.

10.3 An employer participating in a **defined benefit scheme** should refer to Appendix II 'Accounting for retirement benefits: defined benefit schemes'.

11   Provisions, contingent liabilities and contingent assets

11.1 The requirements in paragraphs 11.2–11.7 do not apply to **retirement benefits, deferred tax** and leases, which are covered by more specific requirements of the FRSSE.

Provisions

11.2 A **provision** should be **recognised** when, and only when, it is probable (i.e. more likely than not) that a present **obligation** exists, as a result of a past event, and that it will require a transfer of economic benefits in settlement that can be estimated reliably. The amount **recognised** as a

Appendix 5

provision should be the best estimate of the expenditure required to settle the **obligation** at the balance sheet date. Where the effect of the time value of money is material, the amount of a **provision** should be the present value of the expenditures expected to be required to settle the **obligation**. Where discounting is used, the unwinding of the discount should be shown as other finance costs adjacent to interest.[16]

11.3 Where some or all of the expenditure required to settle a **provision** may be reimbursed by another party (e.g. through an insurance claim), the reimbursement should be **recognised**, as a separate **asset**, only when it is virtually certain to be received if the entity settles the **obligation**. In the profit and loss account, the expense relating to the **provision** may be presented net of the recovery. Gains from the expected disposal of **assets** should be excluded from the measurement of a **provision**.

11.4 **Provisions** should be reviewed at each balance sheet date and adjusted to reflect the current best estimate.

11.5 A **provision** should be used only for expenditures for which the **provision** was originally **recognised**.

Contingent liabilities and contingent assets

11.6 Contingent liabilities and contingent assets should not be **recognised**.

11.7 The following should be disclosed for **contingent liabilities**, except where their existence is remote, and for probable **contingent assets**:

(a) a brief description of the nature of the contingent item; and
(b) where practicable, an estimate of its financial effect.

12 Capital instruments

12.1 **Capital instruments** other than shares should be classified as **liabilities** if they contain an **obligation** to transfer economic benefits (including a contingent obligation to transfer economic benefits). Shares and other **capital instruments** that do not contain an **obligation** to transfer economic benefits should be reported within shareholders' funds.

---

[16] *There are a number of acceptable methods of discounting, and the appropriate discount rate depends on the method adopted. However, if cash flows are expressed in future prices and have been adjusted for risk, it will be appropriate to discount them at a risk-free rate such as a market rate on relevant government bonds. An illustrative example of a provision calculated using discounting is given in Appendix III.*

Financial Reporting Standard for Smaller Entities

12.2 The **finance costs** of **borrowings** should be allocated to periods over the **term** of the **borrowings** at a constant rate on the carrying amount. All **finance costs** should be charged in the profit and loss account.

12.3 **Borrowings** should be initially stated in the balance sheet at the **fair value** of consideration received. The carrying amount of **borrowings** should be increased by the **finance cost** in respect of the reporting period and reduced by payments made in respect of the **borrowings** in that period.

12.4 Where an **arrangement fee** is such as to represent a significant additional cost of finance when compared with the interest payable over the life of the instrument, the treatment set out in paragraph 12.2 should be followed. Where this is not the case it should be charged in the profit and loss account immediately it is incurred.

12.5 Where the entitlement to dividends in respect of shares is calculated by reference to time, the dividends should be accounted for on an accruals basis except in those circumstances (for example, where profits are insufficient to justify a dividend and dividend rights are non-cumulative) where ultimate payment is remote. The amounts accrued in excess of dividends paid or payable should be shown separately in shareholders' funds. All dividends should be reported as appropriations of profit in the profit and loss account.

13 Foreign currency translation

Transactions in foreign currencies

13.1 Subject to the provisions of paragraphs 13.3 and 13.5 each **asset, liability**, revenue or cost arising from a transaction denominated in a foreign currency should be translated into the **local currency** at the **exchange rate** in operation on the date on which the transaction occurred; if the rates do not fluctuate significantly, an average rate for a period may be used as an approximation. Where the transaction is to be settled at a contracted rate, that rate should be used. Where a trading transaction is covered by a related or matching **forward contract**, the rate of exchange specified in that contract may be used.

13.2 Subject to the special provisions of paragraph 13.5, which relate to the treatment of foreign equity investments financed by foreign currency **borrowings**, no subsequent **translations** should normally be made once non-monetary **assets** have been translated and recorded.

13.3 At each balance sheet date, monetary **assets** and **liabilities** denominated in a foreign currency should be translated by using the

Appendix 5

closing rate or, where appropriate, the rates of exchange fixed under the terms of the relevant transactions. Where there are related or matching forward contracts in respect of trading transactions, the rates of exchange specified in those contracts may be used.

13.4 All exchange gains or losses on settled transactions and unsettled monetary items should be reported as part of the profit or loss for the period from ordinary activities.

13.5 Where a company has used foreign currency borrowings to finance, or to provide a hedge against, its foreign equity investments and the conditions set out in this paragraph apply, the equity investments may be denominated in the appropriate foreign currencies and the carrying amounts translated at the end of each accounting period at closing rates for inclusion in the investing company's financial statements. Where investments are treated in this way, any exchange differences arising should be taken to reserves and the exchange gains or losses on the foreign currency borrowings should then be offset, as a reserve movement, against these exchange differences. The conditions that must apply are as follows:

(a) in any accounting period, exchange gains or losses arising on the borrowings may be offset only to the extent of exchange differences arising on the equity investments;
(b) the foreign currency borrowings, whose exchange gains or losses are used in the offset process, should not exceed, in the aggregate, the total amount of cash that the investments are expected to be able to generate, whether from profits or otherwise; and
(c) the accounting treatment adopted should be applied consistently from period to period.

Incorporating accounts of foreign entities

13.6 When preparing accounts for a company and its foreign entities (which includes the incorporation of the results of associated companies or foreign branches into those of an investing company) the closing rate/net investment method of translating the local currency financial statements should normally be used.

13.7 Exchange differences arising from the retranslation of the opening net investment in a foreign entity at the closing rate should be recorded as a movement on reserves.

13.8 The profit and loss account of a foreign entity accounted for under the closing rate/net investment method should be translated at the closing rate or at an average rate for the period. Where an average rate is used, the difference between the profit and loss account translated at an average rate and at the **closing rate** should be recorded as a movement on reserves. The average rate used should be calculated by the method considered most appropriate for the circumstances of the **foreign entity**.

13.9 In those circumstances where the trade of the **foreign entity** is more dependent on the economic environment of the investing company's currency than that of its own reporting currency, the transactions of the foreign operation should be reported as though all of its transactions had been entered into by the investing company itself in its own currency, as stated in paragraph 13.1–13.4.

13.10 The method used for translating the financial statements of each **foreign entity** should be applied consistently from period to period unless its financial and other operational relationships with the investing company change.

13.11 Where foreign currency **borrowings** have been used to finance, or provide a hedge against, group equity investments in **foreign entities**, exchange gains or losses on the **borrowings**, which would otherwise have been taken to the profit and loss account, may be offset as reserve movements against exchange differences arising on the retranslation of the **net investments** provided that:

(a) the relationships between the investing company and the **foreign entities** concerned justify the use of the **closing rate** method for consolidation purposes;
(b) in any accounting period, the exchange gains and losses arising on foreign currency **borrowings** are offset only to the extent of the exchange differences arising on the **net investments** in **foreign entities**;
(c) the foreign currency **borrowings**, whose exchange gains or losses are used in the offset process, should not exceed, in the aggregate, the total amount of cash that the **net investments** are expected to be able to generate, whether from profits or otherwise; and
(d) the accounting treatment is applied consistently from period to period.

Where the provisions of paragraph 13.5 have been applied in the investing company's financial statements to a foreign equity investment that is neither a subsidiary nor an associated company, the same offset procedure may be applied in the **consolidated financial statements**.

14 Post balance sheet events

14.1 Financial statements should be prepared on the basis of conditions existing at the balance sheet date.

Appendix 5

14.2 A material **post balance sheet event** requires changes in the amounts to be included in financial statements where:

(a) it is an **adjusting event**; or
(b) it indicates that application of the going concern concept to the whole or a material part of the entity is not appropriate.

14.3 A material **post balance sheet event** should be disclosed where:

(a) it is a **non-adjusting event** of such materiality that its non-disclosure would affect the ability of the users of financial statements to reach a proper understanding of the financial position; or
(b) it is the reversal or maturity after the year-end of a transaction entered into before the year-end, the substance of which was primarily to alter the appearance of the entity's balance sheet.

14.4 In respect of each **post balance sheet event** that is required to be disclosed, the following information should be stated by way of notes in the financial statements:

(a) the nature of the event; and
(b) an estimate of the financial effect, or a statement that it is not practicable to make such an estimate.

14.5 The estimate of the financial effect should be disclosed before taking account of taxation, and the taxation implications should be explained where necessary for a proper understanding of the financial position.

14.6 The date on which the financial statements are approved by the board of **directors** should be disclosed in the financial statements.

15 Related party disclosures

15.1 Where the reporting entity:

(a) purchases, sells or transfers goods and other **assets** or **liabilities**; or
(b) renders or receives services; or
(c) provides or receives finance or financial support;

(irrespective of whether a price is charged) to, from or on behalf of a **related party**, then such material[17] transactions should be disclosed, including:

    (i) the names of the transacting **related parties**;

---

[17] *The materiality of a related party transaction should be judged in terms of its significance to the reporting entity.*

Financial Reporting Standard for Smaller Entities

   (ii) a description of the relationship between the parties;
   (iii) a description of the transactions;
   (iv) the amounts involved;
   (v) any other elements of the transactions necessary for an understanding of the financial statements;
   (vi) the amounts due to or from **related parties** at the balance sheet date and **provisions** for doubtful debts due from such parties at that date; and
   (vii) amounts written off in the period in respect of debts due to or from **related parties**.

15.2 Personal guarantees given by **directors** in respect of **borrowings** by the reporting entity should be disclosed in the notes to the financial statements.

15.3 Transactions with **related parties** may be disclosed on an aggregated basis (aggregation of similar transactions by type of **related party**) unless disclosure of an individual transaction, or connected transactions, is necessary for an understanding of the impact of the transactions on the financial statements of the reporting entity or is required by law.

15.4 Disclosure, as a **related party** transaction, is not required of:
(a) pension contributions paid to a pension fund;
(b) emoluments in respect of services as an employee of the reporting entity; or
(c) transactions with the parties listed below simply as a result of their role as:
   (i) providers of finance in the course of their business in that regard;
   (ii) utility companies;
   (iii) **government** departments and their sponsored bodies; or
   (iv) a customer, supplier, franchiser, distributor or general agent.

15.5 When the reporting entity is controlled by another party, there should be disclosure of the **related party** relationship and the name of that party and, if different, that of the ultimate controlling party. If the controlling party or ultimate controlling party of the reporting entity is not known, that fact should be disclosed. This information should be disclosed irrespective of whether any transactions have taken place between the controlling parties and the reporting entity.

16 Consolidated financial statements

16.1 Where the reporting entity is preparing **consolidated financial statements**, it should regard as standard the accounting practices and

Appendix 5

disclosure requirements set out in FRSs 2, 6, 7 and, as they apply in respect of **consolidated financial statements**, FRSs 5, 9 10[18] and 11[18]. Where the reporting entity is part of a group that prepares publicly available **consolidated financial statements**, it is entitled to the exemptions given in FRS 8 paragraph 3(a)–(c).

17 Date from which effective and transitional arrangements

17.1 The accounting practices set out in this Financial Reporting Standard for Smaller Entities (effective June 2002) should be regarded as standard in respect of financial statements relating to accounting periods ending on or after 22 June 2002. Earlier adoption is encouraged.

Transitional arrangements – goodwill

17.2 All **goodwill** that was eliminated against reserves in accordance with an accounting policy permitted until 23 March 1999 may remain eliminated against reserves thereafter.[19] Alternatively, in its first accounting period beginning on or after 23 March 1999, an entity may reinstate by **prior period adjustment** all **goodwill** previously eliminated against reserves.

Transitional arrangements – tangible fixed assets

17.3 Where, for its first accounting period ending on or after 23 March 2000, an entity does not adopt an **accounting policy** of revaluation, but the carrying amount of its **tangible fixed assets** reflects previous revaluations, it may:

(a) retain the book amounts. In these circumstances the entity should disclose the fact that the transitional provisions of the FRSSE are being followed and that the valuation has not been updated and give the date of the last revaluation; or
(b) restate the carrying amount of the **tangible fixed assets** to historical cost (less restated accumulated **depreciation**), as a change in **accounting policy**.

17.4 Where, for its first accounting period ending on or after 23 March 2000, an entity separates **tangible fixed assets** into different components with significantly different **useful economic lives** for **depreciation** purposes, the changes should be dealt with as a **prior period adjustment**, as a change

---

[18] FRS 10 and, as directed by FRS 10, FRS 11 need be applied only in respect of purchased goodwill arising on consolidation.

[19] The treatment of such amounts on disposal of a business is set out in paragraph 3.4.

Financial Reporting Standard for Smaller Entities

in **accounting policy**. Other revisions to the **useful economic lives** and **residual values** of **tangible fixed assets** are not the result of a change in **accounting policy** and should be treated in accordance with paragraph 5.28 and not as **prior period adjustments**.

18 Withdrawal of the FRSSE (effective March 2000)

18.1 The FRSSE (effective June 2002) supersedes the FRSSE (effective March 2000).

Appendix 5

C – Definitions

The following definitions shall apply in the FRSSE and in particular in the Statement of Standard Accounting Practice set out in sections 1–18 of Part B.

Accounting policies:

Those principles, bases, conventions, rules and practices applied by an entity that specify how the effects of transactions and other events are to be reflected in its financial statements through

(i) **recognising,**
(ii) selecting measurement bases for, and
(iii) presenting

assets, liabilities, gains, losses and changes to shareholders' funds. Accounting policies do not include **estimation techniques.**

> Accounting policies define the process whereby transactions and other events are reflected in financial statements. For example, an accounting policy for a particular type of expenditure may specify whether an asset or a loss is to be recognised; the basis on which it is to be measured; and where in the profit and loss account or balance sheet it is to be presented.

Actuarial gains and losses:

Changes in actuarial deficits or surpluses that arise because events have not coincided with the actuarial assumptions made for the last valuation or because the actuarial assumptions have changed.

Adjusting events:

Adjusting events are **post balance sheet events** that provide additional evidence of conditions existing at the balance sheet date. They include events that because of statutory or conventional requirements are reflected in financial statements.

Applied research:

Original or critical investigation undertaken in order to gain new scientific or technical knowledge and directed towards a specific practical aim or objective.

Financial Reporting Standard for Smaller Entities

Arrangement fees:

The costs that are incurred directly in connection with the issue of a **capital instrument,** i.e. those costs that would not have been incurred if the specific instrument in question had not been issued.

Assets:

Rights or other access to future economic benefits controlled by an entity as a result of past transactions or events.

Attributable profit (on long-term contracts):

That part of the total profit currently estimated to arise over the duration of the contract, after allowing for estimated remedial and maintenance costs and increases in costs so far as not recoverable under the terms of the contract, that fairly reflects the profit attributable to that part of the work performed at the accounting date. (There can be no attributable profit until the profitable outcome of the contract can be assessed with reasonable certainty.)

Average remaining service life:

A weighted average of the expected future service of the current members of the **pension scheme** up to their normal retirement dates or expected dates of earlier withdrawal or death in service.

Borrowings:

Capital instruments that are classified as **liabilities.**

Capital instruments:

All instruments that are issued (or arrangements entered into) by reporting entities as a means of raising finance, including shares, debentures, loans and debt instruments, options and warrants that give the holder the right to subscribe for or obtain capital instruments. In the case of **consolidated financial statements** the term includes capital instruments issued by subsidiaries except those that are held by another member of the group that is included in the consolidation.

Close family:

Close members of the family of an individual are those family members, or members of the same household, who may be expected to influence, or be

Appendix 5

influenced by, that person in their dealings with the reporting entity.

Closing rate:

The closing rate is the **exchange rate** for spot transactions ruling at the balance sheet date and is the mean of the buying and selling rates at the close of business on the day for which the rate is to be ascertained.

Companies legislation:

(a) in Great Britain, the Companies Act 1985;
(b) in Northern Ireland, the Companies (Northern Ireland) Order 1986; and
(c) in the Republic of Ireland, the Companies Acts 1963–1990 and the European Communities (Companies: Group Accounts) Regulations 1992.

Consignment stock:

Consignment stock is stock held by one party (the 'dealer') but legally owned by another (the 'manufacturer'), on terms that give the dealer the right to sell the stock in the normal course of its business or, at its option, to return it unsold to the legal owner.

Consolidated financial statements:

The financial statements of a group prepared by consolidation. A group is a parent undertaking and its subsidiary undertakings. Consolidation is the process of adjusting and combining financial information from the individual financial statements of a parent undertaking and its subsidiary undertakings to prepare consolidated financial statements that present financial information for the group as a single economic entity.

Contingent asset:

A possible **asset** that arises from past events and whose existence will be confirmed only by the occurrence of one or more uncertain future events not wholly within the entity's control.

Contingent liability:

(a) a possible **obligation** that arises from past events and whose existence will be confirmed only by the occurrence of one or more uncertain future events not wholly within the entity's control; or
(b) an **obligation** at the balance sheet date that arises from past events but

is not **recognised** as a **provision** because:
(i) it is not probable that a transfer of economic benefits will be required to settle the **obligation**; or
(ii) the amount of the **obligation** cannot be measured with sufficient reliability.

Cost (of stock):

Cost is defined as being that expenditure which has been incurred in the normal course of business in bringing the product or service to its present location and condition. This expenditure should include, in addition to cost of purchase, such costs of conversion (including, for example, attributable overheads) as are appropriate to that location and condition.

Current funding level (of a pension scheme):

A current funding level valuation considers whether the **assets** would have been sufficient at the valuation date to cover **liabilities** arising in respect of pensions in payment, preserved benefits for members whose pensionable service has ceased and accrued benefits for members in pensionable service, based on pensionable service to and pensionable earnings at, the date of valuation including revaluation on the statutory basis or such higher basis as has been promised.

Current service cost:

The increase in the present value of the **scheme liabilities** expected to arise from employee service in the current period.

Current tax:

The amount of tax estimated to be payable or recoverable in respect of the taxable profit or loss for a period, along with adjustments to estimates in respect of previous periods.

Curtailment:

An event that reduces the expected years of future service of present employees or reduces for a number of employees the accrual of defined benefits for some or all of their future service.

Deferred tax:

Estimated future tax consequences of transactions and events **recognised** in the financial statements of the current and previous periods.

Appendix 5

Defined benefit scheme:

A pension or other **retirement benefit** scheme other than a **defined contribution scheme**. Normally, the scheme rules define the benefits independently of the contributions payable, and the benefits are not directly related to the investments of the scheme.

Defined contribution scheme:

A pension or other **retirement benefit** scheme into which an employer pays regular contributions fixed as an amount or as a percentage of pay. The employer will have no legal or constructive **obligation** to pay further contributions if the scheme does not have sufficient **assets** to pay all employee benefits relating to employee service in the current and prior periods.

Depreciation:

The measure of the cost or revalued amount of the economic benefits of a fixed **asset** that have been consumed during the period. Consumption includes the wearing out, using up or other reduction in the **useful economic life** of a fixed **asset** whether arising from use, effluxion of time or obsolescence through either changes in technology or demand for the goods and services produced by the **asset**.

Development:

Use of scientific or technical knowledge in order to produce new or substantially improved materials, devices, products or services, to install new processes or systems before the commencement of commercial production or commercial applications, or to improve substantially those already produced or installed.

Directors:

The directors of a company or other body, the partners, proprietors, committee of management or trustees of other forms of entity, or equivalent persons responsible for directing the entity's affairs and preparing its financial statements.

Estimation techniques:

The methods adopted by an entity to arrive at estimated monetary amounts, corresponding to the measurement bases selected, for **assets**, **liabilities**, gains, losses and changes to shareholders' funds.

Financial Reporting Standard for Smaller Entities

Estimation techniques implement the measurement aspects of **accounting policies**. An **accounting policy** will specify the basis on which an item is to be measured; where there is uncertainty over the monetary amount corresponding to that basis, the amount will be arrived at by using an estimation technique.

Estimation techniques include, for example:

(a) methods of **depreciation**, such as straight-line and reducing balance, applied in the context of a particular measurement basis, used to estimate the proportion of the economic benefits of a **tangible fixed asset** consumed in a period;

(b) different methods used to estimate the proportion of trade debts that will not be recovered, particularly where such methods consider a population as a whole rather than individual balances.

Ex gratia *pension*:

A pension that the employer has no legal, contractual or implied commitment to provide.

Exceptional items:

Material items that derive from events or transactions that fall within the **ordinary activities** of the reporting entity and individually or, if of a similar type, in aggregate need to be disclosed by virtue of their size or incidence if the financial statements are to give a true and fair view.

Exchange rate:

An exchange rate is a rate at which two currencies may be exchanged for each other at a particular point in time; different rates apply for spot and forward transactions.

Extraordinary items:

Material items possessing a high degree of abnormality that arise from events or transactions that fall outside the **ordinary activities** of the reporting entity and are not expected to recur. They do not include **exceptional items** nor do they include prior period items merely because they relate to a prior period.

Fair value:

Fair value is the amount at which an **asset** or **liability** could be exchanged in

249

Appendix 5

an arm's length transaction between informed and willing parties, other than in a forced or liquidation sale, less, where applicable, any grants receivable towards the purchase or use of an **asset**.

Finance charge (on a lease):

The finance charge is the amount borne by the lessee over the **lease term**, representing the difference between the total of the **minimum lease payments** (including any residual amounts guaranteed by the lessee) and the amount at which the lessee records the leased **asset** at the **inception** of the lease.

Finance costs (of a capital instrument):

The difference between the net proceeds of a **capital instrument** and the total amount of the payments (or other transfer of economic benefits) that the issuer may be required to make in respect of the instrument other than **arrangement fees**.

Finance lease:

A finance lease is a lease that transfers substantially all the risks and rewards of ownership of an **asset** to the lessee. It should be presumed that such a transfer of risks and rewards occurs if at the **inception** of a lease the present value of the **minimum lease payments**, including any initial payment, amounts to substantially all (normally 90 per cent or more) of the **fair value** of the leased **asset**. The present value should be calculated by using the interest rate implicit in the lease. If the **fair value** of the **asset** is not determinable an estimate thereof should be used.

Foreign entity:

A foreign entity is a subsidiary, associated company or branch whose operations are based in a country other than that of the investing company or whose **assets** and **liabilities** are denominated mainly in a foreign currency.

Foreseeable losses (on a long-term contract):

Losses that are currently estimated to arise over the duration of the contract (after allowing for estimated remedial and maintenance costs and increases in costs so far as not recoverable under the terms of the contract). This estimate is required irrespective of:

(a) whether work has yet commenced on such contracts;

Financial Reporting Standard for Smaller Entities

(b) the proportion of work carried out at the accounting date; or
(c) the amount of profits expected to arise on other contracts.

Forward contract:

A forward contract is an agreement to exchange different currencies at a specified future date and at a specified rate. The difference between the specified rate and the spot rate ruling on the date the contract was entered into is the discount or premium on the forward contract.

Funded scheme:

A **pension scheme** where the future **liabilities** for benefits are provided for by the accumulation of **assets** held externally to the employing entity's business.

Goodwill:

Goodwill is the difference between the value of a business as a whole and the aggregate of the **fair values** of its **identifiable assets and liabilities.**

Government:

Government includes government and inter-governmental agencies and similar bodies whether local, national or international.

Government grants:

Government grants are assistance by **government** in the form of cash or transfers of **assets** to an entity in return for past or future compliance with certain conditions relating to the operating activities of the entity.

Gross earnings (from a lease):

Gross earnings comprise the lessor's gross finance income over the **lease term,** representing the difference between its gross investment in the lease and the cost of the leased **asset** less any grants receivable towards the purchase or use of the **asset.**

Hire purchase contract:

A hire purchase contract is a contract for the hire of an **asset** that contains a **provision** giving the hirer an option to acquire legal title to the **asset** upon the fulfilment of certain conditions stated in the contract.

Appendix 5

Identifiable assets and liabilities:

Identifiable assets and liabilities are the **assets** and **liabilities** of an entity that are capable of being disposed of or settled separately, without disposing of a business of the entity.

Inception (of a lease):

The inception of a lease is the earlier of the time the **asset** is brought into use and the date from which rentals first accrue.

Intangible assets:

Intangible assets are non-financial fixed **assets** that do not have physical substance but are **identifiable** and are controlled by the entity through custody or legal rights.

Interest cost:

The expected increase during the period in the present value of the **scheme liabilities** because the benefits are one period closer to **settlement**.

Investment property:

An investment property is an interest in land and/or buildings:

(a) in respect of which construction work and development have been completed; and
(b) which is held for its investment potential, any rental income being negotiated at arm's length,

but excluding:

(c) a property that is owned and occupied by a company for its own purposes; and
(d) a property let to and occupied by another group company.

Lease term:

The lease term is the period for which the lessee has contracted to lease the **asset** and any further terms for which the lessee has the option to continue to lease the **asset** with or without further payment, which option it is reasonably certain at the **inception** of the lease that the lessee will exercise.

Financial Reporting Standard for Smaller Entities

Liabilities:

An entity's **obligations** to transfer economic benefits as a result of past transactions or events.

Local currency:

An entity's local currency is the currency of the primary economic environment in which it operates and generates net cash flows.

Long-term contract:

A contract entered into for the design, manufacture or construction of a single substantial **asset** or the provision of a service (or of a combination of **assets** or services that together constitute a single project) where the time taken substantially to complete the contract is such that the contract activity falls into different accounting periods. A contract that is required to be accounted for as long-term by the FRSSE will usually extend for a period exceeding one year. However, a duration exceeding one year is not an essential feature of a long-term contract. Some contracts with a shorter duration than one year should be accounted for as long-term contracts if they are sufficiently material to the activity of the period that not to record turnover and **attributable profit** would lead to distortion of the period's turnover and results such that the financial statements would not give a true and fair view, provided that the policy is applied consistently within the reporting entity and from year to year.

Minimum lease payments:

The minimum lease payments are the minimum payments over the remaining part of the **lease term** (excluding charges for services and taxes to be paid by the lessor) and:

(a) in the case of the lessee any residual amounts guaranteed by it or by a party related to it; or
(b) in the case of the lessor any residual amounts guaranteed by the lessee or by an independent third party.

Monetary items:

Monetary items are money held and amounts to be received or paid in money and should be categorised as either short-term or long-term. Short-term monetary items are those that fall due within one year of the balance sheet date.

Appendix 5

Net investment (in a foreign entity):

The net investment that a company has in a **foreign entity** is its effective equity stake and comprises its proportion of such **foreign entity's** net **assets**; in appropriate circumstances, intragroup loans and other deferred balances may be regarded as part of the effective equity stake.

Net investment (in a lease):

The net investment in a lease at a point in time comprises:

(a) the gross investment in a lease (i.e. the total of the **minimum lease payments** and that portion of the **residual value** of the **leased asset**, the realisation of which by the lessor is not assured or is guaranteed solely by a party related to the lessor); less
(b) **gross earnings** allocated to future periods.

Net realisable value (of fixed assets):

Net realisable value of a fixed **asset** is the amount at which the **asset** could be disposed of, less any direct selling costs.

Net realisable value (of stocks and long-term contracts):

The actual or estimated selling price (net of trade but before settlement discounts) less:

(a) all further costs to completion; and
(b) all costs to be incurred in marketing, selling and distributing.

Non-adjusting events:

Non-adjusting events are **post balance sheet events** that concern conditions that did not exist at the balance sheet date.

Obligation:

An obligation may be either a legal obligation (derived, for example, from a contract or legislation) or a constructive obligation, where the entity has indicated to other parties that it will accept certain responsibilities and has created valid expectations in those other parties that it will discharge those responsibilities.

Operating lease:

An operating lease is a lease other than a **finance lease**.

Financial Reporting Standard for Smaller Entities

Ordinary activities:

Any activities that are undertaken by a reporting entity as part of its business and such related activities in which the reporting entity engages in furtherance of, incidental to, or arising from, these activities. Ordinary activities include the effects on the reporting entity of any event in the various environments in which it operates, including the political, regulatory, economic and geographical environments, irrespective of the frequency or unusual nature of the events.

Past service cost:

The increase in the present value of the **scheme liabilities** related to employee service in prior periods arising in the current period as a result of the introduction of, or improvement to, **retirement benefits**.

Pension schemes:

A pension scheme is an arrangement (other than accident insurance) to provide pension and/or other benefits for members on leaving service or retiring and, after a member's death, for his/her dependants.

Permanent differences:

Differences between an entity's taxable profits and its results as stated in the financial statements that arise because certain types of income and expenditure are non-taxable or disallowable, or because certain tax charges or allowances have no corresponding amount in the financial statements.

Post balance sheet events:

Post balance sheet events are those events, both favourable and unfavourable, that occur between the balance sheet date and the date on which the financial statements are approved by the board of **directors**.

Prior period adjustments:

Material adjustments applicable to prior periods arising from changes in **accounting policies** or from the correction of fundamental errors. They do not include normal recurring adjustments or corrections of accounting estimates made in prior periods.

Projected unit method:

An accrued benefits valuation method in which the **scheme liabilities** make

Appendix 5

allowance for projected earnings. An accrued benefits valuation method is a valuation method in which the **scheme liabilities** at the valuation date relate to:

(a) the benefits for pensioners and deferred pensioners (i.e. individuals who have ceased to be active members but are entitled to benefits payable at a later date) and their dependants, allowing where appropriate for future increases; and
(b) the accrued benefits for members in service on the valuation date.

The accrued benefits are the benefits for service up to a given point in time, whether vested rights or not. Guidance on the projected unit method is given in the Guidance Note GN26 issued by the Faculty and Institute of Actuaries.

Provision:

A **liability** of uncertain timing or amount.

Purchased goodwill:

Purchased goodwill is **goodwill** that is established as a result of the purchase of a business accounted for as an acquisition. It represents the difference between the cost of the acquired business and the aggregate of the **fair values** recorded for the **identifiable assets and liabilities** acquired. Positive **goodwill** arises when the acquisition cost exceeds the aggregate **fair values** of the **identifiable assets and liabilities**. Negative **goodwill** arises when the aggregate **fair values** of the **identifiable assets and liabilities** of the entity exceed the acquisition cost.

Pure (or basic) research:

Experimental or theoretical work undertaken primarily to acquire new scientific or technological knowledge for its own sake rather than directed towards any specific aim or application.

Recognised:

Recognition is the process of incorporating an item into the primary financial statements under the appropriate heading. It involves depiction of the item in words and by a monetary amount and inclusion of that amount in the statement totals.

Financial Reporting Standard for Smaller Entities

Recoverable amount:

Recoverable amount of an **asset** is the higher of the amounts that can be obtained from selling the **asset** (i.e. **net realisable value**) or continuing to use the **asset** in the business (i.e. value in use). Value in use is calculated as the present value of the future cash flows[20] obtainable as a result of the **asset's** continued use (including those resulting from its ultimate disposal), or a reasonable estimate thereof.

Regular (pension) cost:

The consistent ongoing cost **recognised** under the actuarial method used.

Related parties:

Two or more parties are related parties when at any time during the financial period:

(a) one party has direct or indirect control of the other party; or
(b) the parties are subject to common control from the same source; or
(c) one party has significant influence over the financial and operating policies of the other party. Significant influence would occur if that other party is inhibited from pursuing its own separate interests.

For the avoidance of doubt, related parties of the reporting entity include the following:

(i) parent undertakings, subsidiary and fellow subsidiary undertakings;
(ii) associates and joint ventures;
(iii) investors with significant influence and their **close families**; and
(iv) **directors** of the reporting entity and of its parent undertakings and their **close families**.

Research and development expenditure:

Research and development expenditure means expenditure falling into one or more of the broad categories of **pure (or basic) research, applied research** and **development** (except to the extent that it relates to locating or exploiting oil, gas or mineral deposits or is reimbursable by third parties either directly or under the terms of a firm contract to develop and manufacture at an agreed price calculated to reimburse both elements of expenditure).

---

[20] *This calculation may not be relevant for fixed assets held by charities and other not-for-profit entities, where they are not held for the purpose of generating cash flows.*

Appendix 5

Residual value:

Residual value is the realisable value of the **asset** at the end of its **useful economic life**, based on prices prevailing at the date of acquisition or revaluation, where this has taken place. Realisation costs should be deducted in arriving at the residual value.

Retirement benefits:

All forms of consideration given by an employer in exchange for services rendered by employees that are payable after the completion of employment. Retirement benefits do not include termination benefits payable as a result of either (i) an employer's decision to terminate an employee's employment before the normal retirement date or (ii) an employee's decision to accept voluntary redundancy in exchange for those benefits, because these are not given in exchange for services rendered by employees.

Scheme liabilities:

The **liabilities** of a **defined benefit scheme** for outgoings due after the valuation date. Scheme liabilities measured using the **projected unit method** reflect the benefits that the employer is committed to provide for service up to the valuation date.

Settlement:

An irrevocable action that relieves the employer (or the **defined benefit scheme**) of the primary responsibility for a pension **obligation** and eliminates significant risks relating to the **obligation** and the **assets** used to effect the settlement.

Start-up costs:

Costs arising from those one-time activities related to opening a new facility, introducing a new product or service, conducting business in a new territory, conducting business with a new class of customer, initiating a new process in an existing facility, starting some new operation and similar items. They include costs of relocating or reorganising part or all of an entity, costs related to organising a new entity, and expenses and losses incurred both before and after opening.

Tangible fixed assets:

Assets that have physical substance and are held for use in the production or supply of goods or services, for rental to others, or for administrative purposes on a continuing basis in the reporting entity's activities.

Tax credit:

The tax credit given under UK legislation to the recipient of a dividend from a UK company.

Term (of a capital instrument):

The period from the date of issue of the **capital instrument** to the date at which it will expire, be redeemed, or be cancelled. If either party has the option to require the instrument to be redeemed or cancelled and, under the terms of the instrument, it is uncertain whether such an option will be exercised, the term should be taken to end on the earliest date at which the instrument would be redeemed or cancelled on exercise of such an option. If either party has the right to extend the period of an instrument, the term should not include the period of the extension if there is a genuine commercial possibility that the period will not be extended.

Timing differences:

Differences between taxable profits and the results as stated in the financial statements that arise from the inclusion of gains and losses in tax assessments in periods different from those in which they are **recognised** in financial statements. For example, a timing difference would arise when tax allowances for the cost of a fixed **asset** are accelerated or decelerated, i.e. received before or after the **depreciation** of the fixed **asset** is **recognised** in the profit and loss account.

Total recognised gains and losses:

The total of all gains and losses of the reporting entity that are **recognised** in a period and are attributable to the shareholders.

Translation:

Translation is the process whereby financial data denominated in one currency are expressed in terms of another currency. It includes both the expression of individual transactions in terms of another currency and the expression of a complete set of financial statements prepared in one currency in terms of another currency.

Useful economic life:

The useful economic life of an **asset** is the period over which the present owner will derive economic benefits from its use.

Appendix 5

Withholding tax:

Tax on dividends or other income that is deducted by the payer of the income and paid to the tax authorities wholly on behalf of the recipient.

D – Voluntary disclosures

The disclosures below are not mandatory and do not form part of the Statement of Standard Accounting Practice. The Board, however, encourages reporting entities voluntarily to include the following disclosures in their financial statements.

Cash flow information[21]

1   Reporting entities are encouraged, but not required, to provide a cash flow statement using the indirect method as explained below.[22]

2   The indirect method starts with operating profit (which is normally profit before income from shares in group undertakings) and adjusts it for non-cash charges and credits to reconcile it with cash generated from operations. Other sources and applications of cash are shown to arrive at total cash generated (or utilised) in the period.

3   Cash is taken as 'cash at bank and in hand' less overdrafts repayable on demand, which should be reconciled to the balance sheet.

4   Cash flows are shown net of any attributable value added tax or other sales tax unless the tax is irrecoverable by the reporting entity.

5   It is recommended that material transactions not resulting in movements of cash of the reporting entity are disclosed by way of note, if disclosure is necessary for an understanding of the underlying transactions.

Adoption of the FRSSE (Effective June 2002) by the Board

Financial Reporting Standard for Smaller Entities (effective June 2002) was approved for issue by the nine members of the Accounting Standards Board.

Mary Keegan	(Chairman)
Allan Cook CBE	(Technical Director)
David Allvey	
John Coombe	

---

[21] The Board's reasoning for including a voluntary recommendation for cash flow information is set out in Appendix IV.

[22] An illustrative example of a cash flow statement using the indirect method is given in Appendix III.

Appendix 5
Douglas Flint
Huw Jones
Roger Marshall
Isobel Sharp
Ken Wild

Financial Reporting Standard for Smaller Entities

Appendix I – Note on legal requirements

Great Britain

Companies Act 1985, sections 247–249

1   The definition of a small company is contained in sections 247 and 247A of the Companies Act 1985. The qualifying conditions are met by a company in a year in which it does not exceed two or more of the following criteria:

Turnover	£2,800,000
Balance sheet total	£1,400,000
Average number of employees	50

For any company, other than a newly incorporated company, to qualify as small, the qualifying conditions must be met for two consecutive years. A company will cease to qualify as small if it fails to meet the qualifying conditions for two consecutive years.

2   Certain companies are excluded by section 247A from the 'small company' criteria for reasons of public interest. These are any entity that is, or is in a group that includes:

(a)   a public company;
(b)   a banking or insurance company;
(c)   a body corporate that (not being a company) has the power to offer its shares or debentures to the public and may lawfully exercise that power;
(d)   an authorised institution under the Banking Act 1987;
(e)   an insurance company to which Part II of the Insurance Companies Act 1982 applies; or
(f)   an authorised person under the Financial Services Act 1986.

3   A parent company shall not be treated as qualifying as a small company in relation to a financial year unless the group headed by it qualifies as a small group.

4   The definition of a small group is contained in sections 248 and 249. The qualifying conditions are met by a group in a year in which it does not exceed two or more of the following criteria:

Aggregate turnover	£2,800,000 net (or £3,360,000 gross)
Aggregate balance sheet total	£1,400,000 net (or £1,680,000 gross)
Aggregate number of employees	50

Appendix 5

'Net' means after the set-offs and other adjustments required by Schedule 4A in the case of group accounts, and 'gross' means without those set-offs and adjustments. A company may satisfy the relevant requirements on the basis of either the net or the gross figure.

Companies Act 1985, Schedule 8, paragraphs 10–14

5   Schedule 8 sets out the accounting principles in the following terms:

> "10. The company shall be presumed to be carrying on business as a going concern.
> 11. Accounting policies shall be applied consistently within the same accounts and from one financial year to the next.
> 12. The amount of any item shall be determined on a prudent basis, and in particular:
>   (a) only profits realised at the balance sheet date shall be included in the profit and loss account; and
>   (b) all liabilities and losses which have arisen or are likely to arise in respect of the financial year to which the accounts relate or a previous financial year shall be taken into account, including those which only become apparent between the balance sheet date and the date on which it is signed on behalf of the board of directors in pursuance of section 233 of this Act.
> 13. All income and charges relating to the financial year to which the accounts relate shall be taken into account, without regard to the date of receipt or payment.
> 14. In determining the aggregate amount of any item the amount of each individual asset or liability that falls to be taken into account shall be determined separately."

Northern Ireland

6   The statutory requirements in Northern Ireland are very similar to those in Great Britain. The following table shows the references to the Companies (Northern Ireland) Order 1986 that correspond to the references in paragraphs 1–5 above.

GREAT BRITAIN	NORTHERN IRELAND
Sections 247–249	Articles 255–257
Schedule 8, paragraphs 10–14	Schedule 4, paragraphs 10–14

Republic of Ireland

7   The following table shows the references in companies legislation in the Republic of Ireland that correspond to the references in paragraphs 1–5 above.

Financial Reporting Standard for Smaller Entities

GREAT BRITAIN	REPUBLIC OF IRELAND
Sections 247 and 247A	Companies (Amendment) Act 1986, sections 2, 8 and 9
Sections 248 and 249	[23]
Schedule 8, paragraphs 10–14	Companies (Amendment) Act 1986, section 5

Status of the FRSSE

8 Legal advice has been obtained that in accounting standards smaller entities may properly be allowed exemptions or different treatment provided that such differences are justified on rational grounds. The Board will have regard to the criteria given in the 'Status of the FRSSE' section in determining whether such rational grounds exist.

9 The summary of advice regarding the status of the FRSSE given by Richard Sykes QC in December 1995 is reproduced below:

"I do not see any conflict with the law or likely weakening of the authority of ASB or FRRP[24] as respects the upholding of Standards provided that

(i) the treatment required by the FRSSE is the same as that required by existing Standards or is a simplified version of that treatment; or

(ii) in a case where a future Standard calls for a new treatment for Big GAAP[25] Companies only and which is also likely to be significant to small companies, ASB is able to justify on rational grounds any lack of a change in treatment for smaller entities when the FRSSE is in due course revised;

(iii) in a case where in the future the FRSSE requires a treatment which is materially different from then existing Standards on a significant matter ASB is able to justify on rational grounds such different treatment in the case of smaller entities.

(iv) it is recognised that the starting point for deciding how a smaller

---

[23] *Small groups are not defined in Republic of Ireland legislation. However, in the Republic of Ireland, for the purposes of the FRSSE, small groups should meet, on a consolidated basis, the conditions for a small company in section 8 of the Companies (Amendment) Act 1986. In addition, a parent company registered in the Republic of Ireland that qualifies as a small company is entitled to adopt the FRSSE only if the group headed by it is also small.*

[24] *Financial Reporting Review Panel*

[25] *Generally accepted accounting practice*

Appendix 5

entity will account for something not covered by the FRSSE will be existing practice and that the smaller entity must be able to justify its departure from such practice on rational grounds related to its size. Where the matter is covered by a Big GAAP Standard, that Standard would provide the obvious source in determining existing practice.

Rational grounds for justifying different treatments might include:
(i) the different nature of entities;
(ii) particularly if the different treatment is in the area of disclosure, the different users of their financial statements; and
(iii) established practices existing at the time of issue of a Standard or FRSSE revision."

True and fair view override – legal requirements

10   The relevant references in companies legislation to the true and fair override are given below.

Great Britain – Companies Act 1985: sections 226(5) and 227(6), and Schedule 8 paragraph 15.

Northern Ireland – Companies (Northern Ireland) Order 1986: articles 234(5) and 235(6), and Schedule 8 paragraph 15.

Republic of Ireland – Companies (Amendment) Act 1986: sections 3(1)(d)–(e) and 6.

Government grants – legal requirements in the Republic of Ireland

11   References below are to the Companies (Amendment) Act 1986 and the Schedule to that Act unless otherwise stated.

12   Note 8 to the balance sheet formats in the Schedule provides that government grants included in the item 'Accruals and deferred income' must be shown separately in a note to the accounts if not shown separately in the balance sheet. However, Note 8 does not impose an obligation to include government grants under 'Accruals and deferred income' and such grants may, therefore, be placed under a separate heading. This separate heading is often placed between liabilities and share capital/reserves. If a new heading is adopted (using section 4(12)), the requirement under Note 8 to have a separate mention of the amount is not applicable.

13   Paragraph 36(2) of the Schedule provides that

"The following information shall be given with respect to any other contingent liability not provided for:

(a) the amount or estimated amount of that liability,
(b) its legal nature, and
(c) whether any valuable security has been provided by the company in connection with that liability and, if so, what."

14 Section 40 of the Companies (Amendment) Act 1983 requires the convening of an extraordinary general meeting not later than 28 days from the earliest day on which it is known to a director of the company that its net assets have fallen to half or less of the company's called-up share capital (that a 'financial situation' exists). The Act also extends the reporting duties of auditors by requiring auditors to state whether in their opinion there existed at the balance sheet date a 'financial situation' in the context of section 40 that would require the convening of an extraordinary general meeting. For the purpose of calculating the net assets of the company, the term 'liability' should be taken to include not only creditors, but also provisions for liabilities and charges, accruals and deferred income. Government grants treated as deferred income should, therefore, be regarded as a liability for the purposes of calculating net assets under section 40.

Appendix 5

Appendix II – Accounting for Retirement Benefits: Defined Benefit Schemes

1   The following requirements should be regarded as standard in respect of financial statements relating to accounting periods ending *before* 22 June 2004 (unless the requirements in paragraph 2 below are adopted early):

(a) The accounting objective is that the employer should **recognise** the expected cost of providing pensions and other post-retirement benefits on a systematic and rational basis over the period during which it derives benefit from the employees' services.

(b) The pension cost should be calculated using actuarial valuation methods. The actuarial assumptions and method, taken as a whole, should be compatible and should lead to the actuary's best estimate of the cost of providing the pension benefits promised. The method of providing for expected pension costs over the service lives of employees in the scheme should be such that the **regular pension cost** is a substantially level percentage of the current and expected future pensionable payroll in the light of the current actuarial assumptions.

(c) Variations from **regular cost** should be allocated over the expected remaining service lives of current employees in the scheme. A period representing the **average remaining service lives** may be used if desired.

(d) Where *ex gratia* pensions are granted the capital cost, to the extent not covered by a surplus, should be **recognised** in the profit and loss account in the accounting period in which they are granted.

(e) Where allowance for discretionary or *ex gratia* increases in pensions is not made in the actuarial assumptions, the capital cost of such increases should, to the extent not covered by a surplus, be **recognised** in the profit and loss account in the accounting period in which they are initially granted.

(f) If the cumulative pension cost recognised in the profit and loss account has not been completely discharged by payment of contributions or directly paid pensions, the excess should be shown as a net pension **provision**. Similarly, any excess of contributions paid or directly paid pensions over the cumulative pension cost should be shown as a prepayment.

(g) A subsidiary company that is a member of a group scheme should disclose this fact in its financial statements and disclose the nature of the group scheme indicating, where appropriate, that the contributions are based on pension costs across the group as a whole. Such a company is exempt from disclosure requirements (vi) and (vii) in paragraph (h), below, and should instead state the name of the holding company in whose financial statements particulars of the actuarial valuation of the group scheme are contained. This exemption applies only if the holding company is registered in the UK or the Republic of Ireland.

Financial Reporting Standard for Smaller Entities

(h) The following disclosures[26] should be made in respect of a **defined benefit scheme:**
    (i) the nature of the scheme (i.e. defined benefit);
    (ii) whether it is **funded** or unfunded;
    (iii) whether the pension cost and **provision** (or **asset**) are assessed in accordance with the advice of a professionally qualified actuary and, if so, the date of the most recent formal actuarial valuation or later formal review used for this purpose;
    (iv) the pension cost charge for the period;
    (v) any **provisions** or prepayments in the balance sheet resulting from a difference between the amounts **recognised** as cost and the amounts **funded** or paid directly;
    (vi) the amount of any deficiency on a **current funding level** basis, indicating the action, if any, being taken to deal with it in the current and future accounting periods;
    (vii) an outline of the results of the most recent formal actuarial valuation or later formal review of the scheme on an ongoing basis;
    (viii) any commitment to make additional payments over a limited number of years;
    (ix) details of the expected effects on future costs of any material changes in the group's and/or company's pension arrangements;
    (x) the **fair value** of the scheme **assets,** the present value of the scheme **liabilities** and the resulting surplus or deficit, determined in accordance with the requirements in paragraph 2, below (without comparatives for the previous period[27]); and
    (xi) where the **asset** or **liability** that would be **recognised** in the balance sheet under the requirements in paragraph 2 differs from the surplus or deficit in the scheme, an explanation of the difference should be given (without comparative disclosure for the previous period[28]).

(i) In addition, for accounting periods ending *on or after* 22 June 2003:
    (i) Comparatives for the previous period should be given in respect of requirements 1(h) (x) and 1(h) (xi) above.
    (ii) An analysis of the movements during the period in the surplus or deficit in the scheme should be given (without comparatives for the previous period).

---

[26] *An illustration of disclosures for a defined benefit scheme is given in Appendix III.*

[27] *Note, however, that comparatives are required for accounting periods ending on or after 22 June 2003 (see (i) below).*

[28] *Note, however, that comparatives are required for accounting periods ending on or after 22 June 2003 (see (i) below).*

Appendix 5

2   The following requirements should be regarded as standard in respect of financial statements relating to accounting periods ending *on or after* 22 June 2004, although earlier adoption is encouraged:

(a) **Assets** in a **defined benefit scheme** should be measured at their **fair value** at the balance sheet date.

(b) **Defined benefit scheme liabilities** should be measured on an actuarial basis using the **projected unit method**. The **scheme liabilities** comprise both any benefits promised under the formal terms of the scheme and any constructive **obligations** for further benefits.

(c) The assumptions underlying the valuation should be mutually compatible and lead to the best estimate of the future cash flows that will arise under the **scheme liabilities**. The assumptions are ultimately the responsibility of the **directors** (or equivalent) but should be set upon advice given by an actuary. Any assumptions that are affected by economic conditions (financial assumptions) should reflect market expectations at the balance sheet date.

(d) **Defined benefit scheme liabilities** should be discounted at the current rate of return on a high quality corporate bond of equivalent currency and term.

(e) Full actuarial valuations by a professionally qualified actuary should be obtained for a **defined benefit scheme** at intervals not exceeding three years. The actuary should review the most recent actuarial valuation at the balance sheet date and update it to reflect current conditions.

(f) The surplus/deficit in a **defined benefit scheme** is the excess/shortfall of the value of the **assets** in the scheme over/below the present value of the **scheme liabilities**. The employer should **recognise** an **asset** to the extent that it is able to recover a surplus either through reduced contributions in the future or through refunds from the scheme. The employer should **recognise** a **liability** to the extent that it reflects its legal or constructive **obligation**.

(g) Any unpaid contributions to the scheme should be presented in the balance sheet as a creditor due within one year. The defined benefit **asset** or **liability** should be presented separately on the face of the balance sheet:
  (i) in balance sheets of the type prescribed for small companies in Great Britain[29] by the Companies Act 1985, Schedule 8, format 1: after item J Accruals and deferred income but before item K Capital and reserves; and
  (ii) in balance sheets of the type prescribed for small companies in

---

[29] *The equivalent statutory provisions for Northern Ireland are in the Companies (Northern Ireland) Order 1986, Schedule 8; and for the Republic of Ireland are in the Companies (Amendment) Act 1986, the Schedule.*

Financial Reporting Standard for Smaller Entities

Great Britain by the Companies Act 1985, Schedule 8, format 2: any **asset** after ASSETS item D Prepayments and accrued income and any **liability** after LIABILITIES item D Accruals and deferred income.

(h) The **deferred tax** relating to the defined benefit **asset** or **liability** should be offset against the defined benefit **asset** or **liability** and not included with other **deferred tax assets** or **liabilities**.

(i) The components of the change in the defined benefit **asset** or **liability** (other than those arising from contributions to the scheme) should be presented separately in the performance statements as follows:
   (i) the **current service cost** should be included within operating profit in the profit and loss account;
   (ii) the net of the **interest cost** and the expected return on assets should be included as other finance costs (or income) adjacent to interest;
   (iii) **actuarial gains and losses** should be **recognised** in the statement of **total recognised gains and losses**;
   (iv) **past service costs** should be **recognised** in the profit and loss account in the period in which the increases in benefit vest; and
   (v) losses arising on a **settlement** or **curtailment** should be **recognised** in the profit and loss account when the employer becomes demonstrably committed to the transaction (gains should only be **recognised** once all parties whose consent is required are irrevocably committed).

(j) The following disclosures should be made in respect of a **defined benefit scheme**:
   (i) the nature of the scheme (i.e. **defined benefit**);
   (ii) the date of the most recent full actuarial valuation on which the amounts in the financial statements are based. If the actuary is an employee or officer of the reporting entity, or of the group of which it is a member, this fact should be disclosed;
   (iii) the contribution made in respect of the accounting period and any agreed contribution rates for future years; and
   (iv) for closed schemes and those in which the age profile of the active membership is rising significantly, the fact that under the **projected unit method** the **current service cost** will increase as the members of the scheme approach retirement.

(k) The **fair value** of the scheme **assets**, the present value of the **scheme liabilities** based on the accounting assumptions and the resulting surplus or deficit should be disclosed in a note to the financial statements. Where the **asset** or **liability** in the balance sheet differs from the surplus or deficit in the scheme, an explanation of the difference should be given. An analysis of the movements during the period in the surplus or deficit in the scheme should be given.

Appendix 5

Appendix III – Illustrative examples and practical considerations

The following is for general guidance and does not form part of the Financial Reporting Standard. The best form of the disclosure will depend on individual circumstances.

Example: Statement of total recognised gains and losses

	2002 £	2001 as restated £
Profit for the financial year	29,000	7,000
Unrealised surplus on revaluation of property	4,000	6,000
Unrealised (loss) /gain on trade investment	(3,000)	7,000
Total recognised gains and losses relating to the year	30,000	20,000
Prior year adjustment (as explained in note x)	(10,000)	
Total gains and losses recognised since last annual report	20,000	

Example: Disclosure – defined contribution pension scheme

The company operates a defined contribution pension scheme. The assets of the scheme are held separately from those of the company in an independently administered fund. The pension cost charge represents contributions payable by the company to the fund and amounted to £50,000 (2001 £45,000). Contributions totalling £2,500 (2001 £1,500) were payable to the fund at the year-end and are included in creditors.

Example: Disclosure – defined benefit pension scheme[30]

The company operates a pension scheme providing benefits based on final pensionable pay. The assets of the scheme are held separately from those of the company, being invested with insurance companies. Contributions to the scheme are charged to the profit and loss account so as to spread the

---

[30] This example does not take into account the guidance added to the FRSSE to reflect FRS 17 (ie paragraphs 1(h)(x), 1(h)(xi), 1(i) and paragraph 2 of Appendix II). A revised example disclosure will be added to the FRSSE when these requirements become mandatory in full (years ending on or after 22 June 2004).

Financial Reporting Standard for Smaller Entities

cost of pensions over employees' working lives with the company. The contributions are determined by a qualified actuary on the basis of triennial valuations using the projected unit method. The most recent valuation was as at 31 December 2000. The assumptions that have the most significant effect on the results of the valuation are those relating to the rate of return on investments and the rate of increase in salaries and pensions. It was assumed that the investment returns would be 8 per cent per year, that salary increases would average 6 per cent per year and that present and future pensions would increase at the rate of 3 per cent per year.

The pension charge for the year was £50,000 (2001 £48,000). This included £5,200 (2001 £5,000) in respect of the amortisation of experience surpluses that are being recognised over ten years, the average remaining service lives of employees.

The most recent actuarial valuation showed that the market value of the scheme's assets was £1,200,000 and that the actuarial value of those assets represented 104 per cent of the benefits that had accrued to members, after allowing for expected future increases in earnings. The contributions of the company and employees will remain at 10 per cent and 5 per cent of earnings respectively.

Practical considerations: Stocks and long-term contracts

Many of the problems involved in arriving at the amount at which stocks and long-term contracts are stated in financial statements are of a practical nature rather than resulting from matters of principle. The following paragraphs discuss some particular areas in which difficulty may be encountered.

The allocation of overheads

1   Production overheads are included in the cost of conversion together with direct labour, direct expenses and subcontracted work. This inclusion is a necessary corollary of the principle that expenditure should be included to the extent to which it has been incurred in bringing the product 'to its present location and condition'. However, all abnormal conversion costs (such as exceptional spoilage, idle capacity and other losses) that are avoidable under normal operating conditions need, for the same reason, to be excluded.

2   Where firm sales contracts have been entered into for the provision of goods or services to customer's specification, overheads relating to design, and marketing and selling costs incurred before manufacture, may be included in arriving at cost.

Appendix 5

3   The costing methods adopted by a business are usually designed to ensure that all direct material, direct labour, direct expenses and subcontracted work are identified and charged on a reasonable and consistent basis, but problems arise on the allocation of overheads, which must usually involve the exercise of personal judgement in the selection of an appropriate convention.

4   The classification of overheads necessary to achieve this allocation takes the function of the overhead as its distinguishing characteristic (e.g. whether it is a function of production, marketing, selling or administration), rather than whether the overhead tends to vary with time or with volume.

5   The costs of general management, as distinct from functional management, are not directly related to current production and are, therefore, excluded from the cost of conversion and, hence, from the cost of stocks and long-term contracts.

6   In the case of smaller organisations whose management may be involved in the daily administration of each of the various functions, particular problems may arise in practice in distinguishing these general management overheads. In such organisations the costs of management may fairly be allocated on suitable bases to the functions of production, marketing, selling and administration.

7   Problems may also arise in allocating the costs of central service departments, the allocation of which should depend on the function or functions that the department is serving. For example, the accounts department will normally support the following functions:

(a)   production – by paying direct and indirect production wages and salaries, by controlling purchases and by preparing periodic financial statements for the production units;
(b)   marketing and distribution – by analysing sales and by controlling the sales ledger;
(c)   general administration – by preparing management accounts and annual financial statements and budgets, by controlling cash resources and by planning investments.

Only those costs of the accounts department that can reasonably be allocated to the production function fall to be included in the cost of conversion.

8   The allocation of overheads included in the valuation of stocks and long-term contracts needs to be based on the company's normal level of

Financial Reporting Standard for Smaller Entities

activity, taking one year with another. The governing factor is that the cost of unused capacity should be written off in the current year. In determining what constitutes 'normal' the following factors need to be considered:

(a) the volume of production that the production facilities are intended by their designers and by management to produce under the working conditions (e.g. single or double shift) prevailing during the year;
(b) the budgeted level of activity for the year under review and for the ensuing year;
(c) the level of activity achieved both in the year under review and in previous years.

Although temporary changes in the load of activity may be ignored, persistent variation should lead to revision of the previous norm.

9   Where management accounts are prepared on a marginal cost basis, it will be necessary to add to the figure of stocks so arrived at the appropriate proportion of those production overheads not already included in the marginal cost.

10   The adoption of a conservative approach to the valuation of stocks and long-term contracts has sometimes been used as one of the reasons for omitting selected production overheads. In so far as the circumstances of the business require an element of prudence in determining the amount at which stocks and long-term contracts are stated, this needs to be taken into account in the determination of net realisable value and not by the exclusion from cost of selected overheads.

Methods of costing

11   It is frequently not practicable to relate expenditure to specific units of stocks and long-term contracts. The ascertainment of the nearest approximation to cost gives rise to two problems:

(a) the selection of an appropriate method for relating costs to stocks and long-term contracts (e.g. job costing, batch costing, process costing, standard costing);
(b) the selection of an appropriate method for calculating the related costs where a number of identical items have been purchased or made at different times (e.g. unit cost, average cost or 'first in, first out' (FIFO)).

12   In selecting the methods referred to in paragraph 11(a) and (b), management must exercise judgement to ensure that the methods chosen provide the fairest practicable approximation to cost. Furthermore, where standard costs are used they need to be reviewed frequently to ensure that they bear a reasonable relationship to actual costs obtaining during the

Appendix 5

period. Methods such as base stock and 'last in, first out' (LIFO) are not usually appropriate methods of stock valuation because they often result in stocks being stated in the balance sheet at amounts that bear little relationship to recent cost levels. When this happens, not only is the presentation of current assets misleading, but there is potential distortion of subsequent results if stock levels reduce and out-of-date costs are drawn into the profit and loss account.

13   The method of arriving at cost by applying the latest purchase price to the total number of units in stock is unacceptable in principle because it is not necessarily the same as actual cost and, in times of rising prices, will result in the taking of a profit that has not been realised.

14   One method of arriving at cost, in the absence of a satisfactory costing system, is the use of selling price less an estimated profit margin. This is acceptable only if it can be demonstrated that the method gives a reasonable approximation of the actual cost.

15   In industries where the cost of minor by-products is not separable from the cost of the principal products, stocks of such by-products may be stated in accounts at their net realisable value. In this case the costs of the main products are calculated after deducting the net realisable value of the by-products.

The determination of net realisable value

16   The initial calculation of provisions to reduce stocks from cost to net realisable value may often be made by the use of formulae based on predetermined criteria. The formulae normally take account of the age, movements in the past, expected future movements and estimated scrap values of the stock, as appropriate. Whilst the use of such formulae establishes a basis for making a provision that can be consistently applied, it is still necessary for the results to be reviewed in the light of any special circumstances that cannot be anticipated in the formulae, such as changes in the state of the order book.

17   Where a provision is required to reduce the value of finished goods below cost, the stocks of the parts and sub-assemblies held for the purpose of the manufacture of such products, together with stocks on order, need to be reviewed to determine if provision is also required against such items.

18   Where stocks of spares are held for sale, special consideration of the factors in paragraph 16 will be required in the context of:

(a)   the number of units sold to which they are applicable;

Financial Reporting Standard for Smaller Entities

(b) the estimated frequency with which a replacement spare is required;
(c) the expected useful life of the unit to which they are applicable.

19 Events occurring between the balance sheet date and the date of completion of the financial statements need to be considered in arriving at the net realisable value at the balance sheet date (e.g. a subsequent reduction in selling prices). However, no reduction falls to be made when the realisable value of material stocks is less than the purchase price, provided that the goods into which the materials are to be incorporated can still be sold at a profit after incorporating the materials at cost price.

The application of net realisable value

20 The principal situations in which net realisable value is likely to be less than cost are where there has been:

(a) an increase in costs or a fall in selling price;
(b) physical deterioration of stocks;
(c) obsolescence of products;
(d) a decision as part of a company's marketing strategy to manufacture and sell products at a loss;
(e) errors in production or purchasing.

Furthermore, when stocks are held that are unlikely to be sold within the turnover period normal in that company (i.e. excess stocks), the impending delay in realisation increases the risk that the situations outlined in (a)–(c) above may occur before the stocks are sold and needs to be taken into account in assessing net realisable value.

Long-term contracts

21 In ascertaining costs of long-term contracts it is not normally appropriate to include interest payable on borrowed money. However, in circumstances where sums borrowed can be identified as financing specific long-term contracts, it may be appropriate to include such related interest in cost, in which circumstances the inclusion of interest and the amount of interest so included should be disclosed in a note to the financial statements.

22 In some businesses, long-term contracts for the supply of services or manufacture and supply of goods exist where the prices are determined and invoiced according to separate parts of the contract. In these businesses the most appropriate method of reflecting profits on each contract is usually to match costs against performance of the separable parts of the contract, treating each such separable part as a separate contract. In such instances, however, future revenues from the contract need to be compared with

Appendix 5

future estimated costs and provision made for any foreseen loss.

23 Turnover (ascertained in a manner appropriate to the industry, the nature of the contracts concerned and the contractual relationship with the customer) and related costs should be recorded in the profit and loss account as contract activity progresses. Turnover may sometimes be ascertained by reference to valuation of the work carried out to date. In other cases, there may be specific points during a contract at which individual elements of work done with separately ascertainable sales and values and costs can be identified and appropriately recorded as turnover (e.g. because delivery or customer acceptance has taken place). The FRSSE does not provide a definition of turnover in view of the different methods of ascertaining it as outlined above.

24 In determining whether the stage has been reached at which it is appropriate to recognise profit, account should be taken of the nature of the business concerned. It is necessary to define the earliest point for each particular contract before which no profit is taken up, the overriding principle being that there can be no attributable profit until the outcome of a contract can reasonably be foreseen. Of the profit that in the light of all the circumstances can be foreseen with a reasonable degree of certainty to arise on completion of the contract, there should be regarded as earned to date only that part which prudently reflects the amount of work performed to date. The method used for taking up such profit needs to be consistently applied.

25 In calculating the total estimated profit on the contract, it is necessary to take into account not only the total costs to date and the total estimated further costs to completion (calculated by reference to the same principles as were applied to cost to date) but also the estimated future costs of rectification and guarantee work, and any other future work to be undertaken under the terms of the contract. These are then compared with the total sales value of the contract. In considering future costs, it is necessary to have regard to likely increases in wages and salaries, to likely increases in the price of raw materials and to rises in general overheads, so far as these items are not recoverable from the customer under the terms of the contract.

26 Where approved variations have been made to a contract in the course of it and the amount to be received in respect of these variations has not yet been settled and is likely to be a material factor in the outcome, it is necessary to make a conservative estimate of the amount likely to be received and this is then treated as part of the total sales value. On the other hand, allowance needs to be made for foreseen claims or penalties payable arising out of delays in completion or from other causes.

Financial Reporting Standard for Smaller Entities

27 The settlement of claims arising from circumstances not envisaged in the contract or arising as an indirect consequence of approved variations is subject to a high level of uncertainty relating to the outcome of future negotiations. In view of this, it is generally prudent to recognise receipts in respect of such claims only when negotiations have reached an advanced stage and there is sufficient evidence of the acceptability of the claim in principle to the purchaser, with an indication of the amount involved also being available.

28 The amounts to be included in the year's profit and loss account will be both the appropriate amount of turnover and the associated costs of achieving that turnover, to the extent that these amounts exceed corresponding amounts recognised in previous years. The estimated outcome of a contract that extends over several accounting years will nearly always vary in the light of changes in circumstances and for this reason the result of the year will not necessarily represent the proportion of the total profit on the contract that is appropriate to the amount of work carried out in the period; it may also reflect the effect of changes in circumstances during the year that affect the total profit estimated to accrue on completion.

Practical considerations – Consignment stock

In determining whether consignment stock is in substance an asset of the dealer, it is necessary to identify whether the dealer has access to the benefits of the stock and exposure to the risks inherent in those benefits. Therefore, to assist in using paragraph 8.5 of the FRSSE, the following table is provided.

Appendix 5

Indications that the stock is not an asset of the dealer at delivery	Indications that the stock is an asset of the dealer at delivery
The manufacturer can require the dealer to return stock (or to transfer stock to another dealer) without compensation *or* Penalty paid by the dealer to prevent returns/transfers of stock at the manufacturer's request.	The manufacturer cannot require the dealer to return or transfer stock *or* Financial incentives given to persuade the dealer to transfer stock at the manufacturer's request.
The dealer has unfettered right to return stock to the manufacturer without penalty and actually exercises the right in practice.	The dealer has no right to return stock or is commercially compelled not to exercise its right of return.
The manufacturer bears obsolescence risk, e.g: – obsolete stock is returned to the manufacturer without penalty *or* – financial incentives given by the manufacturer to prevent stock being returned to it (e.g. on model change or if it becomes obsolete).	The dealer bears obsolescence risk, e.g: – penalty charged if the dealer returns stock to the manufacturer *or* – obsolete stock cannot be returned to the manufacturer and no compensation is paid by the manufacturer for losses due to obsolescence.
Stock transfer price charged by the manufacturer is based on the manufacturer's list price at date of transfer of legal title.	Stock transfer price charged by the manufacturer is based on the manufacturer's list price at date of delivery.
The manufacturer bears slow movement risk, e.g: – transfer price set independently of time for which the dealer holds stock, and there is no deposit.	The dealer bears slow movement risk, e.g: – the dealer is effectively charged interest as transfer price or other payments to the manufacturer vary with time for which the dealer holds stock *or* – the dealer makes a substantial interest-free deposit that varies with the levels of stock held.

Financial Reporting Standard for Smaller Entities

Practical considerations – Debt factoring

To assist in using paragraphs 8.6–8.8 of the FRSSE, the following table is provided.

Indications that derecognition is appropriate (debts are not an asset of the seller)	Indications that a linked presentation is appropriate	Indications that a separate presentation is appropriate (debts are an asset of the seller)
Transfer is for a single, non-returnable fixed sum.	Some non-returnable proceeds received, but the seller has rights to further sums from the factor (or vice versa) whose amount depends on whether or when debtors pay.	Finance cost varies with speed of collection of debts, e.g: – by adjustment to consideration for original transfer *or* – subsequent transfers priced to recover costs of earlier transfers.
There is no recourse to the seller for losses.	There is either no recourse for losses, or such recourse has a fixed monetary ceiling.	There is full recourse to the seller for losses.
The factor is paid all amounts received from the factored debts (and no more). The seller has no rights to further sums from the factor.	The factor is paid only out of amounts collected from the factored debts, and the seller has no right or obligation to repurchase debts.	The seller is required to repay amounts received from the factor on or before a set date, regardless of timing or amounts of collections from debtors.

Appendix 5

Example: Cash flow statement

Entities are encouraged, but not required, to report some cash flow information using the indirect method. An example of a presentation of an indirect method of cash flow statement is given overleaf, as an indication of the type of statements that smaller entities may wish to include in their financial statements. Comparative figures are not shown in the example.

	£	£
Cash generated from operations		
Operating profit/(loss)	(5,050)	
Reconciliation to cash generated from operations:		
Depreciation	245	
Increase in stocks	(194)	
Decrease in trade debtors	67,440	
Decrease in trade creditors	(4,678)	
Increase in other creditors	3,127	
		60,890
Cash from other sources		
Interest received	150	
Issues of shares for cash	5,500	
New long-term bank borrowings	4,500	
Proceeds from sale of tangible fixed assets	50	
		10,200
Application of cash		
Interest paid	(3,000)	
Tax paid	(29,220)	
Dividends paid	(10,000)	
Purchase of fixed assets	(10,500)	
Repayment of amounts borrowed	(3,000)	
		(55,720)
Net increase in cash		15,370
Cash at bank and in hand less overdrafts at beginning of year		(4,321)
Cash at bank and in hand less overdrafts at end of year		11,049
Consisting of:		
Cash at bank and in hand		11,549
Overdrafts included in 'bank loans and overdrafts falling due within one year'		(500)
		11,049

Major non-cash transactions: finance leases

During the year the company entered into finance lease arrangements in respect of assets with a total capital value at the inception of the leases of £2,850.

Example: Discounting when making a provision

A company faces a fine for operating without due regard to safety legislation. The company has been notified of the case and expects to lose it but does not expect the fine (of £100,000) to be payable for five years. How much should be provided for if the amount and timing of the fine is assumed to be certain and the market rate on relevant government bonds is 5 per cent?

The discounted amount for the payment of £100,000 to be made in five years' time is:

$$\frac{£100,000}{(1+(5/100))^5} = £78,353$$

Therefore, in the current year £78,353 is recorded as an expense and a provision in the company's books, rather than £100,000.

In the subsequent years the discount will unwind, increasing the amount of the provision and resulting in a debit to the profit and loss account (shown as a financial expense separate from interest) as follows:

		£
year 1	(78,353 x 5%)	3,918
year 2	((78,353 + 3,918) x 5%)	4,113
year 3	etc	4,319
year 4	etc	4,535
year 5	etc	4,762
		21,647
Add amount originally recorded		78,353
Total provision at end of year 5		100,000

Appendix 5

Appendix IV – The Development of the FRSSE

History

1   For many years there has been different reporting by different types of company: the requirements for listed public companies have been more onerous than for private companies and those for larger companies more onerous than for smaller companies. In particular, the provisions of the EC Fourth and Seventh Company Law Directives have been adopted in the UK and the Republic of Ireland, through which the disclosure requirements for large, medium-sized and small companies have been varied, allowing small companies more extensive exemptions both in the abbreviated accounts to be filed with the registrar of companies and in the statutory accounts for shareholders.

2   The application of accounting standards for smaller companies has also been an issue for standard-setters. The Board, prompted by the concern to reduce burdens on business, asked the Consultative Committee of Accountancy Bodies (CCAB) to establish a Working Party to examine the issue and to undertake wide consultation with a view to recommending criteria for exempting certain types of entity from accounting standards on the grounds of size or relative lack of public interest.

3   The CCAB Working Party published a Consultative Document in November 1994. This proposed that the Board should exempt all entities that met the Companies Act definition of a small company from compliance with all but the five accounting standards and the UITF Abstract noted below, which would continue to apply.

SSAP 4	'Accounting for government grants'
SSAP 9	'Stocks and long-term contracts'
SSAP 13	'Accounting for research and development'
SSAP 17	'Accounting for post balance sheet events'
SSAP 18	'Accounting for contingencies'
UITF Abstract 7	'True and fair view override disclosures'

4   Comments in response to that Consultative Document supported the use of the small companies threshold and a change in the present system whereby small entities were required to comply with almost all accounting standards. However, there was no clear support for the proposal of piecemeal application of a limited number of standards. Analysis of the comments identified a number of recurrent themes, including the need for guidance on measurement issues and the suggestion that a codification of all standards should be undertaken as well as a comprehensive review of those standards that were perceived as needing revision or updating, particularly

in the context of their application to smaller entities. On the latter point, the amount of time needed for this codification and review was recognised, as was the observation that it might not provide a complete solution for the issues faced by smaller entities.

5   Prompted by the comments received, the proposals in the DTI's Consultative Document 'Accounting Simplifications' published in May 1995 and the wish to focus on the needs of smaller entities, the CCAB Working Party proposed in its Paper 'Designed to fit', published in December 1995, that there should be a specific Financial Reporting Standard for Smaller Entities. To demonstrate that this approach was feasible, practical and capable of delivering benefits to those involved with financial statements for smaller entities, a draft FRSSE was included in 'Designed to fit'.

6   Letters of comment received in response to 'Designed to fit' indicated general support for a FRSSE that would apply to small companies and groups, as defined in companies legislation. Accordingly, the CCAB Working Party recommended to the Board that it should publish, as part of its due process, an Exposure Draft containing the proposed FRSSE, amended as appropriate to incorporate comments made on the draft contained in 'Designed to fit'.

7   The Board, largely accepting the CCAB Working Party's recommendations, duly published an Exposure Draft of the proposed FRSSE in December 1996, based on the proposals in 'Designed to fit', but with three main differences. First, the proposed FRSSE in the Exposure Draft was capable of application to small groups, unlike the proposals in 'Designed to fit'. Secondly, guidance on debt factoring arrangements was included in the Exposure Draft. Lastly, the requirement in 'Designed to fit' for a summarised cash flow statement was omitted. This led to the issue of the FRSSE in November 1997.

Link with companies legislation

8   The FRSSE is linked with accounts drawn up in Great Britain under Schedule 8 to the Companies Act 1985[31] for the following reasons:
(a)   it allows the establishment of a clearly distinguishable regime, i.e. the relevant statutory Schedule and the FRSSE. The importance of this was enhanced by the implementation of the Companies Act 1985

---

[31] The equivalent legislation in Northern Ireland is Schedule 8 to the Companies (Northern Ireland) Order 1986 and in the Republic of Ireland is sections 10–12 of the Companies (Amendment) Act 1986.

Appendix 5

(Accounts of Small and Medium-Sized Companies and Minor Accounting Amendments) Regulations 1997 (SI 1997/220), which established a revised Schedule 8, containing all of the provisions applying to small companies; and
(b) it creates the link with the Schedule 8 provisions on a true and fair view, which may be of assistance to standard-setters and others in justifying different disclosure and any simplified measurement regime.

Matters considered in the development of the FRSSE issued in November 1997

Application to small groups

9 Small groups are not required by law to prepare consolidated accounts, and therefore in practice not many do so, at least on a statutory basis. The Board, however, agreed that it would be unfair to those small groups that voluntarily prepare group accounts, if they were not able to take advantage of the provisions in the FRSSE. To import all the necessary requirements from accounting standards and UITF Abstracts into the FRSSE to deal with consolidated accounts would have added substantially to its length and complexity, even though it would have been of interest to only a small percentage of entities. Accordingly, the Board preferred to extend the FRSSE in certain areas and then require small groups adopting the FRSSE to follow those accounting standards and UITF Abstracts that deal with consolidated financial statements. This approach was supported by the majority of respondents to the Exposure Draft commenting on the matter.

Cash flow statements

10 Consistently with the views of the majority of respondents to 'Designed to fit', the Exposure Draft did not propose any cash flow disclosures based on FRS 1 (Revised 1996) 'Cash Flow Statements'. The majority of respondents to the Exposure Draft supported the deletion of the cash flow requirements. However, given that management of cash is fundamental to the success of small businesses, the Board agreed with the minority of respondents, mainly representing users of the financial statements, that a cash flow statement is important. It provides a useful focus for discussions with management, as well as a reference point for subsequent more detailed analysis that users might require. Despite this, the Board recognised the difficulty of mandating a cash flow requirement when, previously, small entities had been exempt from such a requirement. Furthermore, the Board acknowledged that a cash flow format based on FRS 1 (Revised 1996) was not necessarily suitable or appropriate for smaller businesses.

Financial Reporting Standard for Smaller Entities

11   The Board, therefore, while not mandating cash flow statements, strongly encourages smaller entities to provide such a statement voluntarily. Consultations suggested that it would be preferable to advocate only one method of cash flow presentation, for consistency and comparability. The direct method of cash flow statement, in a format similar to an entity's own cash forecasts and management accounts, may provide a link between management's cash projections and the financial statements. However, the indirect method is helpful in understanding the connection between the cash generated during a period and the resulting profit. Following consultation, the Board encourages the presentation of a cash flow statement using the indirect method as it is generally held to be more useful and better understood by many users of financial statements, as well as less costly to prepare.

Related party disclosures

12   About half of the respondents to the Board's Exposure Draft of the FRSSE believed that the FRSSE should not include any of the provisions from FRS 8 'Related Party Disclosures'. They argued that they were unnecessary, given that Parts II and III of Schedule 6 to the Companies Act 1985 require the disclosure of dealings in favour of directors and connected persons. Furthermore, if there was a material transaction with a related party, possibly executed at other than fair value, then, where there was any doubt whether applying any provision of the FRSSE would be sufficient to give a true and fair view, adequate explanation in the notes to the accounts of the transaction or arrangement concerned and the treatment adopted would be required (paragraph 2.2).

13   The Board, however, shared the view of the other respondents that related party disclosures are needed for a proper understanding of an entity's operations and for a true and fair view, given that related party transactions are generally more prevalent in smaller businesses. It also noted that, in respect of dealings in favour of directors and connected persons, the statutory provisions apply equally to companies of all sizes and although the provisions overlapped the disclosure requirements in FRS 8 in many respects, the FRS was broader in scope and, in particular, expressed more clearly than the Act the spirit of Schedule 6. It also clarified, to the benefit of both preparers and auditors, the disclosures necessary to meet the fundamental requirement that accounts should give a true and fair view.

14   The Board, however, accepted that the full requirements of FRS 8 were unduly onerous and could be reduced for smaller entities, without compromising the benefit of the disclosures. Accordingly, the FRSSE requires that only those related party transactions that are material to the reporting entity need be disclosed in the notes to the financial statements,

Appendix 5

even though the FRS requires the disclosure of some transactions that are material only in relation to the other related party.

FRS 5

15 The FRSSE requires regard to be had to the substance of any arrangement or transaction, or series of such, into which an entity has entered. But it does not contain the extensive discussion in FRS 5 'Reporting the Substance of Transactions' on reflecting the substance of transactions. This is because small entities generally do not enter into complex transactions. However, the Board was advised that debt factoring and consignment stock may be a common feature of such entities and accordingly the provisions, principally in FRS 5's Application Notes, are likely to be of value to small entities. The relevant guidance in FRS 5 has therefore been included in the FRSSE.

Subsequent amendments to the FRSSE

The FRSSE (effective March 1999)

16 On issuing the FRSSE, the Board acknowledged that it would need to be revised and updated periodically to reflect developments in financial reporting. The first such revision was issued in December 1998, and incorporated the relevant aspects of FRSs 9–11 and UITF Abstract 18–22. The main changes were to align the requirements for entities applying the FRSSE with the basic measurement requirements of FRS 10 'Goodwill and Intangible Assets', which was issued in December 1997, and FRS 11 'Impairment of Fixed Assets and Goodwill', which was issued in July 1998.

17 The measurement requirements in the FRSSE were simplified, compared with those of FRS 10 FRS 10 and FRS 11, by:

- setting 20 years as a maximum, rather than a presumed maximum that may be rebutted, for the useful economic lives assigned to intangible assets and goodwill arising on the acquisition of unincorporated businesses, thereby removing the need for annual exercises to forecast and discount future cash flows
- removing the exception that allows recognition of internally developed intangible assets with market values and revaluation of any intangible asset with a market value
- omitting the detailed requirements for calculating value in use (as part of recoverable amount) and the subsequent monitoring of cash flows for five years following an impairment review where recoverable amount has been based on value in use.

18 The Board acknowledged that in principle the options for smaller

Financial Reporting Standard for Smaller Entities

entities applying the FRSSE would be more restricted than those for entities applying FRS 10. However, the Board is of the opinion that it would not, in practice, be restricting the options, as smaller entities would rarely be in a position to take advantage of them. The Board has not incorporated the detailed requirements from FRS 11 in the FRSSE, in order to allow smaller entities greater flexibility by enabling simpler calculations to be used where appropriate, given that detailed cash flow projections of smaller businesses are often not readily available.

The FRSSE (effective March 2000)

19   The second revision of the FRSSE was issued in December 1999. It incorporated the relevant aspects, modified and simplified where appropriate for smaller entities, of the four Financial Reporting Standards (FRSs 12–15) that were issued between July 1998 and June 1999.

20   The main changes were to update and add to the material relating to provisions and fixed assets, to reflect the issue of FRSs 12 'Provisions, contingent liabilities and contingent assets' and 15 'Tangible fixed assets'. FRSs 13 and 14, which deal with financial instruments and earnings per share, respectively, were not addressed.

21   The detailed rules of FRS 12 relating to discounting were omitted from the FRSSE, as were the majority of the disclosure requirements. The requirements of FRS 15 were also simplified for inclusion in the FRSSE, particularly those relating to revaluations and the disclosure requirements.

The FRSSE (effective June 2002)

22   The amendments made to the previous FRSSE in producing this document are largely based on those proposed in the Exposure Draft 'Amendment to FRSSE 2001', which was published in June 2001. In developing the revision, the Board was advised by its specialist Committee on Accounting for Smaller Entities.

23   The majority of respondents agreed with the proposal in the Exposure Draft that material relating to defined benefit schemes should be included in an appendix to the FRSSE; however, a number were concerned that small companies would not have adequate time to prepare the information necessary to comply with these requirements. The Board has taken this point and delayed implementation by one year. Small companies will now have a similar length of time to prepare as larger companies had when FRS 17 itself was issued.

24   A number of respondents commented that the four criteria against

Appendix 5

which the appropriateness of accounting policies is judged (as required in FRS 18) should be reflected in the FRSSE. A majority also stated a preference for the definitions of 'accounting policies' and 'estimation techniques' included in FRS 18, over those proposed in the Exposure Draft. Both of these concerns have also been addressed in this final amendment to the FRSSE.

25 Respondents were generally content with the approach adopted in relation to current and deferred tax (FRSs 16 and 19, respectively). However, some did comment that the FRSSE should include guidance covering the deferred tax implications of non-depreciated assets and of 'marking to market'.[32] The Board did not believe that the benefits of including guidance on these specific situations in the FRSSE would justify doing so.

26 Other commentators suggested that the FRSSE should reflect the guidance provided by UITF Abstracts 17 (revised 2000), 26, 29 and 30. These Abstracts address the treatment of share option schemes (17 and 30), barter transactions for advertising (26) and website development costs (29). The Board intends to conduct further research into the relevance of such specific guidance for the FRSSE.

Relationship with other ASB documents

27 The FRSSE is designed to provide smaller entities with a single accounting standard that is focused on their particular circumstances. Smaller entities that choose to adopt the FRSSE are exempt from other accounting standards and UITF Abstracts (with certain exceptions for those small groups preparing consolidated financial statements). The Board accepts that the FRSSE is not comprehensive and that there may be issues of general application on which guidance will be sought. Preparers may come across transactions on which accounting guidance is not provided in the FRSSE. This raises the question of whether, in the absence of guidance within the FRSSE, preparers and auditors would be required to follow all SSAPs, other FRSs and UITF Abstracts to the extent that they provide guidance on transactions of relevance to the smaller entity. The Board's view, formulated after consultation with legal advisers and others, is that users expect financial statements to be prepared using accepted practice. If a practice was clearly established and accepted, it should be followed unless there were good reasons to depart from it. Accordingly, preparers and auditors should have regard to SSAPs, FRSs and UITF Abstracts, not as

---

[32] *i.e. continually revaluing an asset to fair value with changes in fair value being recognised in the profit and loss account.*

mandatory documents, but as a means of establishing current practice.

28 Some respondents asked that there should be specific cross-references within the FRSSE to SSAPs, other FRSs and UITF Abstracts. The Board rejected this suggestion because the inclusion of cross-references would lead to preparers and auditors having to consider those other pronouncements in all cases, as well as the FRSSE, thereby lengthening checklists and adding to the burden. Furthermore, it is recognised that as new FRSs are issued that amend generally accepted accounting practice as it applies to larger entities, it may not be appropriate for such rules to apply to smaller entities. An example that has been frequently cited, but on which the Board has not established a firm position, is that some of the likely proposals on marking to market fixed interest instruments, while appropriate for larger entities, would not be appropriate for smaller entities. Because generally accepted accounting practice had not been established for all in this area then there would not be an expectation that smaller entities should have regard to such a new rule.

Future review of the FRSSE as a whole

29 The issue of the FRSSE in November 1997 introduced a new concept into financial reporting – that of a complete, distinct accounting standard specifically for smaller entities. In the course of the FRSSE's development conflicting views were put forward, ranging from those who believed smaller entities should be exempt from all accounting standards to those who favoured retaining virtually the status quo.

30 Given this divergence of views and the innovative concept behind the FRSSE, it is important that the ability of the FRSSE to respond to perceived needs is carefully monitored. The Board has previously stated its intention to review how the FRSSE, as a whole, is working in practice after two full years of effective operation and to propose amendments as necessary. With this in mind, the Board published a Discussion Paper, 'Review of the Financial Reporting Standard for Smaller Entities' in February 2001. It sought views on the most significant issues affecting the future role of the FRSSE. The responses to the Paper have now been received and analysed and a number of possible developments are being considered.

Appendix 5

Appendix V – Derivation Tables

The following tables are intended to assist readers of the FRSSE in understanding the sources used in its compilation and the changes it makes to the body of accounting standards. They analyse each paragraph of the FRSSE and explain the source, and whether that source has been adopted (a) in its entirety, or (b) with minor amendments, or (c) with major changes. Major changes are deemed to be those where either a disclosure requirement has been lifted, or measurement has been simplified.

FRSSE paragraph	Source: document and paragraph	Complete (a)	Minor changes (b)	Major changes (c)
Objective	ASB's Statement of Principles, Chapter 1		✓ (comment on different balance in financial statements being used for making economic decisions and for assessing stewardship of resources)	
1.1				New paragraph: the scope of the FRSSE
2.1	FRS 5 (14, 16)			✓ (in addition the paragraph refers to the true and fair view and the substance of transactions)
2.2				New paragraph: adequate explanation is needed for a true and fair view
2.3				New paragraph: requirement to state in the accounts whether they have been prepared in accordance with the FRSSE

Financial Reporting Standard for Smaller Entities

FRSSE paragraph	Source: document and paragraph	Complete (a)	Minor changes (b)	Major changes (c)
2.4	FRS 18 (14, 17, 30)		✓(No reference to accounting standards, UITF Abstracts or true and fair view)	
2.5	FRS 3 (62) FRS 18 (45)		✓(the discussion and the disclosure requirements of FRS 3 (62) are omitted)	
2.6	FRS 18 (23, 61(a) and (b))	✓		
2.7	FRS 18 (55(a), (c) and (d))	✓		
2.8	FRS 3 (29)	✓		
2.9	FRS 18 (62)			✓(no reference to departures from the requirements of the FRSSE – this situation is addressed by paragraph 2.2)
2.10	FRS 18(63)		✓(no reference to departures that affect only corresponding amounts)	
3.1	FRS 3 (13)		✓(no reference to other accounting standards)	
3.2	FRS 3 (19)			✓(no reference to continuing or discontinued operations)
3.3	FRS 3 (20)			✓(no reference to continuing or discontinued

293

Appendix 5

FRSSE paragraph	Source: document and paragraph	Complete (a)	Minor changes (b)	Major changes (c)
				operations, and no explanatory text; the term operating profit is described as in FRS 3 (14))
3.4	FRS 3 (21) FRS 10 (71(c) (i))	✓		
3.5	FRS 3 (22)		✓(detail is omitted, additional emphasis of the rarity of extraordinary items)	
3.6	UITF Abstract 21 (17, 18)			✓(excludes specific disclosure requirements (also in companies legislation) and voluntary disclosures)
4.1	FRS 3 (27)			✓(if there are no gains or losses other than those in the profit and loss account no statement is required)
5.1	SSAP 13 (23)	✓		
5.2	SSAP 13 (24)		✓(does not stress that fixed assets for pure and applied research may be capitalised)	
5.3	SSAP 13 (25)	✓		

Financial Reporting Standard for Smaller Entities

FRSSE paragraph	Source: document and paragraph	Complete (a)	Minor changes (b)	Major changes (c)
5.4	SSAP 13 (26)	✓		
5.5	SSAP 13 (27)	✓		
5.6	SSAP 13 (28)	✓		
5.7	SSAP 13 (29)	✓		
5.8	SSAP 13 (32)			✓ (no requirement to disclose movements on deferred development expenditure; disclosure may be given by way of note)
5.9	FRS 10 (7–9, 14)			✓ (no exception allowing recognition of internally generated intangible assets with readily ascertainable market values)
5.10	FRS 10 (10, 13)		✓ (no reference to need to restrict fair values of intangible assets to amounts that do not create or increase negative goodwill)	
5.11	FRS 10 (15, 30)		✓ (no reference to amortisation method reflecting pattern of depletion of goodwill; rather, simply requires a straight-line	✓ (useful economic lives limited to 20 years)

Appendix 5

FRSSE paragraph	Source: document and paragraph	Complete (a)	Minor changes (b)	Major changes (c)
			method unless another is more appropriate)	
5.12	FRS 10 (28)		✓(example added to illustrate circumstances in which a residual value can be regarded as reliable)	
5.13	FRS 10 (33)		✓(consistent with paragraph 5.11, prevents lives from being revised to periods longer than 20 years)	
5.14	FRS 10 (45)			✓(omits exception allowing revaluation of intangible assets with readily ascertainable market values)
5.15	FRS 10 (48–50, 63)			✓(no requirement to show negative goodwill immediately below positive goodwill on the face of the balance sheet)
5.16	FRS 15 (4)	✓		
5.17	FRS 15 (6, 17, 32)	✓		
5.18	FRS 15 (7, 19)	✓		

Financial Reporting Standard for Smaller Entities

FRSSE paragraph	Source: document and paragraph	Complete (a)	Minor changes (b)	Major changes (c)
5.19	FRS 15 (12, 27, 29)		✓ (no reference to construction of a tangible fixed asset being completed in parts)	
5.20	FRS 15 (34, 36)		✓ (no reference to major inspections or overhauls)	
5.21	FRS 15 (42, 43, 59, 61)		✓ (no reference to cases where impossible to obtain a reliable valuation)	✓ (where revalued, tangible fixed assets to be carried at market value or the best estimate thereof, unless judged inappropriate by the directors in which case current value may be used)
5.22	FRS 15 (50)			✓ (valuations may be performed by an experienced valuer, whereas FRS 15 refers to a qualified valuer)
5.23	FRS 15 (65)			✓ (revaluation losses taken to profit and loss account, irrespective of recoverable amount, except falls in market value where carrying amount exceeds

Appendix 5

FRSSE paragraph	Source: document and paragraph	Complete (a)	Minor changes (b)	Major changes (c)
				depreciated historical cost)
5.24	FRS 15 (63, 64)	✓		
5.25	FRS 15 (4)	✓		
5.26	FRS 15 (77)	✓		
5.27	FRS 15 (83, 84)		✓(only life of land included from paragraph 84)	
5.28	FRS 15 (93, 95)		✓(references to impairment and basis on which residual values are priced are omitted)	✓(residual values and useful economic lives for tangible fixed assets to be reviewed regularly and revised when necessary)
5.29	FRS 15 (82)	✓		
5.30	FRS 15 (100)		✓(disclosure of depreciation to be given for (1) land and buildings and (2) other tangible fixed assets in aggregate)	✓(excludes specific disclosure requirements also in companies legislation)
5.31	FRS 15 (102)	✓		
5.32	FRS 11 (5)		✓(no reference to own shares held by an ESOP and unproved oil reserves being excluded from the scope of the impairment requirements)	

FRSSE paragraph	Source: document and paragraph	Complete (a)	Minor changes (b)	Major changes (c)
5.33	FRS 11 (14, 21) FRS 10 (44)		✓ (no reference to the need to review the useful economic life and residual value of the asset when it is impaired)	
5.34	FRS 11 (56)	✓		
5.35	FRS 11 (60)		✓ (no reference to the reversal of an impairment loss on an intangible asset with a readily ascertainable market value)	
5.36	FRS 11 (14, 56, 63)		✓ (slightly simplified treatment of revalued assets)	
5.37	SSAP 19 (10)	✓		
5.38	SSAP 19 (11, 15)			✓ (no requirement to disclose the carrying value of the investment revaluation reserve; disclosure may be given by way of note)
5.39	SSAP 19 (12)	✓		
5.40	SSAP 19 (13)		✓ (no reference to investment companies or property unit trusts, insurance companies or pension funds)	

Appendix 5

FRSSE paragraph	Source: document and paragraph	Complete (a)	Minor changes (b)	Major changes (c)
5.41	SSAP 4 (23, 25)		✓(the discussion in paragraph 23 is not included)	
5.42	SSAP 4 (24)	✓		
5.43	SSAP 4 (27)	✓		
5.44	SSAP 4 (28)		✓(no reference to disclosure of accounting policy)	
6.1	SSAP 21 (31)	✓		
6.2	SSAP 21 (32, 33)			✓(asset and liability to be stated at fair value, rather than the present value of the minimum lease payments, unless fair value is not a realistic estimate)
6.3	SSAP 21 (32, 34)			✓(where grants are received there is no stipulation that the amount to be capitalised should be restricted to the minimum lease payments)
6.4	SSAP 21 (35)		✓(additional emphasis that the straight-line method may be a reasonable approximation)	
6.5	SSAP 21 (37)	✓		
6.6	UITF Abstract 28 (14, 15)		✓(no reference to spreading	

FRSSE paragraph	Source: document and paragraph	Complete (a)	Minor changes (b)	Major changes (c)
			incentives on a basis other than straight-line)	
6.7	SSAP 21 (36)	✓		
6.8	SSAP 21 (38)	✓		
6.9	SSAP 21 (39)			✓ (gross earnings under finance leases should be recognised on a systematic and rational basis)
6.10	SSAP 21 (43)		✓ (no reference to charges for services)	
6.11	SSAP 21 (42)	✓		
6.12	SSAP 21 (45)	✓		
6.13	SSAP 21 (46)	✓		
6.14	SSAP 21 (47)	✓		
6.15	SSAP 21 (48)			✓ (accounting for sale and leasebacks by the buyer/lessor follows the amended treatment for lessors as set out above)
6.16	SSAP 21 (49, 50, 51, 54)		✓ (no requirement to show for finance leased assets, total depreciation for the period by class of asset; disclosure of assets under finance leases	

Appendix 5

FRSSE paragraph	Source: document and paragraph	Complete (a)	Minor changes (b)	Major changes (c)
			required for (1) land and buildings and (2) other assets in aggregate)	
6.17	SSAP 21 (56)			✓(no analysis by type of lease is required)
6.18	SSAP 21 (58, 59, 60)		✓(no reference to disclosure of accounting policy, or of aggregate rentals receivable)	
8.1	SSAP 9 (26)	✓		
8.2	SSAP 9 (28)	✓		
8.3	SSAP 9 (29)	✓		
8.4	SSAP 9 (30)	✓		
8.5	FRS 5 (A11, A12)			✓(omits disclosure requirements)
8.6	FRS 5 (C4, C5, C18)		✓(summarises part of Application Note C relating to derecognition, but with no discussion)	
8.7	FRS 5 (27, C15, C19)		✓(summarises part of Application Note C relating to linked presentation, but with no discussion, and adapts FRS 5(27))	

Financial Reporting Standard for Smaller Entities

FRSSE paragraph	Source: document and paragraph	Complete (a)	Minor changes (b)	Major changes (c)
8.8	FRS 5 (C4, C20)		✓ (summarises part of Application Note C relating to separate presentation, but with no discussion)	
8.9	UITF Abstract 24 (9)	✓		
9.1	FRS 16 (5, 6) FRS 19 (34, 35)	✓		
9.1A	FRS 16 (17) FRS 19 (60)			✓ (Detailed disclosure requirements are omitted and replaced with a broad requirement to disclose the material components of the current and deferred tax charges (or credits))
9.2	FRS 3 (23)			✓ (no specific requirement to disclose special circumstances affecting tax on exceptional items)
9.3	FRS 19 (7(a), 14, 15)	✓		
9.4	FRS 19 (23)	✓		
9.5	FRS 19 (9)	✓		
9.6	FRS 19 (7(b))	✓		
9.7	FRS 19 (37)	✓		

Appendix 5

FRSSE paragraph	Source: document and paragraph	Complete (a)	Minor changes (b)	Major changes (c)
9.8	FRS 19 (42, 44, 60(a)(ii))		✓(FRS 19 states that discounting is "permitted but not required", whereas the FRSSE simply states that it is "not required")	
9.9	FRS 19 (61(a))		✓(Requirement to disclose the 'material components' of the balance replaces the FRS 19 requirement to 'show the amount recognised for each significant type of timing difference')	
9.10	FRS 19 (61(c))			✓(Detailed disclosure requirements are omitted and replaced with a broad requirement to disclose the material components of movement in the net deferred tax balance)
9.11	FRS 19 (64(b))		✓(No reference to tax that may become payable or recoverable in the foreseeable future)	
9.12	FRS 16 (8)	✓		
9.13	FRS 16 (9)	✓		

Financial Reporting Standard for Smaller Entities

FRSSE paragraph	Source: document and paragraph	Complete (a)	Minor changes (b)	Major changes (c)
9.14	SSAP 5 (8, 9)		✓ (no reference to gross turnover)	
10.1	FRS 17 (7)	✓		
10.2	FRS 17 (75)	✓		
10.3				New paragraph: refers the user to Appendix II – 'Accounting for Retirement Benefits: Defined Benefit Schemes'
11.1	FRS 12 (3, 8)		✓ (no reference to financial instruments, executory contracts, long-term contracts or insurance entities)	
11.2	FRS 12 (14, 36, 45, 48)	✓		
11.3	FRS 12 (54, 56, 57)			✓ (no restriction that amounts recognised as reimbursements may not exceed related provision)
11.4	FRS 12 (62)		✓ (emphasis that provisions may need to be reversed omitted)	
11.5	FRS 12 (64)	✓		
11.6	FRS 12 (27, 31)	✓		

Appendix 5

FRSSE paragraph	Source: document and paragraph	Complete (a)	Minor changes (b)	Major changes (c)
11.7	FRS 12 (91, 94)			✓(disclosures relating to uncertainties and reimbursement omitted)
12.1	FRS 4 (24)	✓		
12.2	FRS 4 (28)		✓('debt' is replaced by 'borrowings'; no reference to investment companies)	
12.3	FRS 4 (27, 29)			✓(borrowings initially stated at fair value of consideration received)
12.4				New paragraph: treatment of arrangement fees.
12.5	FRS 4 (43)		✓(the word 'non-equity' has been deleted; it is specified that the dividends should be shown in the profit and loss account and the amounts accrued in excess of dividends should be shown separately in shareholders' funds)	
13.1	SSAP 20 (46)	✓		
13.2	SSAP 20 (47)	✓		

Financial Reporting Standard for Smaller Entities

FRSSE paragraph	Source: document and paragraph	Complete (a)	Minor changes (b)	Major changes (c)
13.3	SSAP 20 (48)	✓		
13.4	SSAP 20 (49, 50)			✓ (references to exceptional and extraordinary items omitted)
13.5	SSAP 20 (51)	✓		
13.6	SSAP 20 (52)	✓		
13.7	SSAP 20 (53)	✓		
13.8	SSAP 20 (54)	✓		
13.9	SSAP 20 (22, 55)	✓		
13.10	SSAP 20 (56)	✓		
13.11	SSAP 20 (57, 58)	✓		
14.1	SSAP 17 (21)	✓		
14.2	SSAP 17 (22)	✓		
14.3	SSAP 17 (23)	✓		
14.4	SSAP 17 (24)	✓		
14.5	SSAP 17 (25)	✓		
14.6	SSAP 17 (26)	✓		
15.1	FRS 8 (2.6, 6, 19)			✓ (the list of transactions is summarised and materiality is in relation to the reporting entity only)
15.2			New paragraph: to clarify that the standard requires disclosure of directors' personal guarantees for their company's borrowings	

Appendix 5

FRSSE paragraph	Source: document and paragraph	Complete (a)	Minor changes (b)	Major changes (c)
15.3	FRS 8 (6)	✓		
15.4	FRS 8 (3, 4)		✓(no reference to exemptions for groups, as given in paragraph 16.1; some explanation omitted)	
15.5	FRS 8 (5)	✓		
16.1				New paragraph: refers the user to FRSs 2, 5–7, 9–11 where group accounts are being prepared and the FRS 8 group exemptions
17.1			New paragraph: effective date	
17.2	FRS 10 (66, 69)			✓(old goodwill previously eliminated against reserves is either wholly reinstated or wholly left in reserves)
17.3	FRS 15 (104)		✓(no reference to testing for impairment)	
17.4	FRS 15 (106, 108)	✓		
18.1				New paragraph: revised FRSSE supersedes previous version

Financial Reporting Standard for Smaller Entities

FRSSE paragraph	Source: document and paragraph	Complete (a)	Minor changes (b)	Major changes (c)
App II paragraph 1(a)	SSAP 24 (77)		✓ (refers to other post-retirement benefits, as well as pensions)	
App II paragraph 1(b)	SSAP 24 (79)	✓		
App II paragraph 1(c)	SSAP 24 (80)	✓		
App II paragraph 1(d)	SSAP 24 (84)	✓		
App II paragraph 1(e)	SSAP 24 (85)	✓		
App II paragraph 1(f)	SSAP 24 (86)	✓		
App II paragraph 1(g)	SSAP 24 (90)	✓		
App II paragraph 1(h)	SSAP 24 (88) FRS 17 (88)			✓ (no reference to disclosure of accounting policy, or funding policy, or circumstances where the actuary is an employee or officer of the company; no explanation of what the 'outline of the results of the most recent formal actuarial valuation' should contain;

Appendix 5

FRSSE paragraph	Source: document and paragraph	Complete (a)	Minor changes (b)	Major changes (c)
				no reference to disclosure of the treatment of refunds)
App II paragraph 1(i)	FRS 17 (88)	✓		
App II paragraph 2(a)	FRS 17 (14)	✓		
App II paragraph 2(b)	FRS 17 (20)		✓(No explanation of constructive obligation)	
App II paragraph 2(c)	FRS 17 (23)	✓		
App II paragraph 2(d)	FRS 17 (32)		✓(No explanation of why the specified rate should be used)	
App II paragraph 2(e)	FRS 17 (35)	✓		
App II paragraph 2(f)	FRS 17 (37)	✓		
App II paragraph 2(g)	FRS 17 (47)		✓(No reference to employers with more than one scheme)	
App II paragraph 2(h)	FRS 17 (49)	✓		
App II paragraph 2(i)	FRS 17 (50, 51, 56, 57, 60, 64)		✓(Only the basic requirements relating to the	

Financial Reporting Standard for Smaller Entities

FRSSE paragraph	Source: document and paragraph	Complete (a)	Minor changes (b)	Major changes (c)
			timing and presentation of gains and losses are included)	
App II paragraph 2(j)	FRS 17 (76)	✓		
App II paragraph 2(k)	FRS 17 (88)	✓		

Appendix 5

Definition: source document and paragraph	Complete (a)	Minor changes (b)	Major changes (c)
Accounting policies FRS 18 (4)	✓		
Actuarial gains and losses FRS 17 (2)		✓(No reference to experience gains and losses)	
Adjusting events SSAP 17 (19)	✓		
Applied research SSAP 13 (21(b))	✓		
Arrangement fees FRS 4 (10)			✓(the FRS 4 definition of issue costs has been used to define arrangement fees)
Assets FRS 5 (2)	✓		
Attributable profit (on long-term contracts) SSAP 9 (23)	✓		
Average remaining service life SSAP 24 (58)		✓(no guidance on the weightings in calculating the weighted average service lives of employees)	
Borrowings FRS 4 (6)		✓(refers to 'borrowings', rather than 'debt')	
Capital instruments FRS 4 (2)			✓(definition extended to specify that it refers to 'arrangements entered into' as well as instruments that are 'issued')
Close family FRS 8 (2.1)	✓		

Financial Reporting Standard for Smaller Entities

Definition: source document and paragraph	Complete (a)	Minor changes (b)	Major changes (c)
Closing rate SSAP 20 (41)	✓		
Companies legislation FRS 5 (10)	✓		
Consignment stock FRS 5 (A1)		✓ (omitted explanation)	
Consolidated financial statements FRS 2 (4, 5, 9)	✓		
Contingent asset FRS 12 (2)	✓		
Contingent liability FRS 12 (2)		✓ (terminology simplified)	
Cost (of stock) SSAP 9 (17)		✓ (attributable overheads are given as an example of conversion costs)	
Current funding level (of a pension scheme) SSAP 24 (59)	✓		
Current service cost FRS 17 (2)	✓		
Current tax FRS 16 (2)	✓		
Curtailment FRS 17 (2)		✓ (Examples omitted)	
Deferred tax FRS 19 (2)	✓		
Defined benefit scheme FRS 17 (2)		✓ (no reference to funding)	
Defined contribution scheme FRS 17 (2)	✓		
Depreciation FRS 15 (2)	✓		
Development SSAP 13 (21(c))	✓		

Appendix 5

Definition: source document and paragraph	Complete (a)	Minor changes (b)	Major changes (c)
Directors APB Statements of Auditing Standards (Glossary of terms)	✓		
Estimation techniques FRS 18 (2)	✓		
Ex gratia pension SSAP 24 (60)	✓		
Exceptional items FRS 3 (5)	✓		
Exchange rate SSAP 20 (40)	✓		
Extraordinary items FRS 3 (6)	✓		
Fair value SSAP 21 (25), FRS 7 (2)	✓		
Finance charge (on a lease) SSAP 21 (27)	✓		
Finance costs (of a capital instrument) FRS 4 (8)			✓ (arrangement fees have been excluded from this definition)
Finance lease SSAP 21 (15)			✓ (there is no supporting definition of the interest rate implicit in a lease)
Foreign entity SSAP 20 (36)	✓		
Foreseeable losses (on a long-term contract) SSAP 9 (24)	✓		
Forward contract SSAP 20 (42)	✓		
Funded scheme SSAP 24 (65)	✓		

Financial Reporting Standard for Smaller Entities

Definition: source document and paragraph	Complete (a)	Minor changes (b)	Major changes (c)
Goodwill FRS 10 (2)		✓(terminology simplified)	
Government SSAP 4 (21)	✓		
Government grants SSAP 4 (22)	✓		
Gross earnings (from a lease) SSAP 21 (28)			✓(no reference is made to the treatment of tax-free grants available to a lessor)
Hire purchase contract SSAP 21 (18)	✓		
Identifiable assets and liabilities FRS 7 (2), FRS 10 (2)	✓		
Inception (of a lease) SSAP 21 (29)	✓		
Intangible assets FRS 10 (2)	✓		
Interest cost FRS 17 (2)	✓		
Investment property SSAP 19 (7, 8)	✓		
Lease term SSAP 21 (19)	✓		
Liabilities FRS 5 (4)	✓		
Local currency SSAP 20 (39)	✓		
Long-term contract SSAP 9 (22)	✓		
Minimum lease payments SSAP 21 (20)	✓		
Monetary items SSAP 20 (44)		✓(no reference to exempt companies)	

Appendix 5

Definition: source document and paragraph	Complete (a)	Minor changes (b)	Major changes (c)
Net investment (in a foreign entity) SSAP 20 (43)	✓		
Net investment (in a lease) SSAP 21 (21, 22, 26)	✓		
Net realisable value (of fixed assets) FRS 11 (2)	✓		
Net realisable value (of stocks and long-term contracts) SSAP 9 (21)	✓		
Non-adjusting events SSAP 17 (20)	✓		
Obligation FRS 12 (2)		✓ (definitions of legal and constructive obligations combined and terminology simplified)	
Operating lease SSAP 21 (17)	✓		
Ordinary activities FRS 3 (2)	✓		
Past service cost FRS 17 (2)	✓		
Pension schemes SSAP 24 (70)	✓		
Permanent differences FRS 19 (2)	✓		
Post balance sheet events SSAP 17 (18)	✓		
Prior period adjustments FRS 3 (7)	✓		
Projected unit method FRS 17 (2)	✓		

Financial Reporting Standard for Smaller Entities

Definition: source document and paragraph	Complete (a)	Minor changes (b)	Major changes (c)
Provision FRS 12 (2)	✓		
Purchased goodwill FRS 10 (2)		✓ (additional explanation that it arises on the purchase of a business accounted for as an acquisition)	
Pure (or basic) research SSAP 13 (21(a))	✓		
Recognised FRS 5 (6)	✓		
Recoverable amount FRS 11 (2, 20)		✓ (wording has been expanded slightly, to include more explanation; definition also includes definition of value in use, which has been given greater flexibility for interpretation)	
Regular (pension) cost SSAP 24 (72)	✓		
Related parties FRS 8 (2.5)			✓ ('influence' is replaced by 'significant influence'; explanation is replaced with straightforward list of common related parties)
Research and development expenditure SSAP 13 (21)	✓		
Residual value SSAP 12 (12)	✓		

Appendix 5

Definition: source document and paragraph	Complete (a)	Minor changes (b)	Major changes (c)
Retirement benefits FRS 17 (2)	✓		
Scheme liabilities FRS 17 (2)	✓		
Settlement FRS 17 (2)		✓(Examples omitted)	
Start-up costs UITF 24 (4)	✓		
Tangible fixed assets FRS 15 (2)	✓		
Tax credit FRS 16 (2)	✓		
Term (of a capital instrument) FRS 4 (16)	✓		
Timing differences FRS 19 (2)		✓(No reference to the fact that timing differences can reverse in one or more subsequent periods)	
Total recognised gains and losses FRS 3 (8)	✓		
Translation SSAP 20 (38)	✓		
Useful economic life SSAP 12 (11)	✓		
Withholding tax FRS 16 (2)	✓		

Financial Reporting Standard for Smaller Entities

Voluntary disclosures: paragraph	Source: document and paragraph	Complete (a)	Minor changes (b)	Major changes (c)
1				New paragraph encouraging entities to give a cash flow statement
2				New paragraph outlining the indirect method of cash flow statement
3	FRS 1 (Revised 1996) (2)			✓(definition of cash loosely based on FRS 1 (Revised 1996) definition; additional proposal to reconcile cash to the balance sheet)
4	FRS 1 (Revised 1996) (39)		✓(included principle but detail is omitted)	
5	FRS 1 (Revised 1996) (46)	✓		

Appendix 5

Appendix VI – Simplifications in the FRSSE

This appendix sets out simplifications that have been made in the FRSSE as compared with the existing body of accounting standards. The analysis below is based on a comparison between the FRSSE and:

(a) the Standard Accounting Practice section in SSAPs;
(b) the Statement of Standard Accounting Practice in FRSs; and
(c) the UITF Consensus in UITF Abstracts.

It therefore does not take into consideration any of the explanatory notes that are included in the SSAPs and FRSs, nor does it attempt to list definitions that are set out in the SSAPs and FRSs but have not been incorporated into the FRSSE.

	Paragraph in source
SSAP 4 *Accounting for government grants*	
• The explanations in paragraph 23 are omitted; only the principle, that grants should be recognised in the profit and loss account to match them with the expenditure towards which they are intended to contribute, is retained. There is no specific statement on dealing with grants made to give immediate financial support, or to finance the general activities of an entity.	23
• No reference to grants relating to leased assets in the accounts of lessors; SSAP 4 cross-refers to SSAP 21.	26
• No reference to the disclosure of the accounting policy.	28
• No reference to disclosure of potential liabilities to repay grants; SSAP 4 cross-refers to SSAP 18.	29
SSAP 5 *Accounting for value added tax*	
• No reference to disclosure of gross turnover.	8

Financial Reporting Standard for Smaller Entities

SSAP 9
Stocks and long-term contracts

- No requirement to subclassify stocks. — 27
- No reference to the disclosure of the accounting policy and the need to apply it consistently. — 32

SSAP 13
Accounting for research and development

- The FRSSE does not stress that fixed assets for pure and applied research may be capitalised. — 24
- No reference to disclosure and explanation of accounting policy. — 30
- No requirement to disclose amounts charged to profit and loss account. — 31
- No requirement to disclose movements on deferred development expenditure. — 32

SSAP 17
Accounting for post balance sheet events

- No differences. — —

SSAP 19
Accounting for investment properties

- No reference to investment companies or property unit trusts, insurance companies or pension funds. — 13, 14
- No requirement to display the investment revaluation reserve prominently in the financial statements. — 15

SSAP 20
Foreign currency translation

- No proviso for restricting exchange gains taken to the profit and loss account on long-term monetary items where there is doubt as to the marketability or convertibility of the currency. — 11, 50
- No references to hyper-inflation. — 26
- No reference to 'exempt companies'. — 35
- No reference to the treatment of exchange gains or losses resulting from extraordinary items. — 49
- No reference to disclosure of accounting policy. — 59

Appendix 5

• No requirement to disclose foreign exchange gains and losses charged/credited to the profit and loss account or offset in reserves under the hedging provisions, in respect of foreign currency borrowings less deposits.	60
• No requirement to disclose movements on reserves arising from exchange differences.	60

SSAP 21
Accounting for leases and hire purchase contracts

• For a finance lease, an asset and liability should be stated at fair value, not the present value of the minimum lease payments, unless that is not a realistic estimate.	32, 33
• For finance leases where grants are received there is no stipulation that the amount to be capitalised should be restricted to the minimum lease payments.	34
• Added emphasis that finance charges may be charged on a straight-line basis as a reasonable approximation.	35
• For lessors, gross earnings under finance leases should be recognised on a systematic and rational basis, with no further guidance given.	39, 40
• No reference is made to the treatment of tax-free grants available to a lessor.	41
• No reference is made to charges for services when recognising rental income from an operating lease.	43
• No reference is made to the treatment of initial direct costs incurred by a lessor in arranging a lease.	44
• Accounting for sale and leasebacks by the buyer/lessor follows the amended treatment for lessors as set out above.	48
• Disclosure of gross amounts of assets and related accumulated depreciation for finance leased assets should be analysed by (1) land and buildings and (2) other assets, rather than by major class of asset.	49
• The requirement to show depreciation for the period in respect of finance-leased assets by major class of asset is not included in the FRSSE.	49
• No requirement for lessees to analyse obligations under finance leases.	52
• No requirement for lessees to disclose finance charges and operating lease rentals charged for the period.	53, 55
• Disclosure of operating lease commitments need not be analysed into land and buildings and other operating leases.	56

Financial Reporting Standard for Smaller Entities

• No reference is made to the disclosure of the accounting policies.	57, 60
• No reference is made to the disclosure of aggregate rentals receivable by lessors.	60
• No definition is given of 'the interest rate implicit in a lease'.	24

SSAP 24
Accounting for pension costs [paragraph 1 of Appendix II to the FRSSE]

• The paragraph setting out the accounting objective has been widened to cover other post-retirement benefits (UITF Abstract 6) as well as pensions.	77
• No reference to circumstances where a significant change in the normal level of contributions occurs because of an adjustment to eliminate a surplus or deficit resulting from a significant reduction in the number of employees covered by the pension scheme.	81
• No provision for recognising a material deficit over a shorter period on the grounds of prudence.	82
• No provision for the accounting treatment of refunds.	83
• No requirement to disclose accounting policy, or funding policy, or circumstances where the actuary is an employee or officer of the company. No explanation of what the 'outline of the results of the most recent formal actuarial valuation' should contain. No reference to disclosure of the treatment of refunds.	88
• No provision for circumstances where a company has more than one pension scheme.	89
• No reference to foreign schemes.	91

SSAP 25
Segmental reporting

• Not covered in the FRSSE.	—

FRS 1 (Revised 1996)
Cash Flow Statements

• There is no requirement for a cash flow statement in the FRSSE. However, a voluntary cash flow statement, presented using the indirect method, is recommended. The only requirements of FRS 1 (Revised 1996) included in the voluntary disclosures are: • the definition of cash (simplified).	— 2

Appendix 5

• the reconciliation between operating profit and operating cash flows.	12
• the treatment of VAT in cash flows.	39
• the disclosure of material non-cash transactions.	46

FRS 2
Accounting for Subsidiary Undertakings

• Not addressed by the FRSSE, except that the user is cross-referred to it, if group accounts are being prepared.	—

FRS 3
Reporting Financial Performance

• No requirement to analyse the turnover, costs, results and exceptional items into continuing operations, acquisitions and discontinued operations.	14–17, 20
• No reference to the consequences of a decision to sell or terminate an operation and the provisions that may be recognised.	18
• No requirement to disclose special circumstances affecting the tax attributable to 'paragraph 20' exceptional items.	23
• No statements relating to computing or disclosing tax on extraordinary and exceptional (paragraph 20) items.	20, 22, 24
• No reference to earnings per share.	25
• No requirement for a note of historical cost profits and losses.	26
• If there are no gains or losses other than those included in the profit and loss account no statement of total recognised gains and losses is required.	27
• No requirement for a reconciliation of movements in shareholders' funds.	28
• No reference to presenting comparative figures.	30
• No reference to investment companies or insurance businesses.	31, 31A

FRS 4
Capital Instruments

• The only parts of FRS 4 that have been included in the FRSSE are:

Financial Reporting Standard for Smaller Entities

• the explanation of which capital instruments should be classified as liabilities and which as shareholders' funds.	24
• the requirement to allocate the finance costs of borrowings to periods over the term of the borrowings at a constant rate on the carrying amount.	28
• the carrying amount at which borrowings should be shown in the balance sheet, amended for the treatment of arrangement fees.	27, 29
• the requirement to account for dividends on an accruals basis (unless ultimate payment is remote) where the entitlement to dividends is calculated by reference to time, and to account for dividends as appropriations of profit.	43
• All other elements of the FRS have been omitted.	
• A new paragraph has been added addressing the treatment of arrangement fees.	—
• The FRS 4 definition of issue costs has been used instead to define arrangement fees and arrangement fees have been excluded from the definition of finance costs.	10
• The definition of capital instruments has been extended to specify that it refers to 'arrangements entered into' as well as instruments that are 'issued'.	2
• The FRS 4 definition of debt has been used to define borrowings.	6

FRS 5
Reporting the Substance of Transactions

• Not covered in the FRSSE, except that:	
• the principle that a reporting entity's financial statements should report the substance of transactions into which it has entered is reflected in paragraph 2.1 of the FRSSE.	14
• a reference to assets and liabilities in determining the substance of a transaction is included.	16
• the user is cross-referred to it, if group accounts are being prepared, to the extent that it addresses group accounts.	—
• Application Note C on debt factoring has been summarised in the FRSSE and the Table in C is reproduced in Appendix III.	C4, C5, C15, C18–C20

Appendix 5

- the treatment of consignment stock and its definition have been included in the FRSSE. The Table in Application Note A is reproduced in Appendix III. | 27, A11, A12
- the definition of 'recognition' has been included in the FRSSE. | 6

FRS 6
Acquisitions and Mergers

- Not addressed by the FRSSE, except that the user is cross-referred to it, if group accounts are being prepared. | —

FRS 7
Fair Values in Acquisition Accounting

- Not addressed by the FRSSE, except that the user is cross-referred to it, if group accounts are being prepared. | —

FRS 8
Related Party Disclosures

- The user is cross-referred to the exemptions available if group accounts are being prepared. | 3
- There is no requirement to consider the materiality of transactions in relation to the other party. | 20
- A new paragraph has been added, clarifying that the standard requires disclosure of directors' personal guarantees for their company's borrowings. | —
- The definition of related party refers to control, common control and significant influence. | 2

FRS 9
Associates and Joint Ventures

- Not addressed by the FRSSE, except that the user is cross-referred to it, if group accounts are being prepared. | —

FRS 10
Goodwill and Intangible Assets

- Simplifications apply only in respect of goodwill and intangible assets arising in the financial statements of an individual entity. (Consolidated financial statements must be based on FRS 10 in its entirety.) | —

Financial Reporting Standard for Smaller Entities

• FRSSE has a requirement, rather than a presumption, that useful economic lives are limited to 20 years. Consequentially, requirements relating to lives in excess of 20 years and indefinite lives are omitted.	17, 19, 37
• Exception allowing recognition of internally generated intangible assets that have a 'readily ascertainable' market value is omitted.	14
• Exception allowing revaluation of intangible assets with a 'readily ascertainable' market value is omitted. Consequential restrictions and requirements relating to revaluation are also omitted.	43, 45, 47
• No reference to need to restrict fair values attributed to intangible assets to amounts that do not create or increase negative goodwill.	10
• No reference to restrictions on useful economic lives to the lives of the underlying legal rights.	24
• Requirements relating to recognition of impairment losses simplified as detailed under the heading for FRS 11.	34, 37, 39–42
• No reference to requirement not to split purchased goodwill arising on a single transaction into positive and negative components.	51
• With the exception of the requirement to disclose the amount and periods over which negative goodwill is being written back in the profit and loss account, the disclosure and presentation requirements are omitted.	48, 52–62, 64, 70(b), 71
• Transitional arrangements for old goodwill previously eliminated against reserves are simplified: it is to be either wholly reinstated or wholly left in reserves.	69
• No specific requirements relating to impairment losses recognised on first implementing the FRS or intangible assets previously included within goodwill.	70(a), 70(c), 74

FRS 11
Impairment of Fixed Assets and Goodwill

• Only the key principle that assets held at above recoverable amount should be written down to recoverable amount and the conditions for recognising the reversal of write-downs are included in the FRSSE.	14, 21, 56, 60, 63

FRS 12
Provisions, Contingent Liabilities and Contingent Assets

• No reference to financial instruments, executory contracts, long-term contracts or insurance entities.	3

Appendix 5

• No reference to rare cases where it is not clear whether there is a present obligation.	15
• No reference to risks, uncertainties and future events being taken into account in measuring a provision.	42, 51
• Detailed rules relating to discount rates omitted.	47
• No restriction that amounts recognised as reimbursements may not exceed related provision.	56
• No reference to provisions and capitalising assets.	66
• No reference to future operating losses, onerous contracts, restructuring or the sale of an operation.	68, 71, 77, 83, 85
• With exception of nature and financial effect of contingent liabilities (unless remote) and probable contingent assets, disclosure requirements omitted.	89–91, 94, 96, 97

FRS 13
Derivatives and other Financial Instruments: Disclosures

• FRS 13 is not addressed by the FRSSE.	—

FRS 14
Earnings per Share

• FRS 14 is not addressed by the FRSSE.	—

FRS 15
Tangible Fixed Assets

• No reference to start-up or commissioning periods.	14
• References to when capitalisation of finance costs should begin omitted.	25
• No reference to construction of a tangible fixed asset being completed in parts.	29
• No reference to major inspections or overhauls for subsequent expenditure.	36
• Bases for revaluation simplified, being market value or best estimate thereof for all tangible fixed assets (unless judged inappropriate by the directors in which case current value used instead). Consequently, detailed valuation requirements for certain tangible fixed assets omitted.	43, 53, 59
• No reference to cases where impossible to obtain reliable valuation.	61
• Treatment of revaluation losses simplified.	65, 66
• Statement omitted that, in determining treatment of gains and losses, material gains and losses within a class should not be aggregated.	67

Financial Reporting Standard for Smaller Entities

• No reference to insurance companies and insurance groups.	71
• Statement omitted that subsequent expenditure does not negate need for depreciation.	86
• No specific requirement for annual impairment review where asset life exceeds 50 years or depreciation omitted as immaterial.	89
• Residual values and useful economic lives to be reviewed regularly, rather than annually, and revised when necessary rather than when expectations significantly different from previous estimates.	93
• No reference to renewals accounting.	97, 98
• With exception of requirement to disclose depreciation methods, useful economic lives or depreciation rates and, where material, financial effect of changes to useful economic lives or residual values, disclosure requirements omitted.	31, 61, 74, 100

FRS 16
Current Tax

• Prohibition of adjustments to income and expenses to reflect notional tax not included.	11
• No reference to tax rates (to be used for measuring current tax).	14
• Detailed disclosure requirements relating to the major components of the charge omitted.	17

FRS 17
Retirement Benefits
[paragraph 2 of Appendix II to the FRSSE]

• No reference to multi-employer schemes.	9
• Requirement to attribute benefits according to the scheme's benefit formula is omitted.	22
• Requirement to reflect expected future events in actuarial assumptions is omitted.	27
• Detailed requirements relating to the treatment of a surplus are omitted.	41, 42, 67, 68, 70
• Detailed requirements relating to the treatment of gains and losses are omitted.	50, 51, 53, 54, 57, 60, 61
• Requirement relating to the recognition of current tax relief on contributions is omitted.	71
• Requirement relating to death-in-service and incapacity benefits omitted.	73

Appendix 5

• Detailed disclosure requirements are omitted.	75[33], 78, 80, 82, 83, 84, 85, 86, 90, 92

FRS 18
Accounting Policies

• No reference to the adoption of accounting policies that enable the financial statements to give a true and fair view.	14
• No reference to departures from accounting standards or UITF Abstracts in exceptional circumstances.	15
• No reference to preparation of financial statements on a going concern basis.	21
• No reference to preparation of financial statements on the accrual basis.	26
• No reference to the constraints that should be taken into account in judging the appropriateness of accounting policies.	31
• No reference to the selection of estimation techniques that enable the financial statements to give a true and fair view.	50
• The requirement relating to accounting for changes in an estimation technique is omitted.	54
• The disclosure requirement relating to significant estimation techniques is omitted.	55(b)
• No reference to SORPs.	58
• No reference to the disclosure required when financial statements are not prepared on a going concern basis.	61(c)
• No reference to departures from accounting standards, UITF Abstracts or companies legislation.	62
• Requirement to cross-reference to disclosures required by companies legislation is omitted.	64

FRS 19
Deferred Tax

• The requirement to provide deferred tax when assets are 'marked to market' is omitted.	12
• The requirement relating to unremitted earnings of subsidiaries, associates or joint ventures is omitted.	21

---

[33] *This reference relates to paragraph 10.2 of the Statement of Standard Accounting Practice of the FRSSE (i.e. not Appendix II).*

- The FRSSE states that discounting of deferred tax balances is not required (but if it is done, it should be done consistently) and does not make any further reference to discounting. | 42, 44, 47, 52, 61(b)
- The presentational requirements of the standard are omitted. | 55, 56, 58, 59
- Detailed disclosure requirements, with the exception of those relating to revalued assets (paragraph 64(b)) and the unwinding of any discount (paragraph 60(a) (ii)), are omitted. | 60, 61, 62, 64

Appendix 5

UITF Abstract 4
Presentation of long-term debtors in current assets

- Not addressed by the FRSSE.

UITF Abstract 5
Transfers from current assets to fixed assets

- Not addressed by the FRSSE.

UITF Abstract 9
Accounting for operations in hyper-inflationary economies

- Not addressed by the FRSSE.

UITF Abstract 10
Disclosure of directors' share options

- Not addressed by the FRSSE.

UIFT Abstract 11
Capital instruments: issuer call options

- Not addressed by the FRSSE.

UITF Abstract 13
Accounting for employee share ownership plan trusts

- Not addressed by the FRSSE.

UITF Abstract 15 (revised 1999)
Disclosure of substantial acquisitions

- Not addressed by the FRSSE.

UIFT Abstract 17 (revised 2000)
Employee share schemes

- Not addressed by the FRSSE.

UITF Abstract 19
Tax on gains and losses on foreign currency borrowings that hedge an investment in a foreign enterprise

- Not addressed by the FRSSE.

UITF Abstract 21
Accounting issues arising from the proposed introduction of the euro

- Only the basic accounting principle is incorporated into the FRSSE.

Financial Reporting Standard for Smaller Entities

- The specific disclosure requirements are not included in the FRSSE.

UITF Abstract 22
The acquisition of a Lloyd's business

- Not addressed by the FRSSE.

UITF Abstract 23
Application of the transitional rules in FRS 15

- Not addressed by the FRSSE.

UITF Abstract 24
Accounting for start-up costs

- No reference to the disclosures detailed in paragraph 10 of the Abstract.

UITF Abstract 25
National Insurance contributions on share option gains

- Not addressed by the FRSSE.

UITF Abstract 26
Barter transactions for advertising

- Not addressed by the FRSSE.

UITF Abstract 27
Revision to estimates of the useful economic life of goodwill and intangible assets

- Not addressed by the FRSSE.

UITF Abstract 28
Operating lease incentives

- No reference to spreading incentives on a basis other than straight-line.
- No reference to investment properties (paragraph 16 of the Abstract) or debtors (paragraph 17).

UITF Abstract 29
Website development costs

- Not addressed by the FRSSE.

UITF Abstract 30
Date of award to employee of shares or rights to shares

- Not addressed by the FRSSE.

Appendix 5

Appendix VII – Amendment to the FRSSE (effective March 2000)

1 The majority of the Financial Reporting Standard for Smaller Entities (effective June 2002) is the same as the previous version of the FRSSE, which it supersedes. New paragraphs or significant revisions have been highlighted in Parts B and C by sidelining the text. Most amendments arise from the incorporation of the relevant aspects of the following FRSs and UITF Abstracts, modified and simplified where appropriate for smaller entities:

		Issued
FRS 16	Current Tax	December 1999
FRS 17	Retirement Benefits	November 2000
FRS 18	Accounting Policies	November 2000
FRS 19	Deferred Tax	December 2000
UITF Abstract 23	Application of the transitional rules in FRS 5	May 2000
UITF Abstract 24	Accounting for start-up costs	June 2000
UITF Abstract 25	National Insurance contributions on share option gains	July 2000
UITF Abstract 17	Employee share schemes (revised 2000)	October 2000
UITF Abstract 26	Barter transactions for advertising	November 2000
UITF Abstract 27	Revision to estimates of useful economic life of goodwill	December 2000
UITF Abstract 28	Operating lease incentives	February 2001
UITF Abstract 29	Website development costs	February 2001
UITF Abstract 30	Date of award to employees of shares or rights to shares	March 2001

2 This appendix sets out all the changes to Part B 'Statement of Standard Accounting Practice' and Part C 'Definitions' of the FRSSE (effective March 2000) that have been incorporated into this version of the FRSSE. In addition, Appendix II 'Requirements for companies subject to taxation in the Republic of Ireland' has been deleted and a new Appendix II 'Accounting for retirement benefits: defined benefit schemes' has been added to the FRSSE.

Current tax (FRS 16)

Amendments to Statement of Standard Accounting Practice

3 Paragraph 9.1 of the Statement of Standard Accounting Practice of the FRSSE is deleted and replaced with the following:

"9.1 **Tax** (**current** and **deferred**) should be **recognised** in the profit and loss account, except to the extent that it is attributable to a gain or loss that is or has been **recognised** directly in the statement of **total recognised gains and losses** (in which case the tax should also be **recognised** directly in that statement).

9.1A The material components of the (**current** and **deferred**) **tax** charge (or credit) for the period should be disclosed separately."

4   Paragraphs 9.19–9.21 of the Statement of Standard Accounting Practice of the FRSSE are deleted and replaced with the following, immediately after the revised paragraphs on deferred tax (as detailed below):

"Tax on dividends

9.12   Outgoing dividends and similar amounts payable should be **recognised** at an amount that includes any **withholding tax** but excludes other taxes, such as attributable **tax credits**.
9.13   Incoming dividends and similar income receivable should be **recognised** at an amount that includes any **withholding tax** but excludes other taxes, such as attributable **tax credits**. Any **withholding tax** suffered should be shown as part of the tax charge."

Amendments to definitions

5   The definitions of irrecoverable ACT and recoverable ACT in Part C 'Definitions' of the FRSSE are deleted. The following definitions are inserted in Part C 'Definitions' of the FRSSE:

"*Current tax*:

The amount of tax estimated to be payable or recoverable in respect of the taxable profit or loss for a period, along with adjustments to estimates in respect of previous periods."

"*Tax credit*:

The tax credit given under UK legislation to the recipient of a dividend from a UK company"

"*Withholding tax*:

Tax on dividends or other income that is deducted by the payer of the income and paid to the tax authorities wholly on behalf of the recipient."

Appendix 5

Retirement benefits (FRS 17)

Amendments to Statement of Standard Accounting Practice

6 Section 10 of the Statement of Standard Accounting Practice of the FRSSE is deleted and replaced with the following:

> "10 Retirement benefits
>
> 10.1 The cost of a **defined contribution scheme** is equal to the contributions payable to the scheme for the accounting period. The cost should be **recognised** within operating profit in the profit and loss account.
>
> 10.2 The following disclosures should be made in respect of a **defined contribution scheme:**
> (a) the nature of the scheme (i.e. defined contribution);
> (b) the cost for the period; and
> (c) any outstanding or prepaid contributions at the balance sheet date.
>
> 10.3 An employer participating in a **defined benefit scheme** should refer to Appendix II 'Accounting for retirement benefits: defined benefit schemes'.

7 In paragraph 11.1 of the Statement of Standard Accounting Practice of the FRSSE, the reference to 'pensions' is deleted and replaced with 'retirement benefits'.

8 The final sentence of paragraph 11.2 of the Statement of Standard Accounting Practice of the FRSSE is deleted and replaced with the following:

> '11.2...Where discounting is used, the unwinding of the discount should be shown as other finance costs adjacent to interest.'

Amendments to definitions

9 The definitions of defined benefit scheme and defined contribution scheme in Part C 'Definitions' of the FRSSE are deleted. The following definitions are inserted in Part C 'Definitions' of the FRSSE:

> '*Actuarial gains and losses*:
>
> Changes in actuarial deficits or surpluses that arise because events have not coincided with the actuarial assumptions made for the last valuation or because the actuarial assumptions have changed.'

Financial Reporting Standard for Smaller Entities

'*Current service cost*:

The increase in the present value of the **scheme liabilities** expected to arise from employee service in the current period.'

'*Curtailment*:

An event that reduces the expected years of future service of present employees or reduces for a number of employees the accrual of defined benefits for some or all of their future service.'

'*Defined benefit scheme*:

A pension or other **retirement benefit** scheme other than a **defined contribution scheme**. Normally, the scheme rules define the benefits independently of the contributions payable, and the benefits are not directly related to the investments of the scheme.'

'*Defined contribution scheme*:

A pension or other retirement benefit scheme into which an employer pays regular contributions fixed as an amount or as a percentage of pay. The employer will have no legal or constructive obligation to pay further contributions if the scheme does not have sufficient assets to pay all employee benefits relating to employee service in the current and prior periods.'

'*Interest cost*:

The expected increase during the period in the present value of the **scheme liabilities** because the benefits are one period closer to settlement.'

'*Past service cost*:

The increase in the present value of the **scheme liabilities** related to employee service in prior periods arising in the current period as a result of the introduction of, or improvement to, **retirement benefits**.'

'*Projected unit method*:

An accrued benefits valuation method in which the scheme liabilities make allowance for projected earnings. An accrued benefits valuation method is a valuation method in which the scheme liabilities at the valuation date relate to:

(a) the benefits for pensioners and deferred pensioners (i.e. individuals who have ceased to be active members but are entitled to benefits payable at a later date) and their dependants, allowing where appropriate for future increases; and

Appendix 5

(b) the accrued benefits for members in service on the valuation date.

The accrued benefits are the benefits for service up to a given point in time, whether vested rights or not. Guidance on the projected unit method is given in the Guidance Note GN26 issued by the Faculty and Institute of Actuaries.'

'*Retirement benefits*:

All forms of consideration given by an employer in exchange for services rendered by employees that are payable after the completion of employment. Retirement benefits do not include termination benefits payable as a result of either (i) an employer's decision to terminate an employee's employment before the normal retirement date or (ii) an employee's decision to accept voluntary redundancy in exchange for those benefits, because these are not given in exchange for services rendered by employees.'

'*Scheme liabilities*:

The liabilities of a defined benefit scheme for outgoings due after the valuation date. Scheme liabilities measured using the projected unit method reflect the benefits that the employer is committed to provide for service up to the valuation date.'

'*Settlement*:

An irrevocable action that relieves the employer (or the defined benefit scheme) of the primary responsibility for a pension obligation and eliminates significant risks relating to the obligation and the assets used to effect the settlement.'

Accounting policies (FRS 18)

Amendments to Statement of Standard Accounting Practice

10   Paragraph 2.3 of the Statement of Standard Accounting Practice of the FRSSE is amended to read as follows (the footnote remains unchanged and therefore has not been reproduced here):

'2.3   The financial statements should state that they have been prepared in accordance with the Financial Reporting Standard for Smaller Entities (effective June 2002).'

11   Paragraphs 2.4–2.6 of the Statement of Standard Accounting Practice of the FRSSE are deleted and replaced by the following:

'2.4   **Accounting policies** and **estimation techniques** should be consis-

Financial Reporting Standard for Smaller Entities

tent with the requirements of the FRSSE and of **companies legislation** (or other equivalent legislation). Where this permits a choice, an entity should select the policies and techniques most appropriate to its particular circumstances for the purpose of giving a true and fair view, taking account of the objectives of relevance, reliability, comparability and understandability.

2.5 **Accounting policies** should be reviewed regularly to ensure that they remain the most appropriate to the entity's particular circumstances for the purpose of giving a true and fair view. However, in judging whether a new policy is more appropriate than the existing policy, due weight should be given to the impact on comparability. Following a change in **accounting policy**, the amounts for the current and corresponding periods should be restated on the basis of the new policies.

2.6 When preparing financial statements, **directors** should assess whether there are significant doubts about the entity's ability to continue as a going concern. Any material uncertainties, of which the **directors** are aware in making their assessment, should be disclosed. Where the period considered by the **directors** in making this assessment has been limited to a period of less than one year from the date of approval of the financial statements, that fact should be stated.

2.7 Financial statements should include:
   (a) a description of each material **accounting policy** followed;
   (b) details of any changes to the **accounting policies** followed in the preceding period including, in addition to the disclosures necessary for **prior period adjustments,** a brief explanation of why each new **accounting policy** is thought more appropriate and, where practicable, an indication of the effect of the change on the results for the current period; and
   (c) where the effect of a change to an **estimation technique** is material, a description of the change and, where practicable, the effect on the results for the current period.'

12   The heading above paragraph 2.3 *'Accounting principles and policies'* is deleted and replaced with a new heading *'Accounting policies'*.

13   Paragraph 2.7 of the Statement of Standard Accounting Practice of the FRSSE is renumbered as 2.8.

14   Paragraph 2.8 of the Statement of Standard Accounting Practice of the FRSSE is deleted.

Appendix 5

Amendments to definitions

15 The definitions of accounting policies and accounting principles in Part C 'Definitions' of the FRSSE are deleted. The following definitions are inserted in Part C 'Definitions' of the FRSSE:

'*Accounting policies*:

Those principles, bases, conventions, rules and practices applied by an entity that specify how the effects of transactions and other events are to be reflected in its financial statements through

(i) **recognising,**
(ii) selecting measurement bases for, and
(iii) presenting

assets, liabilities, gains, losses and changes to shareholders' funds. Accounting policies do not include **estimation techniques.**

Accounting policies define the process whereby transactions and other events are reflected in financial statements. For example, an accounting policy for a particular type of expenditure may specify whether an **asset** or a loss is to be **recognised**; the basis on which it is to be measured; and where in the profit and loss account or balance sheet it is to be presented.'

'*Estimation techniques*:

The methods adopted by an entity to arrive at estimated monetary amounts, corresponding to the measurement bases selected, for **assets, liabilities,** gains, losses and changes to shareholders' funds.

Estimation techniques implement the measurement aspects of **accounting policies.** An **accounting policy** will specify the basis on which an item is to be measured; where there is uncertainty over the monetary amount corresponding to that basis, the amount will be arrived at by using an estimation technique.

Estimation techniques include, for example:

(a) methods of **depreciation,** such as straight-line and reducing balance, applied in the context of a particular measurement basis, used to estimate the proportion of the economic benefits of a **tangible fixed asset** consumed in a period;
(b) different methods used to estimate the proportion of trade debts that will not be recovered, particularly where such methods consider a population as a whole rather than individual balances.'

Financial Reporting Standard for Smaller Entities

Deferred tax (FRS 19)

Amendments to Statement of Standard Accounting Practice

16 Paragraphs 9.3–9.18 of the Statement of Standard Accounting Practice of the FRSSE are deleted and replaced with the following:

- '9.3 **Deferred tax** should be **recognised** in respect of all **timing differences** that have originated but not reversed by the balance sheet date; however, **deferred tax** should not be **recognised** on:
  - (a) revaluation gains and losses unless, by the balance sheet date, the entity has entered into a binding agreement to sell the **asset** and has revalued the **asset** to the selling price; or
  - (b) taxable gains arising on revaluations or sales if it is more likely than not that the gain will be rolled over into a replacement **asset**.
- 9.4 Unrelieved tax losses and other **deferred tax assets** should be **recognised** only to the extent that it is more likely than not that they will be recovered against the reversal of **deferred tax liabilities** or other future taxable profits (the very existence of unrelieved tax losses is strong evidence that there may not be 'other future taxable profits' against which the losses will be relieved).
- 9.5 **Deferred tax** should be **recognised** when the tax allowances for the cost of a fixed **asset** are received before or after the **depreciation** of the fixed **asset** is **recognised** in the profit and loss account. However, if and when all conditions for retaining the tax allowances have been met, the **deferred tax** should be reversed.
- 9.6 **Deferred tax** should not be **recognised** on **permanent differences**.
- 9.7 **Deferred tax** should be measured at the average tax rates that would apply when the **timing differences** are expected to reverse, based on tax rates and laws that have been enacted by the balance sheet date.
- 9.8 The discounting of **deferred tax assets** and **liabilities** is not required. However, if an entity does adopt a policy of discounting, all **deferred tax** balances that have been measured by reference to undiscounted cash flows and for which the impact of discounting is material should be discounted. Where discounting is used, the unwinding of the discount should be shown as a component of the tax charge and disclosed separately.
- 9.9 The **deferred tax** balance and its material components should be disclosed.
- 9.10 The movement between the opening and closing net **deferred tax** balances, and the material components of this movement, should be disclosed.
- 9.11 If **assets** have been revalued, or if their market values have been

Appendix 5

disclosed in a note, the amount of tax that would be payable or recoverable if the **assets** were sold at the values shown should be disclosed.'

Amendments to definitions

17 The definitions of deferred tax, the liability method and timing differences in Part C 'Definitions' of the FRSSE are deleted. The following definitions are inserted in Part C 'Definitions' of the FRSSE:

'*Deferred tax*:

Estimated future tax consequences of transactions and events recognised in the financial statements of the current and previous periods.'

'*Permanent differences*:

Differences between an entity's taxable profits and its results as stated in the financial statements that arise because certain types of income and expenditure are non-taxable or disallowable, or because certain tax charges or allowances have no corresponding amount in the financial statements.'

'*Timing differences*:

Differences between taxable profits and the results as stated in the financial statements that arise from the inclusion of gains and losses in tax assessments in periods different from those in which they are recognised in financial statements. For example, a timing difference would arise when tax allowances for the cost of a fixed asset are accelerated or decelerated, i.e. received before or after the depreciation of the fixed asset is recognised in the profit and loss account'

Start-up costs (UITF Abstract 24)

Amendment to Statement of Standard Accounting Practice

18 The following paragraph is inserted after paragraph 8.8 of the Statement of Standard Accounting Practice of the FRSSE:

'Start-up costs

8.9   **Start-up costs** should be accounted for on a basis consistent with the accounting treatment of similar costs incurred as part of the entity's on-going activities. In cases where there are no such similar costs, **start-up costs** that do not meet the criteria for **recognition** as **assets** under another specific requirement of the

Financial Reporting Standard for Smaller Entities

FRSSE should be **recognised** as an expense when they are incurred. They should not be carried forward as an **asset**.'

Amendments to definitions

19   The following definition is inserted in Part C 'Definitions' of the FRSSE:

'*Start-up costs*:

Costs arising from those one-time activities related to opening a new facility, introducing a new product or service, conducting business in a new territory, conducting business with a new class of customer, initiating a new process in an existing facility, starting some new operation and similar items. They include costs of relocating or reorganising part or all of an entity, costs related to organising a new entity, and expenses and losses incurred both before and after opening.'

Operating lease incentives (UITF Abstract 28)

Amendment to Statement of Standard Accounting Practice

20   The bracketed words '...(and indeed the lessor) ...' are inserted after the word 'lessee' in paragraph 6.6 of the Statement of Standard Accounting Practice of the FRSSE.

Year 2000 and the euro (withdrawal of UITF Abstract 20)

21   Paragraph 3.6 of the Statement of Standard Accounting Practice of the FRSSE is deleted and replaced with the following:

'3.6   Costs involved with the introduction of the euro should be written off to the profit and loss account, except where they meet the conditions to be capitalised as a fixed **asset**. Costs may be capitalised (a) where an entity already has an **accounting policy** to capitalise **assets** of the relevant type and (b) to the extent that the expenditure clearly enhances the **asset** beyond that originally assessed, rather than merely maintaining it. If material, the costs written off to the profit and loss account are **exceptional items** and should be disclosed as such.'

Date from which effective

Amendment to Statement of Standard Accounting Practice

22   Paragraph 17.1 of the Statement of Standard Accounting Practice is amended to read as follows:

Appendix 5

'17.1 The accounting practices set out in the FRSSE (effective June 2002) should be regarded as standard in respect of financial statements relating to accounting periods ending on or after 22 June 2002. Earlier adoption is encouraged.'

Withdrawal of the FRSSE (effective March 2000)

Amendment to Statement of Standard Accounting Practice

23 Paragraph 18.2 is deleted. Paragraph 18.1 is amended to read as follows:

'18.1 The FRSSE (effective June 2002) supersedes the FRSSE (effective March 2000).'

Amendment of FRS 14 and UITF Abstracts 19–22

Amendment to Statement of Standard Accounting Practice

24 Section 19 of the Statement of Standard Accounting Practice is deleted.

Index

References are to Chapters 1–9 and to Appendices 1–5

abbreviated accounts   4.40–4.44
  Companies Act (1985)   4.1
  and directors' statements   4.39
  example   App.2
  and FRSSE   4.39, 4.43
  medium-sized companies   4.50–4.53
    reporting requirements   9.28, 9.37
  public interest companies   3.2
  rejection by Registrar of
    Companies   3.4
  reporting on   9.28–9.37
  small companies   4.45–4.49
  statutory provisions   2.13
Accounting for leases: a new approach
  (G4+1 Group Discussion
  Paper)   6.43
accounting policies
  double counting   5.19
  financial statements,
    example   App.1
  FRSSE (2002)   5.1–5.2, App.5
  principles and   5.18–5.23
  review, need for   5.21
  true and fair view   5.8–5.10
  unincorporated entities   5.3–5.7
accounting principles   5.18–5.23
accounting simplifications
  1996 Regulations   2.15–2.16
  DTI Consultative Document   1.28, 2.17
accounting standards
  in 1970s   1.5–1.6
  in 1980s   1.9
  ASB   1.16–1.18
  harmonisation, international   2.36–2.39
  unincorporated entities   5.3
Accounting Standards Board *see* ASB
  (Accounting Standards Board)

Accounting Standards Committee *see*
  ASC (Accounting Standards
  Committee)
Accounting Standards (Prescribed Body)
  Regulations (1990)   1.32
Accounting Standards Steering
  Committee   1.5, 1.6
ACT (advanced corporation tax)   7.3, 7.4
actuarial gains/losses   App.5
actuarial basis, finance charges   6.35
actuarial valuation methods   7.19, 7.20, 7.23
adjusting events   8.8, App.5
advanced corporation tax (ACT)   7.3, 7.4
amortisation   6.6, 6.8, 6.39
anticipated future income   5.29
APB (Auditing Practices Board)
  Audit of Small Businesses   9.21
  field trials   2.33, 2.34
  FRSSE: Guidance for auditors
    (Bulletin)   9.22, 9.26, 9.30, 9.32, 9.36
applied research   App.5
arrangement fees   7.35–7.37, App.5
ASB (Accounting Standards Board)
  accounting policies, review of   5.21
  accounting standards   1.16–1.18
  auditors, guidance for   9.16
  FRSSE (1992)   App.5
  cash flow information   8.19
  deferred tax   7.7
  development of FRSSE   1.31
  Discussion Papers
    *Leases: Implementation of a new
    approach*   6.43
    *Reporting financial
    performance*   5.36

345

Index

ASB (Accounting Standards Board)—cont.
  financial statements, prepared in accordance with FRSSE (2002) requirement 5.18
  impairment reviews 6.27
  leases 6.36, 6.37, 6.43, 6.44
  related party disclosures 8.11, 8.12
  relationship of FRSSE with other standards 5.15
  retirement benefits 7.17
  share schemes 6.50
  structure of FRSSE 1.32
ASC (Accounting Standards Committee)
  1988 statement 1.12–1.15
    'small', criteria for 1.14
    universality concept 1.13
  Account Standards Board, replacement by 1.16
  accounting standards (1980s) 1.9
  Accounting Standards Steering Committee, replacement of 1.6
  research study (1985) 1.10–1.11
  Working Party, establishment of (1996) 1.11
  see also Accounting Standards Steering Committee
assets
  consignment stock 6.48, App.5
  contingent 7.31–7.33, App.5
  current App.5
  depreciation 6.22–6.23, App.5
  disposal methods 5.30, 5.31, App.5
  factoring of debts 6.47, App.5
  fair value App.5
  foreign currency 8.3
  government grants 6.33, App.5
  impairment reviews 6.27–6.31, App.5
  intangible 6.3–6.10, App.5
  investment properties 6.32, App.5
  leases 6.34–6.44, App.5
  long-term debtors 6.46, App.5
  R & E 6.3–6.5, App.5
  revalued 6.18, 7.12
  share schemes 6.50
  start-up costs and 6.49, App.5
  stocks and long-term contracts 6.45, App.5

assets—*cont.*
  tangible 6.11–6.21, App.5
  website development costs 6.26
  write-down to recoverable amount 6.24–6.25, App.5
  see also leases; liabilities
associated companies
  consolidated financial statements 8.17–8.18
  related party disclosures 8.14
attributable profit App.5
audit exemption 4.19–4.22
  Articles, compliance with 4.21
  Companies Acts 1.7, 4.1
  directors' statements 4.34–4.39
  financial statements 2.22–2.28
  overseas parent, companies with 4.31
  qualifying for 4.23–4.30
  shareholders' objections 4.32–4.33
  'very small' companies 2.12, 2.23
  where audit still carried out 4.20
  wording App.3
audit of financial statements 2.22–2.28
  auditors, guidance for 9.6, 9.12–9.20, 9.23–9.27
  example App.1
  Regulations 2.22, 2.24, 2.25, 2.26
Audit of Small Businesses, APB 9.21
Auditing Practices Board 1.34
auditors, guidance for
  abbreviated accounts
    example App.2
    reporting on 9.28–9.37
  Companies Acts, compliance with 9.10–9.11
  disclosures 9.2
  exemptions, assessment of entitlement 9.5–9.9
  FRSSE, compliance with 9.10–9.11
  general considerations 9.4
  modified financial statements, reporting on 9.23–9.27
  'non-routine' transactions 9.20
  overrides 9.3
  Schedule 8
    adoption by small companies 9.4
    adoption where not entitled 9.8

Index

auditors, guidance for—*cont.*
  statutory obligations 9.1
  voluntary disclosures 9.22
  see also APB (Auditing Practices Board)
average remaining service life App.5

balance sheet total 3.15, 3.23, 4.26
balance sheets
  abbreviated 4.46, 4.50
    example App.2
  audit exemption, directors' statement 4.34
  capital instruments 7.37
  as financial statement 2.3
  financial statements, example App.1
  see also post balance-sheet events
basic research App.5
Big GAAP
  accounting standards 5.16
  deferred tax 7.7, 7.15
  discounting 5.38
  FRSSE, structure 1.32
  leases 6.44
  modified financial statements, true and fair requirement 9.17
  retirement benefits 7.17
  small companies in law 1.8
  taxation 7.3
  see also GAAP (Generally Accepted Accounting Principles); Little GAAP
borrowings App.5

Cadbury Report (corporate governance) 1.17
capital allowances, deferred tax 7.9–7.10
capital instruments 7.34–7.38, App.5
capitalisation of costs 6.12, 6.13
CASE (Committee on Accounting for Smaller Entities)
  challenge for 1.45
  establishment 1.43
  share schemes 6.50
  terms of reference 1.44
cash flow information 4.48, 4, 51, 8.19, App.5

CCAB (Consultative Committee of Accountancy Bodies), Working Party 1.19–1.31
  1994 paper 1.19, 1.20–1.27, 1.42
  1995 paper 1.28–1.31, 1.43, 1.45
  establishment 1.18
  leases 6.35
charities, audit exemption 4.19
close family, defined App.5
closing rates App.5
Commission of European Communities, harmonisation of accounting standards 2.36
Companies Act (1985) 2.2–2.8
  accounting provisions 2.5
  auditors, guidance for 9.1
  concessions to small/medium-sized companies 4.1
  Deregulation Initiative (1990s) 2.7
  directors' statements, audit exemptions 4.35
  evolution of company law, impact 2.6
  financial statements
    circulation requirements 2.4
    meaning 2.3
  general requirement 2.2
  restructuring of schedules to 2.17
  SI 1992/2452 Regulations 2.14
  SI 1994/1935 Regulations 2.22
  SI 1996/189 Regulations 2.15
  SI 1997/220 Regulations 2.17–2.21
  SI 1997/936 Regulations 2.24
companies legislation
  abbreviated accounts 2.13
  accounting simplifications 2.15–2.16
  audit of financial statements 2.22–2.28
  Companies Act (1907) 1.2
  Companies Act (1948) 1.3
  Companies Act (1967) 1.4
  Companies Act (1981) 1.1, 1.7, 1.9
  Company Law Review 2.29–2.31
  compliance with, guidance to auditors 9.10–9.11
  FRSSE 2002 App.5
  harmonisation, international 2.36–2.39

347

Index

companies legislation—*cont.*
  Independent Professional Review
    (IPR)   2.32–2.35
  modified accounts   2.13, 2.14
  regulations
    accounting simplifications   2.15
    audit of financial
      statements   2.22, 2.24, 2.25,
      2.26
    Companies Act 1985, restructuring
      of schedules   2.17–2.21

    see also Companies Act
      (1985)
    modified accounts   2.14
  small and medium-sized
    companies   2.9–2.12
Company accounting and disclosure
  (Green Paper, 1979)   1.7

Company Law Review Steering Group
  establishment   2.29
  Independent Professional Review
    (IPR)   2.32–2.33
  recommendations   2.30–2.31
  unincorporated entities   5.7
components depreciation   7.27–7.30
consignment stock   6.48, App.5
consolidated financial
  statements   8.17–8.18, App.5
Consultative Committee of
  Accountancy Bodies *see* CCAB
  (Consultative Committee of
  Accountancy Bodies), Working
  Party
contingent assets and liabilities   7.31–
  7.33, App.5
contracts, long-term   6.45, App.5
corporate governance, Cadbury
  Report   1.17
costing methods   App.5
current assets   App.5
current service cost   App.5
current tax   App.5
curtailment, defined   App.5

debtors, long-term   6.46
debts, factoring of   6.47, App.5
deferred tax   7.6–7.15, App.5

deferred tax
  Big GAAP   7.7, 7.15
  capital allowances   7.9–7.10
  flow through method   7.7
  FRS19   7.6–7.7, 7.14
  FRSSE (2002)   7.13, App.5
  'material components'   7.7
  permanent differences   7.11
  revalued assets   7.12
  timing differences   7.8–7.10, App.5
defined benefit scheme
  FRSSE   App.5
  new rules, effects   7.22
  popularity of   7.17
  wording   App.3
defined contribution schemes   7.17,
  App.5
definitions
  adjusting events   8.8
  balance sheet total   4.26
  financial statements   2.3
  FRSSE (2002)   App.5
  groups, small or medium-
    sized   3.17–3.27
  public interest companies   3.2–3.5
  size criteria   3.12–3.16
  small or medium-sized, qualifying
    as   3.6–3.11
  timing differences   7.8–7.9
depreciation
  assets   6.22–6.23, App.5
  deferred tax   7.9
  provisions and   7.27–7.30, App.5
  see also finance charges, leases; write-
    downs to recoverable amount
Deregulation Initiative, DTI
  (1990s)   2.7
derivation tables   App.5
*Designed to fit—Financial Reporting
  Standard for Smaller Entities*
  (CCAB paper, 1995)   1.19, 1.28–
  1.31
  FRSSE Exposure Draft   1.31, 1.41
  FRSSE, support for   1.30
  need for   1.28–1.29
  other accounting standards,
    relationship of FRSSE
    with   5.13
  review mechanism   1.43, 1.45

Index

development, defined App.5
directors, defined App.5
directors' report
  example App.1
  financial statements, not part of 2.3
  modifications 4.2, 4.14–4.15
  small companies 4.6–4.8
directors' statement, audit
    exemption 4.34
disclosure requirements
  auditors, guidance for 9.2
  defined benefit/contribution
    schemes App.5
  exemptions 2.13, 4.3–4.5
  leases App.5
  modified accounts, small company
    exemptions 4.6–4.8
  related parties 8.10–8.16
  research and development 6.5
  retirement benefits 7.18, 7.20
  small and medium-sized companies,
    relaxations for *see* exemptions;
    modifications; modified
    accounts; modified financial
    statements
  true and fair view overrides 5.23,
    App.5
  voluntary disclosures App.5
discounting 5.37–5.38, App.5
disposals, profit or loss on 5, 39, 5.31,
  App.5
dividends, tax on 7.4, App.5
DTI (Department of Trade and Industry
  accounting simplifications,
    Consultative Document 1.28,
    2.17
  Deregulation Initiative (1990s) 2.7
  Statutory Audit Requirement for
    Smaller Companies
    (2000) 2.26

estimation techniques 5.20, App.5
euro App.5
European Union, Company Law
  Directives 1.1, 2.5
ex gratia pensions App.5
exceptional items, profit and loss
  account 5.28–5.29, App.5
exchange rates 8.2–8.6, App.5

exempt private companies,
  establishment 1.3
exemptions
  assessment of entitlement 9.5–9.9
  cash flow statements, FRS on 1.17
  cost-benefit test 1.9
  disclosure requirements 4.3–4.5
  group financial statements 4.11,
    4.16–4.18
  see also audit exemption;
    modifications
Exemptions from Standards on
  Grounds of Size or Public Interest
  (CCAB paper, 1994) 1.19, 1.20–
  1.27
  FRSSE, need for 1.42
  main proposals 1.20
  problems identified 1.24–1.27
  as 'quick fix' solution 1.20, 1.24
  standards applicable for all
    companies 1.21
extraordinary items, profit and loss
  accounts 5.27, App.5

factoring of debts 6.47, App.5
fair value App.5
FIFO ('first in, first out') App.5
finance charges, leases 6.34, 6.35,
  App.5
finance leases 6.34, 6.35, 6.40, App.5
Financial Reporting Standard for
  Smaller Entities *see* FRSSE
  (Financial Reporting Standard for
  Smaller Entities)
Financial Reporting Standards App.5
  see also individual FRSs
Financial Services Act (FSA)
  (1986) 3.4
Financial Services and Markets Act
  (FSMA) (2000) 1.38
financial statements
  audit of 2.22–2.28
    auditors, guidance for *see* auditors,
      guidance for
  circulation requirements 2.4
  consolidated 8.17–8.18, App.5
  example App.1
  groups
    abbreviated accounts 4.41

Index

financial statements—*cont.*
  groups—*cont.*
    auditors, guidance for 9.38–9.39
    exemptions and
      modifications 4.11, 4.16–4.18
    intangible assets 6.10
    meaning 2.3
    modified *see* modified financial statements
    notes to App.1
    true and fair requirement 9.12–9.20
fixed assets
  capitalisation of costs 6.12–6.13
  classes of 6.18–6.20
  disposal methods 5.30, 5.31, App.5
  FRS15 requirements 6.11, 6.15, 6.22, App.5
  FRSSE (2002) App.5
  initial measurement 6.12
  provisions 6.15
  repairs 6.15
  subsequent expenditure 6.14
  transitional arrangements 6.21
  valuation 6.16–6.18
  write-downs 6.24–6.25
flow through method, deferred tax 7.7
foreign currency translations
  forward contracts 8.3
  FRSSE requirements 8.2–8.3, 8.5, 8.6
  hedging provisions 8.3–8.4
foreign entities, incorporating accounts of App.5
foreseeable losses App.5
forward contracts 8.3, App.5
FRED22 5.36
FRS1 *Cash flow statements* 4.48, 8.19, App.5
FRS2 *Accounting for subsidiary undertakings* 8.17, App.5
FRS3 *Reporting financial performance* 1.17, 5.24–5.30, 5.34–5.35, App.5
FRS4 *Capital Instruments* 1.17, 7.34, App.5
FRS5 *Reporting the substance of transactions* 5.9, 6.48, 8.17, App.5

FRS6 *Acquisitions and mergers* 8.17, App.5
FRS7 *Fair values in acquisition accounting* 8.17, App.5
FRS8 *Related party disclosures* 8.10, 8.12, 9.22, App.5
FRS9 *Associates and joint ventures* 8.17, App.5
FRS10 *Goodwill and intangible assets* 5.31, 6.6, 6.10, 8.17, App.5
FRS11 *Impairment of fixed assets and goodwill* 6.28–6.31, 8.17, App.5
FRS12 *Provisions, contingent liabilities and contingent assets* 1.21, 6.15, 7.24, 7.30–7.33, App.5
FRS13 *Derivatives and other financial instruments* App.5
FRS14 *Earnings per share* App.5
FRS15 *Tangible fixed assets* 6.11, 6.15, 6.27, 6.22, App.5
FRS16 *Current tax* 7.2, 7.3, App.5
FRS17 *Retirement benefits* 7.17, 7.18, 7.20, App.5
FRS18 *Accounting policies* 1.21, 5.19–5.20, 9.3, App.5
FRS19 *Deferred tax* 7.6–7.7, 7.14, App.5
FRSSE (Financial Reporting Standard for Smaller Entities)
  abbreviated accounts 4.39, 4.43
  accounting policies 5.20
  amendments to original App.5
  ASB publications, other 1.33
  capital instruments 7.35, 7.38
  cash flow information 8.19
  companies legislation, link with App.5
  Company Law Review 2.31
  contents App.5
  controversial issues 1.40
  criteria App.5
  deferred tax 7.13, App.5
  'Definitions' section 1.33, 1.35, App.5
  discounting 5.37–5.38, App.5
  Exposure Draft 1.31, 1.41, 7.15, 7.17, App.5
  foreign currency transactions 8.2, 8.5, 8.6, App.5

Index

FRSSE (Financial Reporting Standard for Smaller Entities)—*cont.*
  general company law exclusions, extension of   1.39
  goodwill   5.31, 6.6–6.10, App.5
  government grants   6.33, App.5
  harmonisation of standards   2.36, 2.39
  history   App.5
  impairment reviews   6.27, App.5
  investment properties   6.32, App.5
  leases   6.34–6.39, App.5
  legal requirements   App.5
  measurement bases   9.17
  modified financial statements, prepared in accordance with   4.12, 9.23, 9.26
  need for   1.28–1.29, 1.41–1.42
  other accounting standards, relationship with   5.11–5.17
  other ASB documents, relationship with   App.5
  post balance sheet events   8.7, App.5
  provisions   7.26, App.5
  related parties   8.10, 8.11, 8.15–8.16, App.5
  research and development   6.3–6.5, App.5
  review   App.5
  scope   1.37–1.38, App.5
  share schemes   6.50, App.5
  simplifications   App.5
  start-up costs   6.49, App.5
  status   App.5
  structure   1.32–1.35
  support for   1.30
  taxation   7.2–7.3, 7.5, App.5
  true and fair view   5.8–5.10, App.5
  unincorporated entities   5.4, 5.7
  see also Designed to fit– *Financial Reporting Standard for Smaller Entities* (CCAB paper, 1995)
FSA (Financial Services Act) (1986)   3.4
FSMA (Financial Services and Markets Act) (2000)   1.38, 3.4
funded schemes   App.5

G4+1 Group   5.36, 6.43

GAAP (Generally Accepted Accounting Principles), *Designed to Fit* (CCAB 1995 paper)   1.45
Glossary of Terms, Auditing Practices Board   1.34
going concern   5.20, 5.22
goodwill   5.31, 6.6–6.10, App.5
government grants   6.33, App.5
Great Britain, legal requirements   App.5
gross earnings, leases   App.5
groups of companies
  acquisitions   3.26
  financial statements
    abbreviated accounts   4.41
    auditors, guidance for   9.38–9.39
    exemptions and modifications   4.11, 4.16–4.18, 9.38–9.39
    intangible assets   6.10
  ineligible   2.9, 3.3, 3.18, 3.27
  small, application of FRSSE   App.5
  small and medium-sized, size criteria   3.17–3.27
  see also parent companies; subsidiaries

hedging provisions, foreign currency translations   8.3–8.4
hire purchase contracts   6.34, App.5

IAS (International Accounting Standards)   2.36–2.39, 6.44
IASB (International Accounting Standards Board)   2.39, 6.44
IASC (International Accounting Standards Committee)   1.34
IBA (industrial building allowance)   7.10
identifiable assets/liabilities   App.5
illustrative wordings   App.3
impairment reviews   6.27–6.31
impairment testing   6.9
inception of leases   App.5
Independent Professional Review (IPR)   2.32–2.35
industrial building allowance (IBA)   7.10

Index

Institute of Chartered Accountants in England and Wales, Committee of   1.5
intangible assets   6.3–6.10, App.5
interest costs   App.5
International Accounting Standards Board   1.34
International Accounting Standards Board (IASB)   2.39, 6.44
International Accounting Standards Committee (IASC)   1.34
International Accounting Standards (IAS)   2.36–2.39, 6.44
investment properties   6.32, App.5
IPR (Independent Professional Review)   2.32–2.35
Irish Republic, legal requirements   App.5

Jenkins Report (1962)   1.4

land and buildings, depreciation method/rate   6.23
leases   6.34–6.44, App.5
Leases: Implementation of a new approach (ASB Discussion Paper)   6.43
leases
 ASB on   6.36, 6.37, 6.43, 6.44
 FRSSE   6.34–6.38
legislation *see* companies legislation
liabilities
 capital instruments   7.34–7.38, App.5
 contingent   7.31–7.33, App.5
 deferred tax   7.6–7.15, App.5
 provisions   7.24–7.30, App.5
 retirement benefits   7.17–7.23, App.5
 taxation   7.2–7.5, App.5
 VAT   7.16, App.5
 see also assets
LIFO ('last in, last out')   App.5
listed companies, accounting policies   5.16
Little GAAP
 accounting standards   5.16
 FRSSE, structure   1.32
 impairment reviews   6.31

Little GAAP—*cont.*
 leases   6.44
 small companies in law   1.8
 see also Big GAAP; GAAP (Generally Accepted Accounting Principles)
local currencies   App.5
long-term contracts   6.45, App.5

medium-sized companies
 abbreviated accounts   4.50–4.53
  reporting on   9.28, 9.37
 Companies Act (1985)   4.1, 4.2
 disclosure relaxations   4.3
 modifications not applicable   4.7
 qualifying as   3.6–3.11
 research and development   6.5
 size criteria   2.11
 see also small companies
minimum lease payments   App.5
modifications
 directors' report   4.2, 4.14–4.15
 small companies   4.6–4.8
 financial statements *see* modified financial statements
 see also exemptions
modified accounts
 meaning   2.13
 public interest companies   3.2
 statutory provisions   2.14
modified financial statements   4.9–4.13
 auditors, guidance for   9.6, 9.12–9.20, 9.23–9.27
 reporting on   9.23–9.27
 small companies   4.6–4.8
 statutory provisions   9.25
 true and fair requirement   9.12–9.20
monetary items   App.5

net investments   App.5
net realisable value   App.5
non-adjusting events   8.9, App.5
non-cash transactions   App.5
Northern Ireland, legal requirements   App.5

obligations   App.5
operating leases   6.34, 6.40, App.5
operating profit   5.27–5.28
ordinary activities   5.29, App.5

Index

overheads
  estimation techniques   5.20
  stocks and long-term
    contracts   App.5
overrides   5.23, 9.3, App.5

parent companies
  audit exemption, qualifying
    for   4.28
  Companies Act (1985)   4.1
  dormant   4.28
  group financial statements
    exemption   4.16
  overseas   4.31
  qualifying as small/medium-
    sized   3.10
  'shell'   3.11
past service cost   App.5
pension schemes, funding levels   App.5
permanent differences, deferred
  tax   7.11
permanent differences   App.5
post balance sheet events   8.7–8.9, App.5
prior period adjustments   7.21, App.5
private companies
  classification by size   1.7, 1.8
  establishment   1.2
profit and loss accounts
  abbreviated   4.50
  example   App.1
  as financial statement   2.3
  FRSSE requirements   5.26, App.5
  group financial statements
    exemption   4.18
  layering format requirement   5.25
  research and development
    disclosure   6.5
projected unit method   App.5
property, investment   6.32, App.5
'Proprietary companies'   1.7
provisions   7.24–7.30
  depreciation   7.27–7.30
  FRSSE requirements   7.26, App.5
  recognition when   7.25
  repairs   6.15, 7.27
public interest companies   3.2–3.5
  qualifying as small or medium-
    sized   3.6

purchased goodwill   App.5
pure research   App.5

R&D (research and
  development)   6.3–6.5, App.5
recognition, defined   App.5
*Recommendations on accounting
  principles*   1.5
recoverable amount, defined   App.5
related parties
  associated companies   8.14
  controlling   8.16
  FRS8   8.10, 8.12
  FRSSE (2002)   8.10, 8.11, 8.15–8.16, App.5
  materiality   8.15
repairs, fixed assets   6.15
reporting
  abbreviated accounts   9.28–9.37
  financial performance   1.17, 5.24–5.32
    see also FRS3 *Reporting financial
    performance*; *Reporting
    financial performance* (ASB
    Discussion Paper)
  modified financial statements   9.23–9.27
Reporting financial performance (ASB
  Discussion Paper)   5.36
Republic of Ireland, legal
  requirements   App.5
research (1985)   1.10–1.11
research and development
  (R&D)   6.3–6.5, App.5
residual value   App.5
retirement benefits   7.17–7.23, App.5
reverse premiums, leases   6.34
Review of the standard-setting process
  (ASC report) 1983   1.9
rollover relief   7.12

sale and leaseback transactions   6.39, App.5
scheme liabilities   App.5
settlements   App.5
share schemes   6.50
shareholders, audit exemptions   4.32–4.33

353

Index

size criteria
  audit exemption, qualifying for   4.24
  definitions   3.12–3.16
  employees, number of   3.16
  groups, small and medium-sized   3.17–3.27
  medium-sized companies   2.11
  private companies, classification by size   1.7, 1.8
  small companies   2.10
small companies
  abbreviated accounts   4.45–4.49
    reporting on   9.28
  Companies Act (1985)   4.1
  directors' report, modifications   4.6–4.8
  disclosure exemptions   2.13, 4.3
    checklist App.4
  financial statements, modifications   4.6–4.8
  meaning   1.1
  qualifying as   3.6–3.11
  Schedule 8, adoption of   9.4
  size criteria   2.10
  see also medium-sized companies
Small company financial reporting (1985 research study)   1.10
SORPS (Statements of Recommended Practice)   App.5
SSAP1 *Accounting for the results of associated companies*   1.5
SSAP3 *Earnings per share*   1.5
SSAP4 *Accounting for government grants*   1.21, 6.33, App.5
SSAP5 *Accounting for value added tax*   7.16, App.5
SSAP9 *Stocks and long-term contracts*   1.21, 6.45, App.5
SSAP10 *Statement of source and application of funds*   1.5
SSAP12 *Depreciation*   6.22
SSAP13 *Accounting for research and development*   1.15, 1.21, 6.3, App.5
SSAP16 *Current cost accounting*   1.6
SSAP17 *Accounting for post balance sheet events*   1.21, 8.8, App.5

SSAP18 *Accounting for contingencies*   1.21
SSAP19 *Accounting for investment properties*   6.32, App.5
SSAP20 *Foreign currency translations*   8.2, App.5
SSAP21 *Accounting for leases and hire purchase contracts*   6.35, 6.36, 6.38, App.5
SSAP24 *Accounting for pension costs*   7.17, App.5
SSAP25 *Segmental reporting* 1.15, App.5
start-up costs   6.49, App.5
Statement of Source and Application of Funds, establishment   1.5
Statement of Total Recognised Gains and Losses (STRGL) *see* STRGL (Statement of Total Recognised Gains and Losses)
Statements of Accounting Practice
  FRSSE 2002 guidance   5.1–5.2, 6.1, App.5
  retirement benefits   7.17
  see also individual SSAPs
Statements of Auditing Standards   9.22
Statements of Recommended Practice (SORPS) App.5
Statutory Audit Requirement for Smaller Companies (DTI)   2.26
statutory instruments
  SI 1992/2452 (Companies Act 1985 (Accounts of Small and Medium-sized Enterprises and Publication of Accounts in ECUs) Regulations (1992)   2.14
  SI 1994/1935 (Companies Act 1985 (Audit Exemption) Regulations (1994)   2.22
  SI 1996/189 (Companies Act 1985 (Miscellaneous Accounting Amendments) Regulations (1996)   2.15
  SI 1997/220 (Companies Act 1985 (Accounts of Small and Medium-sized Companies and Minor Accounting Amendments) Regulations (1997)   2.17–2.21

Index

statutory instruments—*cont.*
  SI 1997/936 (Companies Act 1985 (Audit Exemption) (Amendment) Regulations (1997) 2.24
  SI 2000/1430 (Companies Act 1985 (Audit Exemption) (Amendment) Regulations (2000) 2.26
stock
  consignment 6.48, App.5
  and long-term contracts 6.45, App.5
straight-line method 6.35, 6.36, 6.37
STRGL (Statement of Total Recognised Gains and Losses) 5.33–5.36
  financial statements, example App.1
  FRSSE (2000) App.5
  investment properties 6.32
  tangible fixed assets, revaluation losses 6.11
  write-downs 6.24
subsidiaries
  audit exemption, qualifying for 4.28
  dormant 4.28
  size criteria 3.25
sum of the digits basis, finance charges 6.35

tangible fixed assets *see* fixed assets
taxation 7.2–7.5, App.5
  deferred 7.6–7.15, App.5
  tax credits, 7.3, App.5
  VAT 7.16, App.5
terms of capital instruments App.5
terms of leases App.5
timing differences, deferred tax 7.8–7.10, App.5
total recognised gains and losses App.5
transitional arrangements
  FRSSE (2002) App.5
  intangible assets 6.10
  retirement benefits 7.18–7.19, 7.21
translation, defined App.5
true and fair view
  abbreviated accounts, medium-sized companies 4.52–4.53

true and fair view—*cont.*
  accounting standards (1970s) 1.5
  accounting standards (1980s) 1.9
  ASC statement (1988) 1.12
  auditors, guidance to 9.12–9.20
  directors' statements 4.38
  financial statements
    meaning 2.3
    modified 9.12–9.20
  FRSSE 2002 guidance 5.8–5.10, App.5
  override disclosures 5.23, App.5
  unincorporated entities 5.4, 5.5
turnover
  acquisitions, groups 3.26
  audit exemption, test for 4.24
  comparison 3.14
  defined 3.13
  financial statements, audit of 2.23
  see also size criteria

UITF (Urgent Task Force) Abstracts
  auditors, guidance to 9.22
    true and fair requirement 9.16, 9.19
  CCAB 1994 paper 1.20, 1.21
  debtors 6.46
  FRSSE (2000) App.5
  leases 6.41
  profits and loss accounts 5.16
  share schemes 6.50
  start-up costs 6.49
  website development costs 6.26
unincorporated entities 5.3–5.7, 6.7
universality concept 1.13
Urgent Task Force (UITF) Abstracts *see* UITF (Urgent Task Force) Abstracts
useful economic life 6.8, 6.9, 6.23, App.5

VAT (Value Added Tax) 7.16, App.5

website development costs 6.26
withholding tax 7.3, App.5
write-downs to recoverable amount 6.24–6.25, App.5